ELIZA GAGNON

Mona Harrington was educated at the University of Massachusetts and at Harvard University, where she received
a law degree and a doctorate in political science. She
served as a lawyer in the State Department, taught political science, and raised a family of three children before
turning to writing full-time. She is a contributor to *The
Politics of Ethnicity* by Walzer, Kantowicz, Higham, and
Harrington (1982), and is currently Executive Director
of the Alliance of Independent Scholars in Cambridge,
Massachusetts.

The Dream of Deliverance
in American Politics

MONA HARRINGTON

The Dream of Deliverance
in American Politics

ALFRED A. KNOPF   NEW YORK

1 9 8 6

THIS IS A BORZOI BOOK
PUBLISHED BY ALFRED A. KNOPF, INC.

Copyright © 1986 by Mona Harrington
All rights reserved under International and Pan-American Copyright Conventions.
Published in the United States by Alfred A. Knopf, Inc., New York,
and simultaneously in Canada by Random House of Canada Limited, Toronto.
Distributed by Random House, Inc., New York.

Library of Congress Cataloging-in-Publication Data
Harrington, Mona
The dream of deliverance in American politics.
Bibliography: p.
Includes index.
1. United States—Politics and government—20th century.
I. Title. II. Title : Deliverance in American politics.
E743.H275   1986   973.92   85-19799
ISBN 0-394-54973-2

Manufactured in the United States of America
First Edition

For Paul

Acknowledgments

Nearly everyone I know has served as listener, reader, or questioner during the evolution of this work. There are some whose contributions were vital to its being done at all.

Thomas N. Brown, professor of American history at the University of Massachusetts/Boston, read every chapter of the last two drafts and offered exquisitely thoughtful and informed comment on each. Equally important, he maintained by both example and counsel the constant conviction that the creation of books is worth the vast labor they require.

I am also profoundly grateful to the Alliance of Independent Scholars, which provides a scholarly community for writers working outside the academic profession. I have presented work in progress to the multidisciplinary research colloquium of the Alliance and received helpful comment on cogency and structural clarity. Co-members of a smaller book-finishers group—Natalie Bluestone, Eugenia Kaledin, and Sherrin Wyntjes—provided continuous support and commentary over the period of a year. Nadya Aisenberg, critical reader par excellence, reviewed large portions of the manuscript. In general, my Alliance colleagues, in their always ready friendship and good spirit, provided a crucial antidote to the isolation of writing.

A number of people contributed special help. Stanley Hoffmann, offered encouragement and important advice in the early stages of the work. Glenn Tinder devoted hours to discussions of political theory, which is the ground of the questions from which the book developed. Arthur Kaledin has carried on a lifelong inquiry with students and friends into the meaning of the American experience, and many of his questions—and answers—are woven into these chapters. Frederic Spotts, while laboring on a book of his own, commented on mine with unfailing honesty and humor. And at the end of this process, Jane Garrett, at Alfred A. Knopf, supplied sympathetic and wise suggestions on key points.

Paul Gagnon, to whom this book is dedicated, provided support so multifarious it defies measure and description. My children, Eliza, Benjamin, and Thomas Gagnon asked useful questions, listened to the answers, and also helped to sustain this long effort with crucial cups of tea, jokes, and, perhaps most important, the ordinary exchanges of the day.

Contents

*The Dream of Deliverance
in American Politics*

I

The Promise and the Myth

In their morning newspapers on April 29, 1975, Americans read of the final collapse of South Vietnam, its army unable to withstand the combined forces of North Vietnam and the Vietcong despite still massive support from the United States. With defeat imminent, thousands of South Vietnamese who feared communist retribution for their cooperation with the United States had been evacuated in the preceding weeks. Many, however, frantically sought escape at the last minute. Newspapers carried pictures of frightened people trying to climb onto the walls of the American embassy courtyard and Marine guards pushing them off with rifles. Newspaper stories reported that the last American officials in Saigon, trapped in the embassy, retreated to the roof, where they were lifted off by helicopter as the North Vietnamese closed in on the city.

It was a terrible moment, marking terrible failure—failure of American power, failure of American promises, and, for the Vietnamese pushed off the walls, failure of American decency. Twenty years of American aid, ten years of direct involvement in the war, had accomplished nothing, and the cost both to Vietnam and to the United States was incalculable. There were

the Vietnamese dead and wounded, not only soldiers but thousands of civilians; the American dead and wounded; a countryside
devastated by American bombs and a family and village life
destroyed both by bombing and by relocations imposed by anti-
guerrilla strategies. Moreover, the economic costs—quite apart
from how they may be assessed for the Vietnamese—included an
insidious inflation in the United States that greatly weakened the
economy at home and unsettled other economies as well by
undermining the international strength of the dollar.

After the war, consensus quickly developed that American
policy in Vietnam had been disastrously mistaken. But there was
no consensus about the nature of the mistake and the lessons to
be learned from it. Was the effort in Vietnam well conceived but
badly executed through an unwillingness to commit the force the
strategy required? Or was the strategy badly conceived to begin
with, the enemy misunderstood and the tactics, therefore,
doomed to fail?

In either case, the haunting legacy of Vietnam is the widespread belief that the war and its costs in economic and human
suffering had all been futile. The father of a Marine killed in the
Tet offensive in 1968 expressed this anguish in an interview on
the tenth anniversary of his son's death.

> All of those kids. All those young kids. How many? Fifty-five
> thousand? For what? Why? I still don't know. Who did it
> benefit? . . . The companies that make all the munitions? The
> people of South Vietnam? Who?[1]

In other American wars, grieving parents understood the
reasons for their loss. Some may not have thought the reasons
justified the sacrifice of young lives, but the nation's purposes
were clear and, while challenged and questioned, they were still
widely accepted by the public. In both world wars, the United
States was fighting to curb expansionist nations with authoritarian governments whose imperial designs threatened the survival
of democracy in Europe and an open world order generally. The
need to fight in Korea in 1950 was less clear, but it was at least

a case of resisting clear-cut military assault across an internationally recognized border. North Korean armies had invaded South Korea and, unresisted, would have extended the area in Asia under communist control. This would have placed non-communist Asian countries, including Japan, under increased pressure to accommodate themselves to demands of communist neighbors or internal communist groups. And such accommodation would reduce the areas of Asia politically friendly and economically open to the West. Thus in all three wars, the United States, the largest, strongest democratic nation in the world, fought either to defend established democracies or to protect the potential, threatened by the spread of communism, for developing democratic systems in underdeveloped areas of the world.

For the leaders from Dwight Eisenhower to Lyndon Johnson, whose decisions and commitments led in 1965 to American military engagement in Vietnam, the issues there appeared to be the same as they had been in Korea—stopping communist expansion in Asia and keeping open the chance in Third World countries for development along Western lines. But as the war wore on, the issues became less clear. Americans were in Vietnam to fight the spread of communism, but the enemy, most of the people fighting for the communist cause, were South Vietnamese themselves. The battleground was often the village, and winning battles meant killing villagers, including women and children, burning their homes, destroying their livestock and their fields, whether by bombing or by ground fighting. Defense against communism in Vietnam also meant dealing with a succession of South Vietnamese governments that were at the same time repressive and ineffective and with large numbers of government officials, military officers, and entrepreneurs—Vietnamese and American—who were using the massive war effort to advance or enrich themselves.

Whatever the reasons for the war in theory, it did not seem like the defense of freedom in practice, and the discrepancy between the way officials in Washington explained it and the way it looked to Americans in news reports provoked increasing distress and division at home. Then, with the ultimate defeat of

South Vietnam and the United States, divisions among Americans over the war and what it meant were deepened still further by an inevitable tide of anger, humiliation, bitterness.

The longer-range effect of the Vietnam experience in the United States was to shake the certainty most Americans had felt to that point about the country's political direction—the belief that American commitments in the world were politically and morally sound, a conviction matched by general confidence that the country could make good on its words and intentions. For many, especially among those coming of age in the late 1960s— draft age, college age—the impact of the war went beyond uncertainty to a deep disaffection for their own society, an end to automatic patriotism. The earlier tendency of Americans to accept and follow national government leadership in foreign affairs turned, with Vietnam, to a tendency to doubt or disbelieve or actively to denigrate officialdom.

But if Vietnam was the first powerful shock to the self-respect and self-confidence of Americans, it was not the only one. The killing of John Kennedy in 1963 had been horrifying, but the assassinations of Martin Luther King and Senator Robert Kennedy in 1968 raised more general fears about violence and lawlessness in the society—fears reinforced in the late 1960s by outbreaks of summer rioting, burning, and looting in major industrial cities and by an increase in violent crime of all kinds throughout the country. The Watergate scandal in 1974 revealed a conspiracy among top national officers, including the President, Richard Nixon, to discredit Nixon's Democratic opponents in the 1972 presidential election by various unfair and illegal means, and a further conspiracy to cover the traces of illegality once a judicial investigation had begun.

In addition to the unease caused by shocking episodes of violence and corruption, there was, throughout the decade from 1965 to 1975, chronic and cumulative disappointment with the social experiments of the 1960s, Lyndon Johnson's War on Poverty. The money and energy expended on the wide range of social welfare programs sponsored by the new Office of Economic Opportunity had not succeeded in changing, or changing enough, the conditions that perpetuated disadvantage among both urban and rural poor. Then there was the beginning of a profoundly unsettling economic inflation and a slowdown of economic growth, which together meant that no one could be sure of the future value of money or other assets, that workers could not be sure of employment, and that graduates of colleges and professional schools could not be sure of entry into fields for which they had been trained. The lack of confidence in leadership provoked by Vietnam turned, with these factors, into a more general disintegration of certainty about the health, openness, and promise of the society.

In 1980, the deepening uncertainties and contention about their causes produced an epic paroxysm in the Democratic Party, the party that had shaped, if not always controlled, American politics since the 1930s. Bitter battles in primary elections in which the Democratic President, Jimmy Carter, was challenged by Senator Edward Kennedy revealed wide fragmentation among traditional Democratic constituencies, some of which abandoned their party altogether in the general election. The result was the electoral victory of the Republican Ronald Reagan, a candidate with a conception of government not seriously advocated since the 1920s, when it was already an echo of an earlier era of laissez-faire.

As President, Reagan translated his 1980 victory into legislation radically cutting federal programs and taxes—defunding the Left, his backers called it—supported by majorities in Congress that only fifteen years earlier had set out to create a Great Society precisely through the use of governmental resources and choices.

The 1981 turnaround on federal social programs reflected a broadly held belief that the Johnsonian approach had not worked. It had been expensive, and too often ineffective, but, more seriously, the ineffectiveness of many programs made the expenditure seem to be no more than a payoff to groups with good political leverage, or guilt money. Programs for the handicapped, for retarded schoolchildren, for Vietnam War veterans, for minorities in need of health care, education, and housing, were not funded in amounts great enough to change the basic condition of those receiving benefits, but enough to relieve the consciences of those voting them. Thus Americans turned from the apparent

bankruptcy of federal activism to Reagan's older, simpler prescription for social health—"getting the government off our
backs"—in the hope of regaining lost strength and confidence.

What was ultimately at stake in the twists and turns of
American politics in the post-Vietnam period was a much larger
question than the effectiveness of federal programs. The real
question was whether the fundamental, historical promises of
the American governing system could be redeemed. The promises were those implicit in the political values Americans inherited and accepted from the nation's founders, the values
of Enlightenment liberalism which the eighteenth-century
philosopher-politicians translated into practical form in the
American Constitution. The basic precepts of liberal philosophy
are that individual freedom is the highest social goal and that all
individuals are of equal worth. From those root principles,
Americans have derived the others that form the basis of the
American system: the subjection of the government to direction
by the governed through democratic processes; the right of the
people to remain free from governmental detention or punishment except by due process of law; the right to remain free from
undue governmental encroachments on speech, assembly, and
religious practice; the right to hold property free of governmental restriction except by due process of law; and the right of all
people to equal justice and equal opportunity.

In short, the American governing system stands for the promise of both liberty and equality at the same time, in full measure
and not just as abstractions or pious sentiments. Liberty and
equality are the basic components of the American dream, the
dream of being free, of living by one's own choices. It is a dream
of openness, of possibility, of change. Black or white, rich or
poor, man or woman, Americans are supposed to have the chance
to become what they will and, within the constraints of their
income, choose where they will live, with whom they will
associate, where their children will go to school. In the American
dream, individual choices are not narrowed by governmental
restrictions or unalterably shaped by patterns passed down from
preceding generations.

Of course, there never has been a time in American life when the dream of freedom and equal opportunity for all has been fulfilled or even come close to fulfillment, but it has always seemed that we were making progress. This is what has changed. It is the sense that the promise is receding, the bright dream mocked by seemingly intractable inequalities and divisions, by ineffectual or untrustworthy governments, that is unnerving to Americans.

But why? What has gone wrong? Has the promise of the founders been false from the beginning? Or was a governing system dedicated to their ambitious goals adequate for a simpler time, but inadequate for a technological society of immense size, with vital economic connections running throughout the world?

The answer is that threats to the promise of liberty and equality—threats that have long been serious although not recognized as such by most Americans—have become dangerously serious in recent years in large part because they have never been faced and dealt with in the past. In generation after generation, we have not seen—or admitted to—the deeper problems facing us, have not seen—or admitted to—the deep internal divisions of interest and action among economic and social groups in America and thus have failed to see the rising barriers to the attainment of our fundamental goals.

The greatest barrier has gone unrecognized in part because it has been assumed to be the very source of progress of every sort: the modern industrial system. The threat to liberty and equality at home and to an international order fostering these goals elsewhere arises directly from the very structure and power of the industrialism that is at the base of our economic life. That is, modern industrial economies produce immense wealth and that wealth enhances the possibilities of freedom and open opportunity because the production of needed goods does not require endless labor from most of the population. The more wealth a system produces, the more people should be able to expect enough income and enough free time to be able to make real choices about how they will live. But the structural requirements of the industrial system and its operation in practice do not automatically harness the wealth the system produces to the goals of either liberty or equality. On the contrary, there are elements in it that, without control, militate against those goals in societies living on industrial bounty.

For one thing, industrial systems must operate according to the logic of the machines that liberate human labor and the logic of the markets from which resources are bought and in which products are sold. But new technologies change machines and hundreds of conditions produce changed markets—including their manipulation by strong buyers and sellers. Thus the fortunes of whole industries can change unpredictably. And since in an industrial economy the units of production are large—steel mills, for example—the decline of an industry can affect a whole region, as the decline of American steel has, producing unequal conditions of employment and income in different parts of the country.

Even more damaging, though, to the expectation of expanding freedom and equality for everyone in an industrial order is a conflict in the needs and interests of the groups forming the essential component parts of the economy—and a disparity of power among those groups. Such conflict is often attributed— in the legacy of Karl Marx—to the particular workings of a capitalist order, but it is not peculiar to capitalism, because it stems from causes deeper than a quarrel over ownership of capital. It is a conflict built into industrial systems as such, stemming from the fact that each group in the system has different sources of livelihood and well-being, and conditions promoting the well-being of one group necessarily threaten those of others.

The major lines of conflict run between the professional managers of industrial capital, the most powerful group in the system, and the weaker groups—workers in the industrial sector, the proprietors of small businesses and their workers, and all of those engaged in enterprises, small or large, that are in some important way locally fixed. Historically, farmers have been the most important part of this last category and have been weak in relation to the industrial sector because their capital, fixed in land and farm machinery, cannot be moved around to seek higher returns in bad times.[2]

The interest of capital managers is opposed to that of other groups because, industrial units being large, managers have huge stakes to protect. Thus, whether employed by private corporations or by governments, they must seek a maximum degree of control over the productive and distributive processes. Faced with innumerable chances of loss through mistake, confusion, inefficiency, corruption, high costs, or unpredictable market changes, managers attempt to achieve the maximum possible regularity within their range of responsibility and to maintain control as far as possible over the terms on which they deal with other groups.

The interest of wage earners, on the other hand, is to share power with managers in the distribution of income to which their labor contributes, to insist that it is not a management prerogative alone to set the percentage of income that goes to wages and to various guarantees of security to workers. The interest of small and locally fixed business is to resist the unlimited growth and expansion of business units in the industrial sector—the expansion that capital managers prize for purposes of market predictability. Finally, the interest of the agrarian sector forces it into constant battle against the stronger industrial markets that, if uncontrolled, create a chronic price squeeze for farmers—high costs for the manufactured materials they use, low prices for the farm products they sell.

Then, on some issues, the interests of the weaker groups may be opposed to each other. Historically, for example, industrial managers and workers tend to stand together in opposition to agrarian demands for high tariffs on raw materials, while managers and farmers may unite in efforts to keep the costs of manufacturing down, by opposing worker demands for higher wages. And there is the further complication of divided interest, to some degree, within each major constituency—the most important being the differential in available work, income, and opportunity as between men and women within each group.

Thus the needs of the various interests making up an industrial system inevitably collide, and in such collisions, the weaker groups inevitably suffer. The central challenge for a society committed to liberty and equality, then, is to protect the effective freedoms and opportunities of those in weaker groups, given the disadvantage they inevitably face. My premise here is that to keep the American promise alive for all, to prevent an economic stratification trapping whole groups in a state of permanent disadvantage, deliberate protection of the promise by government is necessary.

To some extent, of course, the American government has adopted such a role. Since the turn of the century, there have been several great moments of governmental reform relieving the pressures of industrialism. There was Woodrow Wilson's New Freedom, Franklin Roosevelt's New Deal, and the anti-poverty programs of the John Kennedy–Lyndon Johnson Great Society. But even the most far-reaching reforms—the National Labor Relations Act of 1935, the Fair Labor Standards Act and the Agricultural Adjustment Act of 1938, the Civil Rights Act of 1964, and Medicare in 1965—dealt only with parts of the problem, only with the most visible forms of trouble.

For effective protections to operate against the kinds of pressures weaker groups have always suffered and have been suffering with a growing sense of hopelessness in recent years, much deeper, system-wide regulators must be attached to the economy. There must be laws based on explicit recognition of the points of conflict among various economic groups, recognition of the source of that conflict, what each group stands to win or lose, and, specifically, how various outcomes to the conflict would affect the liberty and opportunity of the weak. That is, unless laws are designed specifically to protect the goals of liberty and equality against threats from industrial pressures and conflicts, these goals cannot be progressively achieved. Rather, they will recede further and further from our reach.

This will become increasingly true as the economic system becomes more dependent on high technology and less in need of human and especially unskilled labor. In the older, labor-intensive industries, workers were at a chronic disadvantage in that the system did not accord them fairness. But it did employ most of them and thus distributed some income to them. In our highly technologized economy, we cannot count on employment as the sole—and automatic—distributor of income and of opportunity.

But the idea of imposing deliberate and systematic controls on the economy for the purpose of minimizing the effects on the weak of conflict among groups with differing economic interests is an alien idea for Americans. It suggests a fixity of interests defined by economic class or group and elevates the concept of class and class differences to a place of economic and political importance. And Americans have always acted politically out of an opposite tradition which denies the existence of deeply rooted class differences in the society. That is, we deny the existence of class in the sense of fixed interests inevitably at odds with other fixed interests. And thus we deny also the operation of a permanent internal drag against the weak caused by built-in conflicts among groups with different interests and disparities of power among those groups.

Denying the conflict of class or economic interests, Americans cannot deal explicitly with the hardships caused by such conflicts, cannot make the enactment of structural protections for the economically weak an explicit part of the national political agenda. The result has been to approach problems through the much-celebrated American tradition of pragmatism. We give attention to crises or pressing problems but not their underlying causes. We solve problems in a practical way and avoid the deep bog of theory about social reconstruction. But it is the very lack of attention to structural weaknesses that produces the confusion over programs, the vacillation in direction, the ineffectuality of reforms that have come to trouble Americans deeply.

The key question is why this occurs. Why do Americans so strongly resist recognizing the existence and importance of economic interest in the life of the nation? Why do we not see the threat that conflicts among interests pose to the more effective pursuit of fundamental social goals?

The answer begins in a paradox. In spite of our persistent and pervasive denial of significant conflict rooted in economic interest, our political life is shaped by it. The most important political actors *are* interest-based constituencies. That is, each of the three primary interests within the American economy—capital managers, industrial wage earners, and those engaged in small or locally based (including agrarian) enterprise—has a political counterpart, a coherent, cohesive political base. And out of this base, leaders articulate proposals and programs reflecting the interest of the particular group. The important positions on each major issue that arises in American politics emanate from these groups, and our national political debate consists of arguments among them.

But there is a phantom quality to these arguments. The economic constituencies behind particular programs have no formal organization or even a recognizable identity or name. They certainly do not take the form of political parties. Rather, the three interests form coalitions within the two major parties—coalitions that shift from time to time depending on changing issues. And further, the interest-based constituencies do not frame their programs in terms of their own interest. They do not deal explicitly in the economic needs and demands of the group, but in surrogate issues. Therefore, what is in fact a three-sided, interest-based debate does not produce a clear confrontation of conflicts in economic interest and no direct address to problems resulting from the conflict.

Again, why? Why the paradox? How can a group act politically out of common interest without recognizing itself as an interest-based group or its programs as expressive of that interest?

The further answer lies in a mysterious merger in American politics of economic interest and ideas. More specifically, the power of economic interest to shape choices and outcomes combines, for Americans, with a powerful set of ideas and values—a deeply entrenched national political myth. And it is the combination of interest and myth that ultimately shapes American issues—that translates problems rooted in economic differences into surrogate issues and avoids looking at what is really wrong.

My purpose here is to show how this central myth works in our politics, how political myth and economic interest together define the issues we act on, and most important, how they exclude from our attention the issues we should act on—both domestically and in the world.

Myth is an ephemeral concept with different meanings in different usages. Even political, as opposed to literary, myth is less than a precise term. It can refer to ways of understanding particular events or people or epochs. I am using political myth in its broad sense as a general system of belief—a system of values and attitudes that define the general political norms of a nation, its fundamental goals, national conceptions of what is right, and also expectations as to what is achievable.[3]

As a collection of commonly held political values, a broad national myth resembles political theory or ideology, but it is unlike both in that the people of a nation hold mythic tenets in an unexamined way as assumptions, rather than analytically as consciously accepted principles. Mythic beliefs pass from one generation to the next as a given, so obvious and persuasive that it is rarely questioned or even identified as merely one system of values among other possible choices.

The significance of political myth is that it shapes, quietly and only half consciously, the way the people of a society interpret and evaluate their common experience, both past and ongoing events. It provides common ground for evaluating threats to the social norms and expectations the myth itself defines. And it supplies also, if the hold of the myth is broad enough, the political consensus necessary to take action in response to such threats, internal and external.

As important and powerful as it is, however, political myth is not a complete motivational system. It does not by itself determine what political decision makers think and do on specific matters. It does not preclude the operation of individual conscience or the corruption of it, the play of reason or political pressure, the intrusion of accident or luck or wisdom or foolishness in the shaping of particular decisions. Rather, the force of beliefs carried in a national political myth is to determine— usually without explicit discussion or even conscious recognition of the process by policy makers—what matters will appear on the national political agenda in the first place. It serves as a screen, allowing some problems through to receive public attention and excluding others.

The significance of American political myth lies precisely in what it excludes, what it effectively screens out of political vision. Specifically, American political myth denies the existence of economic conflict deep enough to threaten the American promise of individual liberty and equal opportunity. This is not to say that the myth denies the existence of all barriers to the achievement of liberty and equality, but it locates those barriers elsewhere than in serious economic differences. Therefore, national public policy does not directly address the problems that stem from such differences.

What, then, is the substance of the American myth? What are the beliefs that deflect the attention of Americans from the implications of inevitable conflict among them?

At the core of the myth is the conviction that human relations are, by their nature, harmonious, that *serious* conflict in human societies is unnatural and unnecessary. Or to put it another way, differences in interest among different groups in the nation or among nations, while inevitable, are essentially superficial. According to the myth, there exists, beneath such contention, a beneficent natural order within which all interests are complementary. The principles of this order supply the means of resolving the conflicts in interest that necessarily occur. And—most important—the principles of natural order, if properly understood and followed, resolve conflict *without loss to any legitimate interest.*

It is this core belief in an available natural order that supplies for Americans explanations for conflict that does not get resolved fairly, for unfair losses borne by some groups, for serious derogations from the goals of liberty and equality, as well as for conflict that results in violence. When such trouble occurs, when serious conflict among economic interests or races or other groups leaves some in a state of inequity, Americans do not conclude that the differences involved may actually be too great to be resolved without serious loss to anyone. Rather, following the myth, we assume that something has gone wrong, that somewhere in the system there is an abuse of power, deliberate or inadvertent, which is wrongfully distorting natural social harmony. And we further assume that the wrong can be put right.

The active principle of the myth, therefore, is that injustice is abnormal and that justice is always achievable. A people determined to achieve social peace, social fairness, can always do so by locating and removing the abnormal force, the abuse of power that is producing unfair benefit to some groups, unfair loss to others. Thus, shaped by mythic principles, the national political agenda can include searches for wrongdoing or more complicated forms of abnormality, but it cannot include examination of deep-rooted economic differences. There is no need for such examination when it is the removal of abnormality that releases or liberates the natural order of things and allows all groups to work out fair exchanges.

I call this complicated system of belief the myth of deliverance from evil.

The roots of the American belief in deliverance are long and old, going back to the founding of the nation and before. In an incomplete form, the myth arrived in America with the first permanent settlers, the Puritans, who sought a literal deliverance from the social corruptions of the Old World by leaving it for a new promised land, a new Jerusalem. In an unformed, unspoiled virgin land, they believed, free people could live by the just order that was to be found in the will of God. John Winthrop, preaching to his people on the *Arbella* as it sailed toward America in 1630, described the Puritan venture in terms of Matthew's version of the Sermon on the Mount. The new settlers would be, like the early Christians, "as a City on a Hill," Winthrop said, teaching by their example how human beings could build harmonious communities by following God's law.

In the Puritan settlements, the task of defining God's law for earthly societies was given over to the clergy—those best able by training and inspiration to comprehend divine will. In the eighteenth century, however, the theocratic approach to social harmony gave way to a secular vision of order, the Enlightenment vision of a natural order that inspired and guided the nation's founders.

Enlightenment thinkers, like the Puritans, believed firmly in God-given principles of order for human communities—principles which, if followed, would reward all parties to the social contract. And the eighteenth-century philosopher-politicians shared, too, the optimism of the early settlers about the possibility of establishing that order in the open and innocent New World. They, too, saw the tyrannies and oppression and wars of Europe, not as the inevitable lot of human beings on earth, but as the terrible consequence of power misused. European monarchies and aristocracies captured control of a nation's wealth and used it for their own good instead of the good of all. But a society free of these power structures would be free to organize itself according to principles that allowed its people to live in peace with one another.

Most Americans of the eighteenth century, however, saw these principles not so much as emanations of God's will, remote and mysterious, but rather as laws inherent in human nature and the nature of human relations. And as they were embodied in the nature of things on earth, they did not require interpretation by divines. On the contrary, as Thomas Jefferson said in the Declaration of Independence, the laws and rights given to human beings by their Creator were "self-evident." They were discernible to anyone with the capacity to reason. This was why monarchies and theocracies were unnecessary for human government. The people themselves could govern themselves through their own capacities.

Jefferson's confidence in the accessibility of nature's laws to all reasoning people remained strong well past the heady moment of 1776. One of his projects in later life was an attempt to distill through reason the precepts of ultimate moral truth as taught by Christ and recorded in the gospels of the New Testament. Christ's moral teaching, perfect in itself, had been confused, Jefferson thought, by the gospel writers. Therefore, he set himself the task of separating the pure truth of Christ from the misunderstandings of the evangelists by literally cutting out the genuine messages as they appear in the four gospels and pasting them, according to their true logic, in a book of blank pages. The job was not difficult, Jefferson said in a letter to John Adams, because the truth standing out amid the surrounding confusions was as obvious as "diamonds in a dunghill."[4]

It is in its Enlightenment form, in the range of assumptions Jefferson enunciated, that the belief in natural principles of social harmony has been embodied in a broader myth and has lived on in American history. Seen through the myth, the dunghill of history is replete with oppression caused by self-interested uses of power. The diamonds of natural truth, natural law, are ever-present, enduring, and clear to those who would look for them.

The New World, like Jefferson's blankbook, is a place that is unspoiled, open to truth, a place where deliverance from wrongful power is always possible. And deliverance is mainly a task of liberation, of freeing natural patterns of social and economic exchange from any conglomerations of power unfairly controlling them.

This is a simple-sounding commentary—that Americans seek to relieve social injustice by removing and controlling abnormal uses of power—but its implications are profoundly important. It means that the constant focus of American politics is on the wrongdoer and on the removal of wrongdoing as the primary cure for social suffering. It means that we practice—and have from the nation's beginning—a politics of deliverance from evil as the means of achieving liberty and equality. The national theme of deliverance in specific political form begins, again, with the Declaration of Independence. Having declared the enjoyment of certain natural rights as the ground for the order that *should* prevail in America, Jefferson identified numerous abuses of that order by the British king as the cause of American suffering. The cure was to remove the authority of the king.

The themes of power abuse and deliverance from abuse continue throughout the great conflicts of American history. The Civil War erupted out of the different needs, different interests, and different levels of power between the commercial North and the agrarian South. The South produced foods and cotton with slave labor and had relatively little capacity for expansion of population or of wealth. The North, with growing centers of commerce and manufacturing, had great capacity for growth, both in population and in capital, and its voting power and market power threatened eventual domination over the agrarian regions. Northern political power meant northern control over rules governing numerous matters crucial to the South—tariffs, slavery, currency, credit. But neither side perceived the differences between them as deeply serious conflicts in interest. Both saw the widening scope of trouble as caused by abnormal and unnecessary abuses of power by groups in the other region.

From the vantage point of the North, the quarrels between the regions could be settled sensibly and fairly if it were not for the disruptions caused by the slave-power conspiracy, that small minority of wealthy landowners who stood to gain—unfairly— from the status quo. To Southerners it seemed that the trouble was caused by a small group of capitalist power holders in the North seeking to use an increasingly powerful national government to consolidate their unfair hold over *all* of the nation's people. The southern states seceded to escape this abuse and the North fought to defeat the slave power, but the underlying conflict between agrarian and industrial interests dividing the two regions remained unaddressed—and unresolved by the South's defeat.

In the twentieth century, social inequities have been ascribed in different times and by different interests to power abuse by monopolists, grafters, munitions makers, big business, communists, labor unions, welfare cheats, and reformers stifling business with governmental regulations. But, in terms of the myth, once the abuse is brought under control, the groups that were oppressed by it will be free to work out decent and beneficial solutions to their problems. In short, evil in the form of conflict that produces hardship, inequality, or oppression for some groups is not inevitable; it can be excised by preventing or controlling the abuse of power.

The job of government prescribed by the myth is to keep the abuse of power under control. This means rooting out the cause of trouble in times of great conflict, but it also means organizing the society by the rules that will keep the most likely sources of power abuse under ongoing control. It is the right ground rules, rules protecting fair dealing, that will allow a natural just order to operate. Right rules will release the natural principles that allow all social exchange—economic exchange most significantly —to take place on terms that are positive for all parties. But designing the right rules means in turn placing authority to make rules in the right hands, in people and institutions least likely to abuse power and best able to discern and control abuse.

This conception, too, goes back to the nation's founding. In spite of their ebullient optimism, the writers of the Constitution and the early national leaders were not utopians. They were realists in their view of human nature and saw it combining tendencies toward good and evil. Therefore, they did not assume that a new government in a new land, however respectful of self-evident truths and rights, would automatically deliver a whole people into a state of unending peace. They firmly believed that while human nature included the reason and virtue that would make deliverance possible, it also included the selfishness and limits of mind that would make it difficult. Thus they sought to contain weakness and liberate strength and to do so through a careful dispersal and control of power—public and private. They were not attempting to eradicate the evil of power abuse, but to deliver the society from the consequences of that evil by placing controls on its expected manifestations.

What the founders expected, out of their experience with English kings and American states, was trouble of two kinds. One was the strong tendency of the states to retain power for self-interested purposes without regard for the general needs of people in all the states. But the other, exemplified by the British kings, was the danger of excessive power in the head of a national government. Thus the Constitution makers designed a system in which a central government would have authority over matters of common concern to all the states—interstate commerce, currency, foreign policy—but would also be subject to strict controls.

First, the federal government could make rules *only* for those matters specifically designated in the Constitution as its responsibility, a scheme which left the main business of the society to private authority. Then in carrying out its designated functions, the government was to be subject to exquisitely careful divisions of power between federal and state levels and, for the federal government, among its three branches.

Again, the assumption behind the new order was that, with the primary threat of power abuse under control, the welter of competing interests in the society could work out their differences freely and equitably—whether through private bargaining or government action—according to the natural logic of human affairs.

James Madison made this argument explicit in his *Federalist* paper no. 10, part of the series he and Alexander Hamilton wrote seeking support for ratification of the Constitution. The thrust of the *Federalist* papers was to counter opposition from those who thought that the Constitutional Convention had produced a governmental design with too much power at the national level. The promoters of greater decentralization charged that a strong national government threatened to re-create the hierarchies and coercions Americans had rejected together with the authority of the British king. Madison argued on the contrary that an energetic national life, economic and political, would bolster openness and freedom and solid social peace.

American society, like all others, Madison stated, operated mainly through faction, through groups "unified and actuated by some common impulse of passion, or of interest, adverse to the rights of other citizens, or to the permanent and aggregate interests of the community." The function of government was to contain the antisocial tendencies of faction but not, for Madison, through repression of factional competition. Rather, he insisted, the best way to deal with the chronic conflict between self-interest and the common good was to multiply factions so that no single self-serving, power-seeking group could dominate the rest.

Dominance by a particularly powerful faction could occur fairly easily at the local or even state level, but would be much more difficult to achieve in the national arena. There, interests that could not win advantage through domination would have to seek it through bargaining and compromise. This would be true in the marketplace, but also, Madison thought, in the national legislature. Congressmen and senators would all seek to promote the varying interests of their particular regions, but if none could dominate, then all would have bargaining power. It was a system for allocating authority—public and private—under which no group would gain all; all would gain something.

Madison's argument, although addressed to a specific purpose in his own time, has remained the basic explanation and justification for the American governing system down to our own time. Not at all coincidentally, it is also a classic formulation of the myth of deliverance. That is, *Federalist* paper no. 10 was influential at the nation's beginning and remains influential now because it captures and codifies core beliefs Americans have held through the nation's history.

At the center of Madison's scheme is the mythic belief that the right rules will contain the chronic tendency in human affairs toward the abuse of power. And the key to assuring the right rules is to put decision-making authority in such a place and under such controls that no group can use public or private power to promote its own advantage at the expense of others. Then, with the major sources of power under proper control, the ordinary and necessary transactions of a society will work themselves out through their own natural logic to the benefit of all concerned. The result promised by the myth is deliverance to conditions of maximum freedom, openness of opportunity, and prosperity that inevitably follow from self-interested effort.

Most important, however, is the promise of the myth that the right rules will produce deliverance without cost. With deliverance assured through such rules, there is no need for the government to place limits or costs on some groups in their economic transactions in order to protect the freedom of others. The natural logic of mutual benefit will prevail with all groups able to bargain freely and without undue loss if the field of exchange is not blocked by power abuse.

But in spite of the elegance of Madison's argument, and the enduring appeal of the belief in deliverance, a system of multiple interests balancing each other can work only if, in fact, the governing rules effectively ensure that strong interests do not dominate and oppress others. In fact, such conditions of balance have never prevailed, and—given the depth of difference among the interests—could not. Even as Madison wrote, agrarian interests had begun to feel threatened by the growing commercial power of cities and towns and the financial power of banks. It was from primarily agrarian regions that opposition came to the Constitution Madison was defending—opposition from those who feared that a strong national government would respond mainly to the needs of commerce, not farming. By 1860, the clash of those interests had produced the agrarian secession that was ended only by war.

Within the industrial structure prevailing in the twentieth

century, the sharpness of conflict among the interests making up the system has only increased. In the first place, the increased wealth that is the product of industrialism has created levels of power within the society beyond anything Madison could have imagined. And within such a field of power, interests holding an advantageous position—capital managers generally—can extend broad control and inflict great disadvantage on less powerful groups, not only within regions but throughout the nation. But if deliverance has never been achieved, if serious inequalities in opportunity persist, the myth of deliverance nevertheless prevails. We continue to interpret our experience in mythic terms and to believe that the right dispersal of authority will produce just results.

The consequence of this belief, as a practical matter, has been to turn American politics into a perpetual quest for the demon cause that is blocking the operation of natural just exchanges among all interests. And we search simultaneously for the right rules that will keep power abusers under control. More specifically, our attention remains perpetually fixed on the issue of rule-making authority—who should hold authority to make what kinds of decisions under what controls and with what justification.

And here is the crux of the matter. In no era has the common quest of Americans for a rule-making system of deliverance produced common answers as to what the system should be. Rather, the political contestants in all major battles have advanced differing systems for dispersing authority depending on their differing interests, each group arguing for the placement of power in a decision-making body controllable by or answerable to itself. That is, each major economic interest—in the twentieth century, capital managers, wage earners, and those engaged in agrarian and other locally based enterprises—has a different demonology. Each locates the cause of serious trouble in a different place. And to control the demon threat it identifies, each interest seeks to empower decision makers most likely to share its demonology.

Each contestant, however, while battling for a particular system of authority that would advance its own interest, sees its

cause through the conflict-denying myth as the system best designed to achieve deliverance for the whole society and argues for
it in these terms. This stance is not hypocritical, or not necessarily
so. Rather, it stems from deep conviction. The point is that the
belief in deliverance is genuine. At the same time, the press of
interest is inescapable. The mingling of mythic belief and economic interest in arguments over systems of authority is the
genuine, if confusing, result.

This, then, is the way the myth of deliverance, in generation
after generation, displaces arguments over substantive conflicts in
economic or class interest and sets up instead arguments over the
surrogate issue of authority. In the twentieth century, all three
major interests, instead of arguing about the power exerted
throughout the whole society by those who control the largest
conglomerates of capital, argue about the narrower question of
power *abuse*. Instead of confronting their differences over the
disparities of power that work chronic harm on weaker groups,
instead of asking who is bearing the costs of chronic conflict and
who ought to bear these costs, all three groups argue over which
part of the government, which level, which branch is best able
to root out abuse and prevent its recurrence.

Americans, therefore, are dealing with the immense pressures
exerted by an industrial economy on the furtherance of the
American promise, but are fixed in this effort—seriously con-
strained—by a politics of deliverance. The solutions we are able
to propose as each set of problems arises are limited to three. And
they are always the same three because they consist of the rule-
making solutions that are the constant responses of the three
major interests to problems they perceive as evidences of power
abuse. None of the solutions—which the later chapters explicate
in detail—is as wide as the actual problems. None, even if
adopted intact, could provide more than partial answers.

But the most devastating effect of the myth on American
politics is that it precludes real bargaining, real compromise of
deep differences, because the myth prevents us from seeing how
deep our differences are. Although we pride ourselves on our
genius for pragmatic compromise, the level at which compromise
takes place is superficial and the results can produce only superfi-

cial or temporary benefits. In the long run, by denying the seriousness of differences in the society, the myth solidifies those differences and polarizes the groups bearing them.

That is, conflicts occur—between managers and workers, big and small business, industry and agriculture, labor and agriculture —but as the political process does not clarify or address the deep issues at stake, neither can it control or temper the outcome, or impose controls on it protective of fundamental goals and values. Rather, the results of conflict among economic interests are determined by the comparative strength of those interests. The strong protect themselves. The weak suffer losses in income, security, liberty, and equality.

To a degree, the harshness of this inexorable logic has been tempered throughout the industrial century by an ever-expanding economy. If the strong have held on to their percentage of the pie, the size of the pie has increased, benefiting the weak as well. But the rate of expansion in the advanced industrial economies has slowed markedly. Economic growth no longer provides a comfortable margin for political error or blindness. In these conditions, lack of deliberate protections for freedom and equality necessarily results in the diminution of those goals. Superficial solutions are increasingly ineffective and their inadequacy is the cause of the confusion, the deepening unease of Americans in the last few decades.

To compound the difficulty, the same mentality—the same impress of the myth on political choice—applies to foreign affairs as well and with the same results: incoherent policies. As in the domestic sphere, the myth prevents us from assessing the full depth and complication of the conflicts that cause trouble internationally.

To begin with, the age-old sources of war among peoples are still terribly active—racial, ethnic, and religious differences, factional and individual drives for power, and national, imperial, and messianic impulses to conquer. But added to them all, making each more dangerous, is the new and main source of animosity and violence among nations in the twentieth century—the spread throughout the world, as at home, of industrial systems of production. Out of the new stresses and needs produced within nations by industrialism—and with the new wealth and power produced by it—grounds for conflict among nations multiply.

At the base of the problem is the fact that the logic of industrialism is international, not national. Its efficient operation requires the constant movement of resources, labor, products, and capital across national boundaries. But this movement of wealth in one form or another is threatening to national economies in a number of ways. Governments of nations with a large and strong industrial base must be concerned with keeping markets elsewhere open to their own corporations. They must protect against the possibility that other strong nations may attempt to preempt or close off important markets. At the same time, internal stresses require governments to adopt policies at home that limit imports or exclude foreign labor or capital in order to protect home interests from international market pressures. Thus perpetual competition and perpetual grounds for conflict prevail among the economically strong.

Another set of pressures afflicts smaller or less developed countries. They require capital from developed countries in order to industrialize. But they must also deal with internal pressures to protect against the massive, indiscriminate effects of outside capital on their labor force, on small local enterprise, on established power holders, and on agrarian-based social and cultural patterns. The result is chronic conflict between highly developed and less developed nations.

The point is, the needs of all nations, large and small, conflict when governments deal as they must with the pressures of industrialism. These conflicts are unavoidable and the stakes are often high. Then to complicate matters, the wealth produced by industrialism has given all nations the means to build or buy huge military arsenals. The two together, the tangled lines of opposed interest, plus vastly heightened military capacities, are the main generators of the century's many wars—the world wars, the local wars.

But the world, seen from the United States through the prism of the myth of deliverance, has a different appearance. According to the myth, conflict among nations is not normal or inevitable. It is not the result of desperately serious differences in interest.

Rather conflict is caused by abnormal or evil abuses of power—variously ascribed, depending on the viewer, to fascists, communists, imperialists, nationalist politicians, or multinational corporations. And as with domestic politics, the focus of policy is on removing and controlling abuse, with the consequence that policy cannot address explicitly the deeper levels of conflict involved.

In a further parallel to domestic policy, the American tradition in foreign affairs is to try to control power abuse internationally—in an ongoing, systematic way, that is—by constructing the right kind of international order. This means an order in which the authority to use power, and thus to control power abuse, is properly organized. But, again, in this sphere, Americans do not agree on the proper placement of rule-making power. Instead, the major interests, the major actors in American politics, advocate policies abroad that are projections of the procedural solutions they advance at home. Thus, as the succeeding chapters describe in detail, we have three perpetual approaches to foreign problems—a managerial policy, a wage earner policy, and a localist policy—and all are based on the premise of deliverance through right rules, none addressing the full depth of international issues. The policy we follow shifts around among the three, depending on which interest dominates the national government at a particular time.

This is a gloomy picture—a great nation expending its energies on a futile quest for deliverance, at home and abroad, and apparently locked into its quest by an unchanging political myth. There are, however, signs of change. The slowing of economic growth, the greater competition for resources internationally, the danger to the planet from industrial wastes, the danger to the species from nuclear weapons, are problems increasingly apparent to everyone. They are problems forcing us to examine the consequences of our choices and the consequences of not making choices. If new directions for policy have not yet emerged, there is at least a growing call for new directions.

Still, the myth of deliverance, which enters our thinking in ways we do not recognize, gets in the way. An important step toward moving beyond a politics of deliverance is to be able to recognize the myth and to separate it out from the actual forces at play in the society—the conflict among interests that the myth denies. The point of the chapters that follow is to render our invisible politics visible, in order to clarify our actual choices and their costs.

II

Localists, Functionalists, Majoritarians

To see the myth of deliverance in operation, to see the limits it imposes on overall political choice, it is necessary to recognize its three distinct patterns, the three different forms it takes as it combines with the interests of managers, wage earners, and those in locally fixed enterprise. And these patterns are hard to see, given the fact that the major interests, while holding distinctive political outlooks, have no clearly demarcated political identity.

The political actors we are used to seeing are Democrats and Republicans, or sometimes liberals and conservatives, or ethnic groups, or highly specialized interests such as the American Medical Association or the National Rifle Association. But beneath this variegated surface, the most important initiatives and responses in American politics *are* rooted in the respective belief systems, the value systems, of the three major economic constituencies. Each group shares the mythic belief in a natural order that should prevail in the society. But each holds a different political position because it maintains different principles, based in its interest, concerning the achievement of that order.

Specifically, each identifies differently: (1) the source of order in the society, the system that, if not suppressed, would produce fairness; (2) the force or evil that prevents the system or order from operating; (3) the best means of controlling that evil or disruptive force—in each case, a matter of placing authority to make rules for the society in trustworthy hands; and (4) the general policies that the rule makers should follow to keep the evil under control.

The problem, of course, is to define coherent systems of belief in political groups that have no tangible form. What is the evidence that such groups, such belief systems, exist at all, let alone as fundamental touchstones of American politics? My evidence consists of the words of political leaders who represent constituencies based in the major economic interests, and the correspondence of these words with the political action backed by each group. Leaders, in appealing to their constituencies or justifying to others the positions of their groups, necessarily articulate the group's key convictions, and do so repeatedly. It is from the repetition of the same words, the same principles, by influential leaders in different generations, and from political actions consistent with their principles, that the political beliefs and positions of each group become clearly identifiable.

The story begins in this chapter with the words of turn-of-the-century leaders grappling with the new forces of industrialism and formulating responses to them for the first time responses that will, however, in their basic principles, mark the position of each group on major issues throughout the century.

To aid in characterizing and discussing the three major interests and their systems of thought, I have given each group a name. In each case, the name reflects the type of rule-making authority the particular group consistently seeks, the rule makers it considers the most trustworthy holders of power. Thus the interest made up of agrarian and other locally based enterprise, I refer to as "localist" because it seeks to place authority at the grass roots, in common, ordinary people making decisions about their daily business privately in their local communities. For the wage earner interest, I use the term "majoritarian" because it is the conviction of this group that the proper locus of authority is the great majority of the country's people, counted not locally but nationwide. The managers of capital I call "functionalists" because they would vest authority in functional experts, people trained and experienced in carrying out important social functions, from running a steel company to running an army.

The localist interest is disparate in that it includes a variety of occupations and people with great variations in wealth. Farming —including farmers with much or little land and farm workers —has always been a central component, but the interest includes also small mining operations, small-town retailers, lawyers, and other purveyors of services in agrarian areas, as well as enterprise not related to farming but still, in some important way, locally fixed.

The political interest that rural and locally fixed enterprises have in common is the need to protect the well-being of whatever systems or conditions contribute to local order and prosperity against threatening conditions in the outside world. Such interests suffer a double bind in relation to the larger industrial economy; they cannot affect to any great degree the prices, demands, conditions, or tastes of the markets they deal with, but they are themselves subject to the powerful forces exerted by these markets.

This general configuration of interest marks an age-old tension between country and city economies, but in the late nineteenth century, under the pressure of rapid industrial expansion, American localists moved their attitudes and grievances into the political arena in sharpened form. The Granger movement, the Greenback Party, the Farmers' Alliance, and finally, in 1892, the People's Party sprang up in rural areas as carriers of agrarian demands. The special aim of the Farmers' Alliance and its political arm, the People's Party, was to unite the rural interests of the West, Southwest, and South in a cross-regional drive for the general protection of agrarian interests. They aimed both for cooperative self-help—the establishment of cooperatives for banking, buying, and selling—and for government controls reducing the power of big business in relation to farming and other local enterprise. They sought especially regulation of railroad rates, anti-monopoly laws, and various mechanisms for loosening credit and increasing the supply of currency.

Agrarian cooperation as a concerted political movement failed, inevitably and fairly quickly, in the face of the very force that produced the movement in the first place—the intensity of highly diverse local interests. The most intransigent was the interest of the old Confederate states in maintaining, on terms they defined themselves, the economic and social relations of blacks and whites. Further, in the West as well as the South, the established power of the traditional parties, in which agrarian interests already had a recognized if not wholly comfortable place, promised more certain, immediate protection than any new organization could.

In 1896, the People's Party succumbed to this reality and disintegrated as a separate political force when it nominated as its presidential candidate the already chosen Democratic nominee, William Jennings Bryan. From this point on, the localist interest is not discernible politically through its own party organization. With Bryan's defeat by William McKinley, the various elements of the localist coalition moved back into the traditional parties. The West and Southwest became more firmly Republican while the South retained its deeply entrenched Democratic identity, and, thus divided, the movement lost some of its clarity of purpose. But its disappearance was more apparent than real.

Cloaked by Democratic and Republican party labels, the positions formulated by the People's Party and other groups— the first clear localist response to the pressures of industrialism— lived on. That is, a coherent politics of localism has persisted, pressed by Democrats and Republicans alike from states with primarily agrarian economies. This group of states has remained essentially the same—in its agrarian character *and* politics—from the turn of the century to the present. It comprises: in the South, Alabama, Arkansas, Florida, Georgia, Louisiana, Mississippi, North Carolina, South Carolina, and Virginia; in the West, Colorado, Idaho, Montana, North Dakota, South Dakota, Utah, Wyoming, and Nevada; and in the Southwest, Arizona, New Mexico, Texas, and Oklahoma. There are strong localist traditions also in the agrarian regions of the Midwest, but the semi-agrarian, semi-industrial character of the midwestern states tugs their political representatives in different directions. Thus voting patterns in the Midwest are not so distinctly localist as those from states in the agrarian heartland.

The most powerful articulator of the localist political stance in its turn-of-the-century formulation was, without question, the defeated People's Party/Democratic Party candidate William Jennings Bryan. In spite of his loss in 1896—when he won every solidly agrarian state, except North Dakota, and lost nearly all the others—his popularity in the West and South remained high. It propelled him into two more presidential campaigns—in 1900 and 1908—and into Woodrow Wilson's Cabinet as Secretary of State from 1913 to 1915. He propagated his views in a weekly newspaper, *The Commoner,* which he published from 1901 to 1922, and he spoke indefatigably throughout the country in support of his causes, virtually until the day he died in 1925.

A Nebraska lawyer and politician, and a wholehearted Christian fundamentalist, Bryan was popularly called the Great Commoner. His central political theme, delivered with boundless optimism, was the coming of peace in the nation and the world through the agency of the common man. In spite of his repeated defeats for the presidency by big-money Republicans—McKinley twice and William Howard Taft—he remained convinced that the era of aristocratic, elitist, monopolist control of societies everywhere was coming to an end, to be replaced by popular rule. Bryan saw the United States as the vanguard of a future when power would devolve in all countries to ordinary citizens who would use it responsibly out of their innate moral sense and common sense.

At the base of Bryan's position was the mythic conviction that no essential interest divided person from person, class from class, or even nation from nation. He was certain that, in spite of great differences in the specific interests of city workers, farmers and farm workers, big business and small business, great and small nations, there were no differences that could not be resolved harmoniously—and quite easily—through mutual goodwill.

The ground for social harmony in Bryan's thought was a universally shared morality that naturally motivates human be-

ings to fair behavior. That is, he saw human nature created by
God as a moral nature, producing natural inclinations that are
loving, generous, decent, sensible. Further, Bryan reasoned, as a
matter of common sense, there is more to be gained for all by
cooperation than by discord. Each person, he insisted, "finds his
greatest security in the intelligence and happiness of his fellows
—the welfare of each being the concern of all." In the good
society, therefore, each person would "exert himself to the ut-
most to improve conditions for all and to elevate the level upon
which all stand."[1]

It followed, then, that since harmony among members of a
society is humanly possible, endorsed by human nature, and
advantageous to all, achieving it is only a matter of will. People
divided by interest but united by goodwill can work out peaceful
relations devoid of exploitation, of unfair advantage and disadvantage, relations defined essentially by the freedom and equality
of all members of society.

Further, for Bryan, there was nothing in the worldly environment that would necessarily block natural human inclinations
to construct peaceful societies. On the contrary, it was God's
beneficent design that human beings should use the physical
resources of nature creatively to produce what they needed for
life and comfort, and that human workers should receive from
such efforts a return measured by the quality of their work. The
"law of rewards given us by the Creator," Bryan said, is: "Go,
work, and your reward shall be proportionate to your diligence,
intelligence, and perseverance." Thus human beings, utilizing the
resources nature had provided—their own talents and energies
and the materials in their physical environment—should be able
to work together in conditions of mutual profit, under a general
law of natural justice: the better or harder the work, the greater
the reward.

The glaring fact that this was not so for Americans in the
early twentieth century, that for most workers on farms or in
factories twelve- or sixteen-hour days of hard labor produced a
return of bare subsistence while a new and growing capitalist class
enjoyed incredible wealth, Bryan insisted, was unnatural, and
therefore temporary or alterable. This reversal of God's intent "is

due to man-made privileges and immunities—to law-made
inequalities in distribution," he said, and "the most imperative
duty resting upon the citizen is to bring the government as nearly
as possible into harmony with Divine Law."[2] That is, "the man-
made privileges and immunities" and especially "the man-made
giant which we call corporation" must be remade to rid the
system of the unnaturally accumulated power, corporate monopoly primarily, that allowed the heads of monopolized business to
charge unfair prices, pay unfair wages, in general to distribute
unfairly the wealth cooperatively produced by all those involved
in the enterprise.[3]

If not all localists saw the evil of monopoly in Bryan's terms
as a defiance of divine law, they did see it as an evil attributable
to something unnatural and wrong. This was, in fact, the way
they saw all large institutions, private and public. The localist
vision of a healthy society was one in which ordinary people
provide for themselves, as well as available resources allow,
through direct transactions in which everyone's position and
interest are clear. The natural form for economic exchange is the
relatively small local business unit responding directly to local
needs and to the natural laws of competition which keep business
transactions orderly and wages and prices fair. Other community
needs could be met by local social and political organization. In
such a society there would be no need for giant corporations or
for large institutions of any kind, such as government bureaucracies, distant banks, or church hierarchies, to organize the people's
affairs.

For localists, the primary consequence of organizing huge
institutions was to transfer to the people running them advantages
that the unorganized common people did not have. Large corporations, large institutions of any kind, were power systems, and
their organizers and directors must be suspect as power seekers,
wrongdoers, deliberately and willfully manipulating the ordinary citizenry on farms or in factories, small businesses, and banks
or in the offices of local government throughout the country.

The localist version, then, of the American mythic belief in
natural social harmony is distinguished by the assumption that
disharmony is caused by deliberate, wrongful power seeking

behind the façade of large, legitimate-seeming institutions, of which the most threatening at the turn of the century were monopolies and big business generally. That is, localists did not see their plight as the inevitable product of a differential in power between industrial and agrarian economies. Rather, they saw stolen power, stolen authority, as the cause of their suffering. Their enemy, their demon—which they saw plaguing the entire country, not just themselves—was bigness as such and its deliberate manipulation by wrongdoers.

The localist solution to the country's ills was to reform the misplacement of authority by breaking up bigness, breaking up monopoly with anti-trust laws, and, for those necessary monopolies like railroads and other utilities, regulating them if not nationalizing them. Some localists sought to control corporate size by an even more direct means proposed by Senator Gilbert Hitchcock, a Democrat from Nebraska. This was a graduated tax on corporations proportionate to their product which would, very simply, make big business unprofitable.

Another regulating mechanism favored by localists was publicity, or what later generations would call sunshine rules, designed to expose behind-the-scenes malefaction. Bryan, for example, championed the solution of labor-management disputes by referring such problems to investigating tribunals that could find all facts and claims on both sides and make them known to the public. He was sure that "the very existence of such a tribunal would tend to restore harmony between the two classes" because publicity would expose and thus discourage the deliberate wrongdoing he assumed always lay behind such conflict.[4]

By these various mechanisms, the usurpers of power, in localist belief, would be dispersed or controlled, and economic power would naturally devolve to the local level, where it could be exercised by individuals privately and monitored by the natural laws of the free market. For problems that defied such controls, the people themselves would find solutions through their own experience and sense of moral decency—as long as political authority remained firmly within their control at the local level.

Thus the localist agents of deliverance, the necessary holders of authority, are the common citizens, acting either on their own or through local authorities and locally elected representatives to Congress. Bryan said, in a 1907 *Commoner* article, "The heart of mankind is sound, the sense of justice universal. Trust it, appeal to it, but do not violate it. . . . I fear the plutocracy of wealth, I respect the plutocracy of learning, I thank God for the democracy of the heart."[5]

To the next group—the functionalists—"the plutocracy of wealth" presented different problems. The functionalists are a business interest but different from the business interest that had prevailed through the nineteenth century, the individual owners of the pre-industrial era and the individualist tycoons of early industrialism. Functionalists are a new breed, a new class of paid professionals who manage capital they do not themselves own.

They emerged as a group with common interests out of the organization of capital on a scale too large for individual management. Industrial corporations bought and sold in markets extending nationwide if not internationally. They used complicated technology, employed thousands of people, and the integration of such activity required teams of executives, lawyers, accountants, economists, researchers, and administrators. Later, the same would become true in the public sector as well. That is, government functions, still small at the turn of the century, would later develop wide and complicated scope and require the same kind of managerial teams as those running industrial corporations.

Capital managers, whether in the private or public sector, hold strong common interests. The well-being of managers depends on their ability to utilize the capital in their control to accomplish the complicated ends to which it is assigned. In the private sector, they must do so at a profit; public managers must work within budgetary constraints supplied by lawmakers. But both must be concerned with economic conditions and relations of the broadest scope as their success depends on the stability and predictability of transactions locally, nationally, even globally.

The essential interest of managers is to maintain smoothly flowing transactions over the widest possible sphere, which they try to accomplish, traditionally, by maintaining the widest possible range of control over the processes for which they are responsible. They mount constant resistance against claims to share in the control of capital by people or groups whose interests are not primarily the enhancement of capital productivity—most importantly, labor groups, farmers, and entrepreneurial interests and political factions or institutions representing such interests.

The belief in deliverance for the capital managers starts, as it does for localists, with the assumption that there are natural social processes capable of producing the conditions all Americans seek —order, prosperity, freedom, equality. And both groups believe that the key to a good and just society is to follow rules that will control whatever evils are operating to disrupt or suppress those natural processes. But capital managers and localists have a wholly different sense of what those evils are and therefore what rules need to be in place to suppress them.

For localists, the laws capable of producing harmony are the natural inclinations of unspoiled, uncorrupted human beings to deal sensibly and honestly in carrying out the ordinary transactions of ordinary business and community life. Their enemies are forces that flourish in the artifice and sophistication of the city —corporate intricacies arranged by the lawyer servants of business, leagues of power built by adroit politicians and their tamed theoreticians bought from the academic and professional worlds. The social vision of the capital managers is almost completely the reverse, and not surprisingly, as they are themselves the powerful sophisticates, the dealers in big business, high finance, and high politics so mistrusted by the localists.

For capital managers, the human heart is not the repository of simple, natural laws providing directions for human harmony; quite the contrary, it is full of turbulent emotion, prejudice, impulses to self-gratification and violence. To follow the heart is to find chaos.

What managers see as the natural sources of order and fairness in human affairs are natural principles implicit in the functions —including business functions—of human societies generally. These functions vary with varying levels of technology, but in the managerial view, all human enterprise, from growing food to manufacturing cars, has an inherent logic that dictates the most efficient way to accomplish it. And that logic, in itself, supplies terms of fairness in the dealings among all groups involved in an enterprise. That is, if all groups involved, for example, in the manufacture of cars understand, respect, and follow the rules that dictate the most efficient methods of production, then all—owners, managers, workers—will derive the maximum possible benefit from the process, as will the purchasers. This is true, in functionalist belief, because the interests of all the groups are by nature complementary and the rules of functional efficiency—the managerial rules of deliverance—disclose the terms that simultaneously serve the interests of all.

The key steps to deliverance, then, are: first, to discern the logical patterns producing efficiency in each general social function, a process depending on reason and expert knowledge, not the heart's dictates or common sense; and second, to allow the functional imperatives to operate without disruption by groups using some sort of power leverage to extract special benefit for themselves at the expense of the overall beneficial process.

The identification of functionalist demons follows from these conditions for deliverance. Functionalist demons are groups or forces that interrupt functional logic. One such force is the mass or the mob, untutored, swayed by emotion, shortsighted, and selfish—dangerous in the United States insofar as it uses political power to gain its ends, or is used by political leaders to gain theirs. To put it another way, functionalists fear the demon politics in a democracy because it is a power system with no intrinsic order behind it—only the pressures of an emotional electorate.

But a second major force regarded as a demon threat by functionalists is disorder and unrestrained power within the business world itself. This threat is the use of economic power for short-term calculations of self-interest—essentially the old laissez-faire ethic—operating at the expense of the economic logic that would, if followed, produce long-term gain for all.

Economic power as an enemy to capital managers sounds paradoxical, as does their opposition to self-interest as the motive force behind economic exchange, but, in fact, the old rules of laissez-faire were not well suited to the managerial function in the new industrial era. The problem was that the old system based on unrestrained calculations of gain by each firm worked only if such transactions were kept fair by market laws of supply and demand—which was more or less the case in the pre-industrial era of small business. The massed capital of industrial corporations, however, could at times flout market laws and, without other restraints, could gouge, exploit, and maraud at will.

Functionalist managers, requiring order and predictability, could no longer accept old beliefs in the unqualified beneficence of the market or the omniscience of the invisible hand. Of course, they retained belief in the general principles of a free market economy, but they no longer maintained as an unquestioned class creed that natural guidelines to efficient production and just distribution would be identified through the blind forces of the market alone. More deliberate efforts were necessary to uncover the logic of functional efficiency and to clear the way for that logic to prevail as the basis for doing business throughout the nation.

But how? How could a fairly primitive system of blind competition be displaced nationwide by a sophisticated system of functional logic?

One answer produced by turn-of-the-century managers was the movement to convert business management from a pragmatic operation to a science. The high priest of scientific management in its early stages was Frederick Winslow Taylor, an engineer and businessman whose Winslow and Taylor forebears in Philadelphia provided a long heritage of entrepreneurial success as well as high-minded concern for reform. Taylor's *Principles of Scientific Management,* published in 1911, gained immediate notice among the engineers and professional managers coming into their own as business leaders in a fast-developing system of industrial bureaucracy.[6]

The key to Taylor's principles and the source of the excitement they provoked was his message that conflict in a capitalist order was not only unnecessary but also counterproductive. The essential capitalist conflict between management and labor was unnecessary, Taylor insisted, because the real interests of the two sides were actually complementary. Both stood to benefit from maximum levels of production, and an enterprise could best achieve such levels through careful cooperation rather than competition. What were needed were labor policies that matched aptitude to task, that provided decent, safe working conditions, incentives for good work, and generous returns to labor out of increased productivity.

What divided management and labor, Taylor thought, was a misunderstanding of their differences by both sides. He preached, therefore, a "revolution . . . in the mental attitude of the two parties." They had to be persuaded to "take their eyes off the division of the surplus as the all-important, and together turn their attention toward increasing the size of the surplus until this surplus becomes so large that it is unnecessary to quarrel over how it shall be divided."

In organizing his own business and in consulting with others, Taylor turned his attention to the most minute parts of the productive process—the weight of a shovel in relation to the size of the man using it, the system of records to measure the precise results of different methods of production. However, his overall vision was nothing less than revolutionary. What he sought and what scientific management could produce, Taylor told a congressional committee in 1911, was a complete change in industrial relations—"the substitution of peace for war; the substitution of hearty brotherly cooperation for contention and strife . . . both [sides] pulling hard in the same direction rather than pushing apart . . . replacing suspicious watchfulness with mutual confidence . . . becoming friends instead of enemies."[7]

To achieve this state of hearty cooperation, it was necessary only to find and follow the natural logic of the function being carried out by the particular enterprise, and this was a matter of scientific experimentation and definition. Taylor's "principles" were instructions for discovering, scientifically, the procedures for optimum productivity in any given enterprise. Other guides included Harrington Emerson's *Twelve Principles of Efficiency*[8] and the better-known time and motion studies of Frank and Lillian Gilbreth, which would reveal "the one best way" to organize any process.

But promising as the movement for scientific management

seemed to be, even its most ardent proponents among progressive managers did not regard the self-reform of business as sufficient to cure the economic and social ills of the day. They recognized that additional controls on powerful corporations were necessary to curb practices producing throughout the country unfair competition, unfair prices, and unfair wages. That is, they knew that some kind of governmental monitoring of the world of business was essential, but the question for functionalist managers was: what kind of monitoring and who would do it? More specifically, how could the abuse of power in business be monitored by government without the abuse of power by government becoming a problem?

Government, after all, takes its direction from elected officials, and elected officials must be responsive to the people who elect them. But the electorate, in the functionalist view, reacts to social problems viscerally, not knowledgeably, making political power a dangerous instrument to unloose on a business world in need of logical ordering.

The functionalist solution to this dilemma—a solution advanced by the Progressive reform movement, which was important at the turn of the century—was the invention of a *non-political* instrument of government, the independent regulatory agency. Regulatory agencies, such as the Interstate Commerce Commission, established in 1887, keep tabs on corporate behavior in various ways. They review records, hear complaints, issue regulations concerning rates, charges, and corporate practices, sit in judicial-like judgment on breaches of their regulations, and impose penalties on corporate regulation-breakers.

But, according to the design of the agencies, all of this regulation, judgment, and punishment is conducted on professional, not political, lines. To ensure independence from political pressure, appointments to the agencies are made, like judicial appointments, on the basis of professional standing and for terms exceeding those of the President or governor making them. Further, agency members can be removed only for cause, not for political reasons.

Most important, however, the regulators, in making judgments about reasonable and unreasonable corporate behavior, necessarily look to standards of functional efficiency as their guides. In examining railroad rates, for example, they would allow rates that would be fair *if* the railroad were operating according to reasonable standards of efficiency. The presumption —the mythic presumption—is that such a rate would necessarily provide a fair return to the railroad and, at the same time, be fair to railroad users.

Freed from politics, using reason to uncover the inherent logic of efficiency in particular industries, the regulatory commissions and agencies are, for the functionalists, less an arm of government than an arm of nature. They impose needed regulations on corporations, not through the dictates of political power, but through the rule of reason. Thus, both in business and in government, the functionalist answer to the problem of controlling the abuse of power is to trust in reason. The functionalist agent of deliverance in both spheres is the user of reason. Authority in business should be placed in the hands of scientific managers, and in government, in the hands of disinterested experts.

This position appears, eloquently articulated over decades of public service, in the words of the progressive Republican leader Charles Evans Hughes. Although best remembered now as Chief Justice of the Supreme Court in the 1930s, Hughes was an important shaper of functionalist principles and practice in other roles —as a reform governor of New York from 1907 to 1910, Republican presidential candidate running against Woodrow Wilson in 1916, and then Secretary of State under Presidents Harding and Coolidge in the 1920s. In fact, Hughes made the issue of the need to base public decision making on disinterested reason the focal point of his whole political career. His own entrance into politics dramatized, almost caricatured, this central concern.

For the first twenty years of his adult life, Hughes practiced law in New York City, where he gained a reputation for great skill, integrity, and hard work, and where he engaged in no political activities at all. It was a combination of these attributes that prompted a request in 1905 by state Republican leaders that he head a committee investigating corruption in the gas industry in New York, and especially corruption in dealings between the industry and state officials. Hughes accepted the position reluctantly, as a public duty, insisted on assurances that he would not be subject to political pressure, then set about the task before him with meticulous, conscientious concern for fact.

He collected masses of documents, digested and organized their contents, for the most part by himself, and then interrogated witnesses—according to contemporary accounts—with the inexorable logic of an adding machine. He did not engage in histrionics, did not badger witnesses or raise his voice. He simply pressed for factual answers, one after another, until the patterns of corruption connecting business and politics were completely clear and proven. He then submitted a report to the legislature recommending forms of regulation adequate to control the practices uncovered, and many of his proposals were enacted into law.

For this contribution to efficient, effective good government, Hughes became a hero in New York overnight. Republicans, tarred by scandal and desperate to win back the confidence of the voters, appealed to Hughes to run for governor in 1906, and the public, much taken with a political figure both honest and personally attractive, swept him into office only months after his first foray into public life.

In his inaugural speech, Hughes defined the primary qualification for public service as "the capacity for . . . close examination without heat or disqualifying prejudice" of the many-faceted problems dealt with by government.[9] At considerable political cost to himself and the programs he favored, he remained true to this principle as governor, doing constant battle with his own party leaders over patronage demands, insisting on professional, not political, qualifications in his appointees, even seeking to remove from office Republican officials he considered incompetent.

As the Republican presidential nominee in 1916, Hughes again affirmed his faith in professional experts as the people in the society most to be trusted with power. "It is an extraordinary notion that democracy can be faithfully served by inexpertness," he declared in his speech accepting the nomination. "Democracy needs exact knowledge, special skill, and thorough training in its servants." Indeed, he made trust in experts part of the definition of "Americanism" he set out in the first paragraph of the address.

Citing "expert knowledge and thorough organization as the indispensable conditions of security and progress," he described his patriotic vision served by these qualities as "America first and America efficient."[10]

A second necessary attribute of authority holders in the functionalist view was a moral one—adherence to a code of ethics, unwritten but well understood, that treated decision-making authority as a matter of highest trust. For Hughes this meant that government officials must be technically qualified, but must also be "men of single-minded devotion to the public interest, who make unselfish service to the state a point of knightly honor."[11] Of course, Hughes and his fellow progressive Republicans did not invent the concept that selfless public service is a citizen's duty. It is an old principle, going back at least to the beginning of the Republic, but it took a new twist in the thought of functionalists of the Progressive era in that they saw a capacity for selflessness as a quality particularly linked to professionalism, rather than a trait to be found generally dispersed in the society.

Their sensitivity to the forces of emotion, greed, predation, even violence, in human nature led functionalists generally to assume that the power of these elemental impulses could be curbed only by cultivation, the deliberate discipline of the patiently tutored will. Thus the capacity for selfless service was necessarily a capacity of the educated citizenry, but this made it also a condition of their authority throughout the society, in the private as well as the public realm. Hughes insisted that Americans would not be able to achieve the full promise of their system "until the meaning of trusteeship sinks deep into the American consciousness and its realization controls our activities both in business and in political affairs." Their role as trustees of economic power "must seize the conscience of the directors of corporations." They must come to recognize that modern business is not made up of individuals dealing with their own fortunes. Rather, it is "simply a gigantic series of sacred fiduciary obligations."[12]

A third qualification of decision makers, public and private, in functionalist thought, was an extension of the first two. Officials with training appropriate to their functions and guided by a sense of honor or trusteeship would properly use their authority only to advance professionally defined goals, only to serve the ultimate purpose of efficiency, never of particular interests.

Hughes as governor of New York attempted to carry out his function by placing all decisions in the lap of reason. He dealt with issues that came before him as the state's chief executive by gathering all available data, basing proposals on an analysis of data, and seeking support for them through reasoned argument alone—just as he had done as investigator of the gas industry. He refused, in the words of his secretary, Robert Fuller, to employ the usual methods by which governors tried to implement their programs, which was "practically to bribe and bully legislators into carrying out their wishes."

Hughes would not promise appointments in return for votes, or threaten to punish legislators who were not supporting his program by holding up their bills, nor did he remove from office friends of legislators who denied him support. Rather, in his legislative proposals as in his appointments, he tried to convert the medium of exchange in state government from power to merit, appealing, as his secretary said, "directly to the constituencies with his proposals and his reasons for supporting them."[13]

Going to the constituencies was the last step in the process of governing, the step of submission to the people as the final arbiters of policy in a democracy. For functionalists, however, the most important steps preceded this one, the steps in which experts sorted out the welter of evidence on an issue, made sense of it, and set out the best methods they could devise for dealing with it.

For Hughes, the model of the skilled, analytical, disinterested public servant was, not surprisingly, the socially responsible lawyer. Speaking to an audience of federal government lawyers in 1931, he described their function and their qualities in terms reminiscent of Old Testament hymns of praise. "[You] are the interpreters of the law, not in selfish interest but in the public interest," he began. "You are not the wards of politicians but the guardians of society." As administrators of the law, "you deal with its unavoidable complications; you seek to resolve its ambiguities; you subject the endless and sometimes burning controversies that come before you to cool and impartial analysis. You give no favors and you fear no antagonists; you unmask pretensions, expose fallacies, and frustrate evasions."[14]

This, then, is the functionalist agent of deliverance from irrationality, confusion, and greed in both private and public sectors—the rational, knowledgeable, honorable professional. In present-day electoral politics, as in Hughes's time, the representatives of functionalist belief, are, for the most part, Republicans from the industrial areas of the North, the Northeast, and the West Coast. That is, Republicans in these areas tend to represent the views of professionals, white-collar workers, suburbanites— often people who regard themselves as political independents rather than party members out of a distaste for partisanship and an attachment to objectivity, people who are part of the industrial sector but in managerial not wage-earning capacities.

For the third group, the majoritarians, the problem of deliverance begins with yet another set of premises and requires yet another solution. The majoritarian interest is made up of the workers of the nation—not only the blue-collar, lunch pail, labor union members the word "worker" often conjures up, but all non-professional employees of enterprises, private and public, that function in some way as part of the interdependent system of an industrial economy.

This definition excludes workers in the kinds of business that are localist in character—enterprises tied in important ways to local conditions which induce workers as well as owners to seek protections for their position through localist forms of politics. The workers making up the wage-earning interest are, by contrast, part of an economic system that operates nationally or internationally. As such, they are subject to economic forces so broad in scope as to affect the welfare of workers over very broad areas in similar ways—factors such as competing supplies of resources or labor, changes in technology, national energy or transportation patterns and costs, and openings or blockages in international trade.

Like the managers, workers must be concerned with the

stability and strength of national and international economies. But workers must also be concerned with controlling the broad economic forces that affect their welfare, or at least with protecting themselves as far as possible from the harmful effects of such forces. Beyond mutual self-protection, wage earners share a common interest in ensuring that as high a percentage as possible of the society's product is distributed to workers, either directly in wages or indirectly through social or community benefits.

There is some difficulty in drawing the exact bounds of the interest in that the outlook and behavior, for example, of white-collar wage earners and salaried managers often overlap in the bureaucracies of large corporations or government agencies. But the general distinction between the two lies in their ability, or lack of it, to make decisions about placement of capital and distribution of income. Managers have the authority to make such decisions as part of their normal range of work, and wage earners do not. Whatever control wage earners are able to exercise over the large economic forces affecting them, they must exert, therefore, through channels beyond their workplace and beyond their locality.

That is, wage earners are commonly affected—for good or ill—by economic forces generated within a giant corporate industrial system over which they have no direct control. However, like the managers but unlike the localists, they do not seek to dismantle the system to make it more controllable. Their interest lies in leaving the industrial system in place and even enhancing its growth, but also in subjecting it to some kind of restraint that will ensure fair terms in dealings between managers and workers.

Wage earners cannot accept the system of restraint proposed by functionalists—placing primary authority in experts—because experts are, in fact, part of the managerial interest. Negotiating matters vital to their welfare, wage earners cannot trust reason alone to overcome the pull of managerial interest and power. In common with the localists, industrial workers see the *fact* of power held by large corporations as the paramount element in the problem of fair dealing. They see greater power in the hands of one bargaining party as a situation necessarily producing unfair bargains.

For wage earners, then, the demon in the system, the evil preventing the fairness that would otherwise be possible for everyone, is an *imbalance* of power. As with the localists, their central concern is to right the balance, but, again, to do so without attacking corporate size as such.

In their search for a balance of power between labor and management—and this is an important point to see—American wage earners depart significantly from the dominant political focus of workers in other industrial nations. By the early years of the century, workers in England and Europe had clearly identified themselves as members of a class in the sense of a group with interests different from and antagonistic to those of other classes—most importantly, the capitalists. European workers do not see their interests and those of corporate managers as complementary; rather, they see them as unalterably at odds. One side cannot gain, in this view, without the other side losing. European working-class movements, therefore, seek political power as a means of imposing on the managers the losses that would ensure working-class gains.

American workers, on the other hand, seeing their situation through a myth of deliverance in which loss is *not* inevitable and interests *are* complementary, seek political power only to counteract the bargaining advantage of the managers. That is, American wage earners seek to curb the economic power of the managers with the countervailing power, in John Kenneth Galbraith's phrase, of the government. Wage earners do not control capital, but they do exercise political power through their votes and, comprising a majority of the electorate, they can elect officials to make rules advancing their interest. Government rules responsive to the needs of the majority can limit the power of corporations or enhance the power of wage earners, or both. But in either case, what majoritarians seek is a power balance between the two parties. It is this balance, in majoritarian belief, that ensures fair negotiations over terms of work and thus ensures the deliverance of workers from unfair wages and conditions—unfair constraints on liberty and equality.

Historically, the evolution of a majoritarian position in the terms just outlined was slower than the formation of localist and functionalist systems of thought and political programs. Wage earners were slower than farmers or managers to see the commonality of their interest and to translate it into political terms.

In part, this was due to the extraordinary disparateness of the wage-earning interest in the years when industrialism was becoming the predominant shaper of workers' lives. Much of the work force in the late nineteenth and early twentieth centuries consisted of newly arrived immigrants. Many did not speak English. Many were illiterate in any language. And among them were groups with inherited burdens of mutual suspicion—Catholics and Jews, Russians and Poles, Asians and whites, English and Irish. Further, the labor force was spread over wide areas from the ports of the Northeast and the West Coast to the rapidly growing cities of the Midwest. The conditions of work and specific problems of wage earners varied greatly in different regions.

Identifying common interests and goals among workers across this range of difference—cultural and geographic—called for unusually acute and persuasive leadership and leaders whose voices reached nationwide. The first efforts to establish such links came from the trade union movement at the turn of the century, but there were sharp differences within the movement at that time over labor's proper political goals. Socialist and communist unions sought outright nationalization of industries. Other groups favored extensive but non-socialist uses of government such as the passage of laws providing for minimum wages, maximum hours, retirement pensions, unemployment insurance, and workplace safety.

The largest single union—although still representing only a small percentage of workers—was the American Federation of Labor, led for decades by Samuel Gompers. A fervent believer in industrial growth and large-scale corporations to accommodate it, Gompers opposed the use of government to break up large business units through anti-trust laws. And he opposed also seeking direct governmental protections, such as minimum wages and social security, because he thought such programs were too likely to be influenced and watered down in the legislative process by business interests. For Gompers, the only sure protection for workers was that provided by unions through the process of collective bargaining—a process in which the power of organized capital was balanced by the power of organized labor. In his view, therefore, the primary role of government was to protect the process of collective bargaining, and this single issue was the center of his lifelong crusade.[15]

Thus divided among themselves, union leaders in the early years of the century were ineffective in defining for workers a common political ground, a broadly accepted approach by which workers could use the power of government to offset the power of industry. The first effective articulation of such a majoritarian position came from the world of politics itself and was supplied by an unlikely-seeming champion for the nation's workers—Woodrow Wilson.

Wilson had no personal connection to the labor movement or the plight of workers generally. He was, before entering politics, a professor of political science and later president of Princeton University. Through most of his life in academe, he retained a belief in the economic principles of laissez-faire and opposed collective bargaining by unions as violating market principles. In spite of his lack of association with labor, however, Wilson as a politician became a spokesman for what was essentially a wage earner interest. In fact, he became a definer of the interest and its necessary political stance. The explanation of this paradoxical position was his intellectual and moral concern with community and especially with national community.

At the center of his work as a scholar was a vision of the good society as a well-functioning whole—one in which individual citizens recognize a moral responsibility toward the larger community and in which public policy is formulated on the basis of general needs, a balanced assessment of the general good. He expressed this ideal in an early book called *Cabinet Government in the United States.* And in his *Congressional Government,* he demonstrated that the then prevailing dominance of national policy by Congress produced an opposite and deplorable result —an uncoordinated mix of responses to special interests with no assessment of general need at all.[16]

When, with the reputation of a reformer, he moved out of

the presidency at Princeton to the governorship of New Jersey and then, in 1912, to the Democratic nomination for President, he began to cast his theoretical principles into specific political terms. His positions as a presidential candidate on the question of corporate abuses and the need for new and stringent government regulation were close enough to those of William Jennings Bryan to win Bryan's support both for the nomination and for the election. However, in the campaign of 1912, it became clear that Wilson was not speaking from Bryan's localist perspective. It was at this point that he became the spokesman for what he called explicitly the *majority* of the people, the country's workers, "the backbone of the Nation."

He shared with Bryan the general mythic view that the country's troubles were abnormal, not inevitable, and were thus susceptible to relatively easy solutions. "The nation has been unnecessarily, unreasonably, at war with itself," he declared in his speech accepting the Democratic nomination in August 1912. "Interest has clashed with interest when there were common principles of right and fair dealing which might and should have bound them all together, not as rivals, but as partners." Declaring that a government by Democrats "will set us free again," he went on to insist that the necessary reform would have "no flavor of tragedy to it." Instead, "it will be a chapter of adjustment, not of pain and rough disturbance. It will witness a turning back from what is abnormal to what is normal."

The abnormality Wilson identified was also much the same as Bryan's and that of functional reformers as well. What had gone wrong, he said, was the result of new forms of business organization—huge corporations and trusts—that put unorganized labor at a great disadvantage in protecting its position, and it was this imbalance that had to be righted, not as part of a class war, but in ministration to the health of the society. But Wilson's reference point for reform, the group whose suffering was the measure of wrong and whose well-being would be the measure of right, was different from that of both localists and functionalists. Wilson's constant attention was on the people as a whole, the people making up a *national* community.

The people of the nation, he said in the same speech, are made up of all "sorts and conditions of men." They are "mixed, of every kind and quality," but together they "constitute somehow an organic and noble whole, a single people," and "they have interests which no man can privately determine without their knowledge and counsel." The point of representative government, he said, "is nothing more or less than an effort to give voice to this great body through spokesmen chosen out of every grade and class."

In explicit commitment to the needs of the people, he stated, "The working people of America—if they must be distinguished from the minority that constitutes the rest of it, are, of course, the backbone of the Nation," and therefore, "no law that safeguards their life, that makes their hours of labor rational and tolerable, that gives them freedom to act in their own interest, and that protects them where they cannot protect themselves, can properly be regarded as class legislation or anything but as a measure taken in the interest of the whole people, whose partnership in right action we are trying to establish and make real and practical."[17]

The central theme of his campaign was that the voice of the people stating their needs and expressing their positions and choices on the nation's issues had not been sufficiently heard. There was no effective channel for the people's will and would not be if business-oriented Republicans held national office. Wilson continually portrayed the presidency he would conduct as an instrument serving the people's interest in their struggle against what had become overpowerful forms of capital. He also came out explicitly in favor of union organizing for the first time. He stated that equality might better be achieved by disallowing the right of capital to be organized in massive quantities in corporations, but dismissed that possibility as impractical. "Imagine the howl that would create," he said. But if capital is organized then labor must have the right to organize to equalize the balance. "What is sauce for the goose is sauce for the gander." But he added that the federal government must regulate what both can do with their organized strength.[18]

This, then, is the heart of the majoritarian position: the national government must be the essential agent of deliverance for the people generally from overweening private power. But there was, in Wilson's formulation of this approach, a further refinement. In order for the national government to be effective in the control of private power, primary authority had to be lodged in the presidency. The Congress, as Wilson had cogently charged in his *Congressional Government,* represents a patchwork of local interests and is unable to produce policy responsive to nationwide problems, nationwide constituencies. The President, on the other hand, is elected by the people of the nation as a whole and is, therefore, necessarily responsive to the needs of the whole.

One important facet of the presidency, claimed and practiced by Wilson and later developed to a high degree by Franklin D. Roosevelt, was the role of the active leader, the interpreter of national needs. This was a crucial role for an official seeking to assess and respond to the interests of a vast national majority because millions of people across a continent-nation could not themselves define a program for action simply through their votes. The mandate that majorities gave national leaders was necessarily general; the leaders themselves had to give it specific shape. The presidency, Wilson thought, supplied its occupant a vantage point well situated for the exercise of such leadership.

The President, moving through the entire country, speaking and listening, was exposed to needs and attitudes expressed in all areas and, putting them together, could show the people everywhere how their particular needs fit into the general picture. This perspective—available to no other elected official—enabled the President to translate the pattern of what was wrong across the nation into a program that would put it right—a program that all parts of the constituency would recognize as responsive to their interests. That is, the politically expressed will of the people was the source of needed social balance for majoritarians, but the effective interpretation of their will required a strong and sensitive leader.

The complicated relation between leader and constituency in a democracy was another issue that Wilson the scholar had analyzed before moving into public life. The function of a leader, Wilson said in an 1890 address, was to articulate the needs and needed direction of a society. But great leaders or statesmen do not simply present personal points of view; rather, they read "the common thought" and give it shape. In fact, Wilson said, leaders cannot move effectively in any direction "for which the major thought of the nation is not prepared." On the contrary, "every successful reform movement has had as its efficient cry some principle of equity or morality already accepted well-nigh universally, but not yet universally applied in the affairs of life." The leader is the catalyst that moves the principle from an inchoate state to the basis for political action.[19]

Thus for Wilson and majoritarians generally, it was the two-way movement of messages between leader and people that made the leader—in the American system, the President—the key to deliverance for the majority. The President or presidential candidate sent messages to the people through direct address or through the media, and the people sent messages back through the ballot box. The presidency, therefore, had a built-in corrective for any serious mistakes its occupant might make in interpreting the people's will.

Another important element of the majoritarian presidency, however, was its deliberate embrace of political power—a position completely and directly at odds with that of the functionalists. Mistrusting popular judgment and political power based on it, functionalists would entrust governmental authority only to highly trained, disinterested experts. The experts would establish order and fairness through reason. Majoritarians, however, would ensure the reasonable behavior necessary to order and fairness through a careful balance of power—public vs. private. Far from suppressing politics, majoritarians would use it deliberately as the path to deliverance.

Wilson made this issue explicit in the 1912 campaign, railing in speech after speech at the Progressive trust in experts. "God forbid that in a democratic country we should give the government over to experts," he declared in one such address. "What are we for if we are to be scientifically taken care of by a small number of gentlemen who are the only men who understand the job? Because if we don't understand the job, then we are not a free people."[20] And further, experts are people who "don't see anything except what is under their microscope." Their knowledge cannot provide answers to general questions involving judgments about what is good or bad for general conditions. They can supply only factual answers within the compass of specific questions.[21]

Drawing an analogy between experts and kings, Wilson declared that even kings have only twenty-four hours in the day. "And no brain in its twenty-four-hour day can comprehend the complex business of a nation. Representative government, representative assemblies are necessary; not because their individual units are wise, but because their individual units are various, because, picked out of every class and condition, they speak what no ordinary man can speak—the voice of all classes and conditions."[22]

Republicans generally, he claimed, saw government as another board of trustees, consisting of "a selected number of the big businessmen of the country who know a lot that you don't know, and who take it for granted that your ignorance would wreck the prosperity of the United States." He added that it was the ambition of both William Howard Taft, the Republican candidate, and Theodore Roosevelt, a Republican running as a Progressive, to be elected "president of the board of trustees."[23] The province of experts and trustees was to achieve efficiency, Wilson said repeatedly throughout his campaign, but the goal of the nation was not efficiency. It was improvement in the lot of the majority, and to reach this goal, the people themselves had to serve as guides, expressing their needs and opinions through the people they elected. "My interest in politics is to enlarge as much as possible the number of men thought to be qualified to advise the government," he declared.[24]

And in stark contrast to the vision of Charles Evans Hughes, Wilson as chief executive saw it as his proper role to use power deliberately for the purpose of putting the people's needs and wishes into practical effect. Thus where Hughes as governor would not play politics with the legislature because it was an abhorrent exercise of power, not reason, Wilson as President set about immediately to enhance presidential leverage over the legislative process. One of his first acts on assuming the presi-

dency, for example, was to present a major piece of legislation
—a bill for tariff reform—in a message delivered to both houses
of Congress in person. His biographer, Arthur S. Link, notes that
Wilson's action caused great shock, as it was the first time a
President had challenged Congress in this way in over a hundred
years. George Washington had addressed Congress directly, but
Thomas Jefferson had ended the practice because he thought it
smacked of royalty.[25]

Wilson continued his personal introduction of legislation,
however, and he usually followed up this initiative by meeting
frequently with House and Senate leaders in charge of steering
a particular bill through committee hearings and floor debate.
He also appeared informally on occasion in the Capitol building
to press his cause with key legislators. Furthermore, Wilson suffered none of Hughes's philosophic compunction or personal distaste for the deliberate use of favor and patronage to advance
his programs. Immediately on taking office in 1913, he began
to oversee the distribution of federal jobs at the local level—
postmasterships, for example—for the purpose of rewarding or
encouraging those factions within the Democratic Party organization that supported his policies in Congress.[26]

Another technique of Wilson's was to go over the head of
Congress, as he said, with a direct appeal to the people for support
if a bill got stuck somewhere in the legislative process. He used
this approach to great effect when his tariff bill was stalled by
lobbyist pressures for particular industries, or so Wilson claimed
in several strongly accusatory public statements. Exposed to the
glare of national publicity on the question of improper influence
by special interests, Congress quickly passed the tariff package
Wilson wanted.

In all of these ways, Wilson deliberately fashioned the presidency into a point of leverage, a point at which the power of
the majority could be concentrated. From this point, the legislature could be instructed in the needs and wishes of the people and
be made more responsive and responsible to the needs of the
whole. And laws then passed by the legislature, in the majoritarian view, could change an abnormal situation in the country
—an imbalance of power between managers and wage earners—

to a normal, healthy relation in which one could not dominate the other.

Since Wilson's time, the political base of majoritarianism has been in the Democratic Party, in those areas—the North and the West Coast primarily—where industry and therefore the interest of wage earners is politically important.

Majoritarians, localists, functionalists—throughout the century, the major debates in American politics have stemmed from competition among these three constituencies. And in this competition, the position of each—what it seeks, what it opposes—has been defined by the political principles outlined here. That is, the specific positions of each group change with changing times and issues, but its guiding principles do not change, because they derive from a myth that does not change and from basic economic interests that, by their nature, cannot change. Thus, in decade after decade, a stubborn system of belief marks the bounds of what each group sees and how each is prepared to respond.

This fixity of belief is crucial to the story that unfolds in the following chapters, not only because of the limits it imposes on the overall range of policy choice in different periods, but also because of its effect on the dynamics of American politics—the way policy is formed and put into effect.

Such political movement occurs at the national level through coalitions of interests behind particular leaders and policies. The reason for the coalitions is that no one group—not even the managerial interest with its economic predominance—can act effectively at the national level on its own. To elect a President or effect important policy change, at least two of the three major interests must act together, and this is possible because the needs of the different groups do coincide in various ways at various times. Furthermore, the emphasis of the myth on mutuality of interest facilitates cooperation among the groups by obscuring the extent to which their purposes differ. But beneath the apparent consensus within any coalition, the fixed differences in interest and belief remain, putting coalition partners at chronic cross-purposes. The effect on policy making of this phenomenon—the

cooperation between groups with deep but unrecognized differences—is to render major programs, domestic and foreign,
chronically vulnerable to internal incoherence or to change imposed by the collapse of coalitions.

Thus the impact of the myth is both general, in its limits on
the thought of all groups, and particular, in its effects on their
relations and decisions. It is a complicated story.

III

"The Promise of the Best Things":
New Freedom, New Deal

On the face of it, the movement of American domestic politics from the early reforms of the Wilson administration through Franklin Roosevelt's New Deal looks like a literal unfolding of the promise of deliverance—if anything, a validation of mythic beliefs. In the first two years after his election in 1912, Wilson won from Congress passage of four major bills, all designed to control excessive corporate power—the Underwood Tariff Act, the Clayton Anti-Trust Act, and the laws setting up the Federal Trade Commission and the Federal Reserve Board. With these curbs on monopoly, on unfair trade practices, on private control of credit supplies in place, Wilson exulted that "the future is clear and bright with the promise of the best things."

Casting his success unambiguously in terms of deliverance, Wilson went on: "While there was agitation and suspicion and distrust and bitter complaint of wrong, groups and classes were at war with one another, did not see that their interests were common, and suffered only when separated and brought into conflict. Fundamental wrongs once righted, as they may now easily and quickly be, all differences will clear away." The future then will be "a time of healing because a time of just dealing and co-operation between men made equal before the law in fact as well as in name."[1] Wilson believed, that is, that the power of the contesting groups had been balanced or "made equal" by governmental restraints on the power of corporations. Therefore the dealings between corporations and less powerful groups—notably wage earners—would, in the future, be fair.

Of course, Wilson's high hopes were not "easily and quickly" realized, but then his programs scarcely had time to prove themselves one way or the other. The confusions of a wartime economy intervened, to be followed by a period in the 1920s of efforts by functionalists in the federal government to encourage the self-reform of business through scientific management. And then there was the devastation of the Great Depression. With the election of Franklin Roosevelt and the passage of the New Deal reforms, however, it appeared that the efforts begun by Wilson to right serious wrongs through governmental controls on corporate power had come to fruition.

It took Roosevelt the better part of two terms, not two years, but he succeeded in imposing on private corporations the obligation to accept collective bargaining by labor unions, basic fair employment standards (minimum wages, maximum hours) set by the federal government, social security insurance, regulation of the stock exchanges, further regulation of banks and insurance of savings deposits, the precedent of a government owned and run public utility (the Tennessee Valley Authority), and government price supports for farm products.

These prodigious accomplishments, like Wilson's, were cast at the time, and have been understood since, in classically mythical terms. That is, the New Deal reformers saw the problems they faced as stemming from an abnormality in the society, an eradicable evil which was the operation of wrongly used corporate power. In response, they developed a broad consensus throughout the country behind governmental efforts to curb corporate power abuse and designed programs effective in doing so. And these programs were pragmatically organized. They were seen by their formulators as experimental responses to the problems at hand as opposed to ideologically based designs. More to the point, the New Dealers did not base their work on an explicit premise of class conflict. And the outcome of the programs—although mistrusted by many at the time, especially in the business world—has been generally accepted as beneficial to all interests, including business.

But such a reading of American history through the New Deal, the assumption that it is a story of reform based on a wide consensus among the various economic interests, is, in important respects, mistaken. And the lesson usually drawn from this reading, the lesson that America has escaped the history of division among interests that plagues other countries, that free from deep divisions we can solve our problems pragmatically and without serious cost to any legitimate interest, is also mistaken.

The political movement producing the New Freedom–New Deal programs was a movement based primarily in the wage-earning constituency and was propelled by the needs and demands of wage earners for relief from adverse conditions organized by capital managers. As such, it was a movement parallel to those mounted in the same period by working-class constituencies in all the industrial countries, and the issues were essentially the same. They stemmed from the enduring conflict in interest between workers and managers, with greater power in the hands of managers and with complications introduced by the enduring conflict between industrial interests—comprising both managers and workers—and agrarian interests. That is, workers throughout the industrial world confronted these conflicts, suffered inequity, and engaged in political action seeking change. And this was no less true in the United States.

The reason that it *seemed* less true, the reason that the American experience looked different and sounded different from political contests elsewhere, was that the American debate over interest-based demands was cast—as American political discourse is always cast—in mythic terms. Filtered through the myth of deliverance, the political issues produced by workers' demands did not focus explicitly on conflicts in economic interest. Rather they focused, as always, on the surrogate issue of authority. The American argument in the 1930s was over the authority to make important rules and where that authority should be placed. Should it be in the private sector or the public? And if the public, should it be at the national or state level? And at either level, should primary authority be in the executive, in the legislature, or in independent agencies or commissions?

Removing the debate still further from a focus on deep conflicts among different interests was the fact that the champions of each form of authority argued for it as the best system for all, the best means of suppressing the wrong or abnormality that threatened all. But in fact the argument over authority did divide by interest. Beneath the emphasis on common interest and practicality—the argument over which system would work best to curb abuse—the debate was actually three-sided. It was a debate among managers, workers, and localist interests, with each arguing for the system of authority that was in fact best suited to *its* needs. Thus the United States did not escape the pulls and pressures of conflicting interests. Rather, it escaped addressing them—or even admitting they were there.

The impact on Americans of the deeper problems not addressed because of this avoidance was postponed by the advent of war in 1940. An expanding wartime economy provided higher returns to all groups and blunted their differences and problems, reinforcing the assumption of the absence of conflict among them. And this assumption—the basic assumption of the myth of deliverance—remains to confound Americans in later generations who must deal with mythic promises in a period of economic limits. To see the actual nature of our present problems, then, it is necessary to disentangle them from a reading of history that obscures their roots, to separate the mythic reading of our reform tradition from the actual experience.

The first key point is that Roosevelt, like Wilson, led essentially an interest-based movement. His primary constituency was the wage earner interest and his programs reflected primarily the needs of that group. Further, the conception of the major New Deal programs was firmly rooted in wage earner or majoritarian beliefs concerning what was going wrong and what system of authority would put it right.

In the tradition already forged by Wilson, Roosevelt waged an unceasing campaign for the increased authority of the national government. He argued for national-mindedness in general, for an understanding of the relatedness of needs across the nation and for national rules responding to interrelated nationwide conditions. And like Wilson also, Roosevelt stressed the goal of serving the *whole* people and also of recognizing the importance to the whole of new economic forms, new technologies that in fact linked the whole nation into an interrelated system. The enemy depicted by Roosevelt was often what was old, what was past, primarily the old approach to business through narrow self-interest instead of the new approach that recognized interconnections and required intelligent responsibility.

Thus Roosevelt appealed in literal terms for a broadened conception of common interest across the nation and across economic interests within it. But in effect, his appeals were, as Wilson's had been, appeals for consensus *within* the wage-earning interest, across the great gulfs imposed on it by differences in ethnicity, religion, race, and regional interests.

Wilson had faced the problem of ethnic divisions in an especially intense way because, during his presidency, the homelands of many Americans were engaged in bitter, devastating war in Europe. There were two sources of danger in this. One was that various groups of Americans, out of loyalty to their homelands, would put pressure on the American government to enter the war. The other was that the divisions in Europe would spill over to the United States, creating division among Americans—which indeed occurred, especially in hostility directed at German-Americans.

In the face of these dangers, Wilson preached the transcending of difference through a common commitment to shared values. In an address to a group of newly naturalized citizens in 1915, Wilson called the process of becoming an American "a rebirth" and the motivation of people to become Americans a universal longing "for liberty and justice" and "some vision of a new kind of justice." In swearing allegiance to the United States, Wilson told the new citizens, "you have taken an oath of allegiance to a great ideal, to a great body of principles, to a great hope of the human race." And the ultimate allegiance of Americans, he went on, is not to the nation as such but to the common aspirations of humanity, because the purpose of the United States is to give life to basic human values and particularly the love of liberty.

Thus the tendency in the Old World to think of people as belonging to separate groups had to be left behind. "You do not love humanity if you seek to divide humanity into jealous camps," he said. "Humanity can be welded together only by love, by sympathy, by justice—not by jealousy and hatred. . . . We came to America, either ourselves or in the persons of our ancestors, to better the ideals of men . . . to get rid of the things that divide, and to make sure of the things that unite." And anyone "who seeks to divide man from man, group from group, interest from interest in the United States is striking at its very heart."[2]

Roosevelt, looking in the 1930s at a Europe again at odds with itself, virtually repeated Wilson's message, insisting that Americans "shared a deep purpose to rid themselves forever of the jealousies, the prejudices, the intrigues and the violence, whether internal or external, that disturbed their lives on the other side of the ocean."[3]

But the primary focus of Roosevelt's teaching concerning shared interest was the economy. In the midst of the Great Depression, it was not difficult to convince the people that they must turn their attention to economic reform, but Roosevelt still faced the problem of convincing people in different regions and in different ethnic groups that they did indeed hold common interests and could be helped by common solutions.

In his teaching of this lesson, Roosevelt supplied a central metaphor—the figure of the "neighbor"—to describe the bond linking people across their differences. It is a bond of a common predicament imposed by a common environment, but it is also a moral bond that allows people to understand and accept active mutual responsibilities in order to ensure mutual benefit.

In an extemporaneous talk at Vassar College, close to his home at Hyde Park in New York's rural Dutchess County, Roosevelt developed the theme of the neighbor at length. He was speaking in August 1933, halfway through his first year in office, and he described those months as filled with effort to extend to the nation "the old principle . . . that no individual, man, woman or child, has a right to do things that hurt his neighbors." In the old days, he said, this meant keeping cattle fenced in because it was unfair to allow them "to roam on our neighbor's land," but in modern society, "it became unfair to our neighbors if we . . . sought to make unfair profits from monopolies in things that everybody had to use." Then it became necessary, he went on, for the government to tax higher profits at higher rates "because of a simple principle that very large profits were made at the expense of neighbors" and through taxes those profits would go back to "the benefit of the neighborhood." And that meant to "the people of the United States as a whole." It did not work any more to count them "just by sections or by states" because actions in one section could affect people everywhere in a complex industrial economy.[4]

Wilson's appeal to universal values and Roosevelt's to a principle of neighborly responsibility are scarcely interest-based messages in any literal sense. They do not sound like a radical call to the nation's workers to recognize a common oppressor and to unite in throwing off their chains. But an emphasis on the interest of the whole people or the whole nation and on the interconnectedness of such interests is necessarily a majoritarian appeal—an appeal, in effect, to wage earners—because no other interest is served by it. On the contrary, the interests of both localists and functionalists are threatened by the formation of a nationwide constituency conscious of common interest and interested in national legislation—localists because national rules, by definition, override local choices, and functionalists because any politically defined rules concerning the economy necessarily reduce the scope of their own control. In the name of national unity, therefore, both Wilson and Roosevelt were serving the particular cause of wage earner unity.

Their great battles, however, and Roosevelt's particularly, were battles over specific issues of authority—the authority of the federal government and the authority of the President. Again, the terms of debate centered on the needs of the people as a whole for a modern conception of government to deal with modern forms of business. But again, the issue of authority was a surrogate for the issue of interest, because the national government in general and the presidency in particular are, by their nature, instruments for the power of wage earners, channels for the power of their votes.

Roosevelt raised the issue of authority squarely in his first inaugural address with its unavoidable focus on the deep economic depression he was elected to combat. The depression had made the people of the nation newly aware of their "interdependence," Roosevelt said. They had become aware that their actions could no longer be based on self-interest alone, but had to take account of the needs of others. And, he said, the federal government, too, had to take new forms of action to meet the "extraordinary needs" created by the emergency. He hoped that such action could be framed within the "normal balance of executive and legislative authority." But if congressional responses were not adequate, he warned, "I shall ask the Congress for the one remaining instrument to meet the crisis—broad Executive power to wage a war against the emergency as great as the power that would be given to me if we were in fact invaded by a foe."[5]

Roosevelt never did ask for such a general redefinition of the powers of the executive, but a number of New Deal measures delegated to the President a wide range of discretion over the problems at hand—for example, the early emergency banking laws and the Reciprocal Trade Agreements Act, which increased presidential authority over tariff rates. However, the New Deal legislation that went the furthest toward broadening the scope of effective federal—and executive—authority was the National Industrial Recovery Act.

The NIRA, passed in 1933, claimed for the federal government the authority to set prices and wages and to control unfair competition through specific regulations or codes drawn up for each industry. The codes were to be written by representatives of management and labor within each industry subject to the supervision and approval of the executive but with no requirement of review or approval by Congress. Thus, the result would be—as the law was designed—extensive regulation of national industries within the control of the executive alone.

This first major program of the New Deal produced outrage in the business world, both from remaining proponents of laissez-faire and, for different reasons, from the functionalist organizers of huge industries. Opponents of the law brought immediate challenges in the courts and, in 1935, the Supreme Court found it unconstitutional—on two points, both of which struck at key majoritarian premises.

First, the Court found—as it had in decisions going back to the 1890s—that the right of the federal government to regulate the economy at all was extremely limited. The constitutional provision in question was Article I, section 8, which provides that "Congress shall have Power . . . To regulate Commerce with foreign Nations, and among the several States, and with the Indian tribes"—as opposed to commerce within a particular state, which, presumably, was to remain the responsibility of state governments to regulate. The New Dealers contended that, by the 1930s, commerce "among the several States" meant the nation's commerce generally, because in a modern economy all economic transactions had interstate aspects to them. But the Court continued to read the commerce clause as meaning that the states held the right to regulate all economic activity within them and the federal government had authority only over commerce crossing state lines—that is, over goods in transit, which was an extremely limited economic sphere.

Further, the Court found, to the extent that the federal government *did* have authority to make rules affecting commerce, it was Congress that must make them. By providing for code making subject to executive approval only, Congress had improperly delegated its legislative responsibilities to the executive, so that the NIRA was invalid on this ground as well.[6]

On both counts the Supreme Court decision seriously undermined Roosevelt's efforts to establish a national-minded approach to policy making. Therefore it was, as Roosevelt saw it, a serious and unwarranted frustration by the judiciary of the clearly expressed will of the people. It was the Court that had overstepped its authority, not the executive, he thought, and shortly after the Court's decision on the NIRA, he launched a campaign against the Court itself. Again, the argument was cast in terms of constitutional authority. But again, the underlying implication was how much power wage earners as a group with common needs could wield.

The Supreme Court's view of interstate commerce was antiquated, Roosevelt said repeatedly in the succeeding months. Its logic would subject the immense industrial economy of the United States to the separate laws of forty-eight states, as if they were forty-eight different countries. "Nationwide thinking, nationwide planning and nationwide action are the three great essentials to prevent nationwide crisis for future generations to struggle through," he declared.[7]

After his landslide election to a second term in November 1936, Roosevelt was insistent on the point that it was simply wrong in a democracy for the Court to frustrate programs that a majority of the nation's people clearly wanted. The 1936 election was the third time in the preceding five years, he said, that "great majorities have approved what we are trying to do." And in his inaugural address that year, he came back to his attack on the Court's decisions as frustrations of the proper power of the nation's people. "Nearly all of us recognize that as the intricacies of human relations increase, so power to govern them also must increase—power to stop evil; power to do good."[8]

Roosevelt's conclusion was that the power of the Court to block the political determination of "nearly all of us" had to be reduced. This he proposed to do by giving the President authority to appoint additional judges for every judge over retirement age who refused to resign. Life tenure, Roosevelt said, produced a Court of men too elderly to examine changed conditions with sufficient vigor. "Little by little, new facts become blurred through old glasses fitted, as it were, for the needs of another generation; older men, assuming that the scene is the same as it was in the past, cease to explore or inquire into the present or the future."[9]

A Court expanded according to Roosevelt's plan would, as a rule, give each President a greater chance to place on the Court justices who reflect the presidential viewpoint—which presumably reflects the dominant outlook of the country at large at any particular time. Thus by enhancing the power of the President in relation to the judiciary, the Court-packing plan, as its detractors called it, would enhance the power of the majority as well.

Congress, expressing great alarm over the independence of

the courts, defeated Roosevelt's judiciary bill. But between February 1937, when the bill was submitted, and July, when it was voted down, the Court shifted its position on the meaning of interstate commerce and therefore on the authority of the national government to regulate commerce.

Reviewing the constitutionality of the National Labor Relations Act, passed in 1935, the Court accepted Roosevelt's view that a modern economy was so intricate and interconnected that virtually all elements were part of interstate commerce and thus properly subject to federal regulation. It was Charles Evans Hughes, then Chief Justice, who wrote for the Court, declaring, "When industries organize themselves on a national scale, making their relation to interstate commerce the dominant factor in their activities, how can it be maintained that industrial relations constitute a forbidden field into which Congress may not enter . . . ?"[10]

Thus after 1937 the way was legally clear for wage earners to exert their increasingly united and organized strength in political demands on Congress—funneled through the presidency— for laws setting nationwide requirements for fairness in employment. That is, Roosevelt had waged and won a battle over a constitutional issue of authority—the authority of the national government to regulate national commerce—and this was a victory presumably benefiting all of the people, whatever their role in the nation's economy. It was a victory, presumably, for modernity. But actually Roosevelt had won a victory for wage earners, a victory that gave them a more powerful instrument in the form of a more powerful federal government to use in their ongoing battle against the nation's managers.

Another crucial point in the reading of the New Deal experience as a peculiarly American success with pragmatic compromise, as a successful escape from the problems of class divisions, is the fact that New Deal programs were supported by a coalition of wage-earning *and* agrarian interests. Roosevelt, and Wilson before him, had put together majorities in Congress that depended on substantial support from agrarian as well as industrial regions, and this broad consensus appears to confirm strongly the tenets of the myth. It appears to place beyond contention the belief that differences in economic interest are superficial and can be transcended with benefit for all if skillful negotiators are at work.

But in the Wilson-Roosevelt coalitions, it was the consensus and not the differences between the cooperating groups that was superficial. They cooperated because to a degree they shared an *interest* in restraining capital managers, but the basic differences in their interests remained, serving as a constant source of friction for both Wilson and Roosevelt and ultimately ending the coalition completely.

From the time of William Jennings Bryan, localists had conducted a crusade to place governmental controls on corporate operations crucial to rural interests, most particularly the operations of banks, railroads, slaughtering and meat-packing monopolies, and electric companies. And to this end a majority of senators and congressmen from states with predominantly localist constituencies voted in favor of the major New Freedom and New Deal reforms.

There was strong localist support for Wilson's anti-trust law, banking reform, and regulation of unfair trade practices, and even stronger and more enthusiastic backing for Roosevelt's New Deal. The Great Depression had hit the farm sector of the economy early and badly, and by the 1930s many farmers were losing their land because they could not maintain mortgage payments. Roosevelt quickly won from Congress a moratorium on farm mortgage debt and the establishment of the Federal Farm Credit Administration, providing low-interest mortgage money specifically for farm loans. Further, a long localist campaign for government engagement in the supply of electricity to farmers, blocked for years by the opposition of eastern Republicans and the succession of Republican Presidents in the 1920s, came to spectacular fruition in the Tennessee Valley Authority, established in 1933.

Even more important was the passage of the Agricultural Adjustment Act in 1938, putting into effect a federally subsidized system for the parity pricing of farm products. This supplied the final stroke of independence from the price squeeze traditionally afflicting farmers—high prices for the supplies and services they had to buy in city markets, low prices for the products they had to sell. With the establishment of the Securities and Exchange Commission to control the operation of the stock market and Roosevelt's promise of strict anti-trust enforcement, the localist definition of the enemy of deliverance and strategy for achieving it were more firmly implanted in federal policy than they had ever been before. And with such assiduous attention from Roosevelt to their own needs, localists and their representatives in Washington responded with support for the administration's efforts to aid wage earners, backing such programs as protection for collective bargaining, social security, and fair employment practices.

But underlying this long and successful collaboration for reform was the fact that the localist enemy and the majoritarian enemy were not actually the same. And the ultimate purposes of the allied groups, the results they wanted and expected from the reforms they backed, were not the same. The majoritarians wanted to balance the power of labor and management within the context of a national economy growing through the development of complex industrial production. The localists wanted to limit the size and complexity of industrial units so that the entire economy could operate according to classical principles of market competition—principles that would prevent local economies from being swamped by corporate giants.

In the majoritarian scheme, the national government would have an ongoing role in maintaining a balance between stronger and weaker segments of the economy. In the localist scheme, the national government would do nothing other than maintain controls over corporate size and regulate key areas such as banking that perpetually threaten the health of localist enterprise. Any additional social or economic regulation, in the localist view, lies properly in the province of the states or local communities.

Through the 1930s, the common needs of the two groups outweighed their differences sufficiently to maintain a strong voting coalition in Congress, but still the lines of dissent were clearly visible. The congressional debates on New Freedom and New Deal programs are replete with questions, anxieties, warnings, and sometimes outright opposition on the part of localists concerned over the growth of national authority, however badly they needed that authority for their own purposes.

In both periods, the most eloquent voice articulating these concerns was that of William Borah, Republican senator from Idaho from 1907 to his death in 1940. A farm boy from Illinois, Borah headed West as a young lawyer in 1890, literally to seek his fortune. He had no fixed destination, but simply rode the trains until his money ran out in Boise, Idaho, where he settled and set up a law practice. As a young lawyer, he quickly became involved in the Idaho Republican Party as an advocate of classically localist causes. He ran unsuccessfully for Congress in 1896 as a Silver Republican, taking many of the same positions Bryan championed as the Democratic presidential candidate—the foremost being opposition to the tight credit policies of the eastern Republicans. In 1902, as chairman of the state convention platform committee, he pressed localist reforms scarcely distinguishable from those of Bryan's Democrats—direct election of senators, government ownership of railroads, restrictions on trusts, tariff protection for farm products.[11]

But Borah's embrace of the localist system of belief is perhaps best seen in his response to a crisis that occurred early in his political life. In 1905, the governor of Idaho, Frank Steunenberg, a personal and political friend of Borah's, was killed by a bomb rigged to his own front gate. Steunenberg had been under attack for enforcing anti-union labor laws and it was widely assumed that the killing was done by a radical labor group associated with the Western Federation of Miners. Borah, hearing the news in a neighboring town, rushed to the governor's home, saw the mangled body, the blood on the snow, torn clothes strewn on the ground.

In the succeeding days, the state was alive with fury and talk of recrimination, but Borah, delivering the funeral eulogy for his friend, refused—even under this bitter provocation—to accept implications of class hostility in the killing. He asked the community not to believe "it is the crime of any class or any portion of our citizens, or that it finds sympathy with anyone other than the actual perpetrator." Rather, he urged his listeners to "hope that when mystery yields up her secret it will be found that it is someone irresponsible to all others . . ."[12]

That is, Borah insisted on portraying the murderer as a deliberate wrongdoer, someone acting out of malice or possibly madness. He refused to read into the killing broad patterns of social or economic complication. This reading is politically important in that an act of "someone irresponsible to all others" generally calls for nothing more complicated than local action as a response. It does not assume the need for broad authority to deal with far-reaching and complicated social forces.

And this is the political outlook that Borah, once elected to the Senate, brought to national problems as well—the view that most social trouble stems from deliberate wrongdoing and can be controlled by straightforward measures often best organized at the local level. For over three decades he outlined, in carefully reasoned argument, the dangers to local authority implicit in complex national reforms, even while himself supporting the national programs localists badly needed.

The focus of Borah's criticism in the Wilson years was on the instrument of government central to the New Freedom reforms. This was the independent regulatory commission, fervently extolled for its non-political character by Charles Evans Hughes and the functionalists. Wilson had accepted regulatory commissions as the basis for his reforms, not because he prized government by experts—he had, after all, attacked this concept strongly in the 1912 campaign—but because he prized regulation and he could get functionalist backing for regulation by experts. But in courting functionalists, Wilson had to overcome suspicion by the localists—suspicion directed precisely at the non-political character of such agencies as the Federal Trade Commission and the Federal Reserve Board. Placing great power in governmental commissions, Borah said, was undemocratic because the commissions were run by staffs of experts "which the people neither select, elect, nor can they recall."[13]

In the 1914 debate on new anti-trust legislation, Borah pointed out that the transportation system of the country was already in the hands of the Interstate Commerce Commission, the country's currency was controlled by the new Federal Reserve

Board, and with the Clayton Anti-Trust Act, control over the nation's great industries would also be given over to a commission. This, he warned, would "leave a mere shell of the Government, the mere outward form . . . in the hands of the people to flatter and satisfy their pride, while the great essential elemental powers which deal with and control their destinies are in the hands of 25 or 30 men."[14]

What Borah and the localists feared in delegating to experts the job of controlling corporate power was that experts would analyze problems from the corporate viewpoint and not that of the ordinary citizen. Some saw such danger in simple conspiratorial terms. In the 1914 debate over the Federal Trade Commission, Senator Harry Lane, a Democrat from Oregon, announced that he would vote for the bill but only because it was the best available measure, not because he liked it. What he feared, he said, was the lack of public control over the acts of the proposed Trade Commission. Describing the big business interests of the nation as exploiters, with the ordinary people their prey, Lane exclaimed that the new commission "may be entirely in sympathy and harmony with such predatory interests," and with unchecked regulatory authority, "they can make and enforce a mandate that the people of this country shall continue to be robbed as they are now being robbed, and by the same set of criminals."[15]

Borah was also concerned about the potential for direct wrongdoing in the close, continuing, yet unpublic relation between business and government officials in the new commissions, but he saw a more broadly encompassing danger as well. The underlying problem, he said, arguing against Wilson's Federal Reserve System, was a centralizing tendency that had been running in the nation for the preceding twenty years. "Centralization of industry, centralization of commerce, centralization of banking, centralization of credits, and all in private hands, and the Government yielding to them little by little from time to time its sovereign powers and duties."

Centralization, for Borah, meant the transfer of power from one class to another, from people running small-scale enterprises in their own communities, organized to respond to clear needs and demands, to people operating business empires organized to amass power and through it exorbitant profit. The job of the government, Borah insisted, was to prevent the class of profiteers from dominating the economy and the society, or rather, by removing the profiteers from the picture, to deliver Americans from the curse of class divisions altogether. And what the government should *not* do was to try to accommodate a powerful business class within the nation's life. If the government was to remain truly representative and responsive to the people, "it can not be fitted to classes," he said. "It can not adjust itself to an industrial life grounded in inequality; it can not be fitted to monopoly; though strong enough to destroy, it can never be powerful enough to regulate monopoly." Therefore, he concluded, "we ought to . . . cease our efforts to adjust our Government to the centralizing, monopolizing tendencies of business and compel business to adjust itself to the fundamental principles of democracy."[16]

Borah's position was that the government should break the power of bigness by literally breaking big business up into units small enough to be controllable by the market expressing directly the needs and interests of the people. Any attempt by the government to control business while leaving it large would result in making government the servant of the managerial class, engaged with it and through it in the utilization of the society's resources, the employment of its labor, and the distribution of its product, and implicated also in the terms, the wages, the prices at which these transactions take place—terms necessarily disadvantageous to the people generally.

Those aspects of the New Deal that placed government and business in a regulatory rather than strictly adversarial relation provoked the same reaction from Borah that Wilson's programs had. His greatest outrage was directed against the NIRA with its delegation of code-making authority to administrative boards composed of delegates from business, labor, and government, subject only to presidential approval. This was a clear delegation of substantial legislative authority to non-elected officials and, said Borah, the provision for presidential review did not change the situation because the President could not possibly go over each proposed code in detail, or comprehend their intricacies even if he did. Therefore approval by the President meant in practice approval by some official acting for the President, "an individual whom we do not know and for whom we furnish no rule or law."[17]

Borah was particularly horrified by the power delegated to the code writers to prevent destructive price wars by fixing prices above the cost of production, but with no standards specified anywhere as to what the cost of production should be. Furthermore, the only provision for review of the figures used to determine the cost of production for a particular industry or region was an appeal to the National Recovery Administrator, or as Borah said, "the dictator . . . the coordinator, or whatever we may choose to call him." The judgment of Congress, and through it the judgment of the people, was to play no role in what was to be a major experiment in national economic planning. "Shades of Stalin!" Borah expostulated. "Stabilization, what crimes are to be committed in thy name?"[18]

As the Supreme Court later asserted, the delegation of legislative authority to the executive in the NIRA was extreme, but Borah was alarmed at seemingly more innocuous delegations as well. He opposed, for example, the Fair Labor Standards Act in 1937, the purpose of which was to set standards for minimum wages and maximum hours, not because he opposed such standards, but because they were to be set by a board on the basis of hearings on conditions in particular industries and areas. This would mean, Borah said, that the standards set would necessarily be most responsive to the interests of large corporations because they had the resources to prepare extensive materials and persist in their presentation, which small business did not. Thus the Fair Labor Standards Board, in spite of itself and its pro-labor mission, would end up an effective accomplice of big business in strengthening its position and power as an organizing force in the nation's economy.

Such a combination of government and business power, Borah warned, rendered the American people increasingly powerless over the forces affecting their daily lives, and the programs creating this new power bloc were particularly dangerous because they did not seem to be doing so. Americans tend to think of dictators, he said, as "some strutting colonel at the head of a ragamuffin army" or of a "person of extraordinary ability who, appealing to the homeless and the hungry, undertakes openly to seize the reins of arbitrary power." But in the United States, dictatorship was more likely to take another form, the form of "institutions set up, often for a perfectly good purpose, which secretly, silently, remorselessly undermine and sap the character and the stamina, the self-reliance, and the self-governing capacities of the people."[19]

Borah's answer to the problem of minimum wage was to have the standard set by the Congress, subject to the pressures that could be exerted directly by the people's representatives. This was the localist answer generally to the problem of having the government set social standards of any kind, and the majoritarian objection to it was that a legislature could not review the kind of detail necessary to set a minimum wage level knowledgeably or to make sound judgments about similarly complicated issues. Such matters necessarily had to be delegated to administrators working full time on the problem and bringing to it special knowledge of the subject. Legislative give-and-take was too crude a process for such a task. Localists, however, rejected the basic premise that the government should involve itself at all in rule making so complicated that it required formulation by experts. Any matter that was beyond the capacity of the legislature to evaluate was, by definition, beyond the proper scope of the government to deal with.

Further, in the localist view, whatever governmental regulation is necessary for the protection of social groups with weak bargaining power is usually best organized by local government responsive to specific local conditions. Any attempt at broad-scale regulation at the national level, informed by expertise but not close knowledge of local conditions, is unlikely to accomplish its stated purposes. As Senator Charles Thomas, a Democrat from Colorado, said in 1914—using terms that have been a staple in localist rhetoric ever since—"You can not govern a hundred million people ... from a great central point like Washington."[20] Any attempt to do so, therefore, is actually a power grab, and

worse, a power grab directed against the only legitimate power
holders in a democracy, the people themselves doing business in
their own communities.

This, then—the insistence of people from agrarian regions
on local autonomy—was the fault line running underneath the
localist-majoritarian coalition for national reform. And on issues
where there was no overlapping interest between the two groups
—notably the non-economic issue of civil rights—localists flatly
opposed majoritarian efforts to establish rules of fairness running
nationwide. In the years following the First World War, reform
efforts grew for federal government protection of the rights of
black citizens in southern states and on this issue there was
concerted resistance from localists in all regions, the West and
Southwest as well as the South. The major issue was anti-lynching
legislation.

Beginning in the 1920s and continuing in the 1930s, majoritarian Democrats repeatedly submitted anti-lynching bills in
Congress, bills that would have made lynching, like kidnapping,
a federal crime, prosecuted by federal district attorneys in federal
courts. Repeatedly, they were defeated by majorities in which the
combined localist vote made up the bulk of the opposition. For
example, in 1938, a cloture motion to end a Senate filibuster
against an anti-lynching bill was defeated 51–37. Of the 51 nay
votes, 32 were from the localist heartland—18 from the South,
14 from the West and Southwest.

The non-southern regions had no direct interest in the race
question as such, but as Borah said in the 1938 debate, "The
constitutional feature of this bill . . . is just as vital to Idaho as
to Alabama; it is of just as much concern to Massachusetts as to
Georgia. If the Federal Government can send a United States
Marshal into the State of Tennessee to arrest a sheriff because he
has failed to protect a colored man from violence, it can . . . send
a United States Marshal into the State of New York to arrest a
sheriff . . . because he neglected to protect the life of a citizen
against the violence of thugs."[21]

Out of similar sentiments, Borah opposed the idea, circulat-
ing in the 1920s, of establishing a federal Department of Education and a Department of Conservation. Why not establish as

well departments of athletics, hygiene, and matrimony? he asked. "Why not confess at once that we have become a people utterly without initiative, self-reliance, or self-help and fall down like savages of old before some bureaucratic head and ask for salvation?"[22]

Borah was often pictured in the eastern press as something of a buffoon, a wild man from the Far West—unpredictable, idiosyncratic, sometimes backing his Republican Party leadership, sometimes deserting them to offer enthusiastic support to the Republican archenemy, Roosevelt. But he was not a buffoon. He was a serious, even scholarly man who did his own research, wrote his own speeches, avoided alike the social round in Washington and the play of patronage and power games at home.[23] And he was anything but idiosyncratic. He maintained a philosophic position that was internally logical and consistent from the beginning of his career to the end—a position, moreover, that expressed not just personal principles but principles held by constituencies in all primarily agrarian states.

What is most significant about Borah's principles and positions, however, is that their importance to agrarian constituencies did not end with the end of the New Deal. Rather, Borah's backing of local autonomy and resistance to national authority foreshadowed what would later become open dissent by the localists to the continued press by majoritarians for expanded national agencies, national rules, and national taxes in aid of a national constituency of industrial wage earners. As later chapters show, the coalition for domestic reform that held through the late 1930s began to splinter after 1945 and by 1965 had collapsed completely.

The third important voice in the shadow debate of the 1930s —the three-sided debate among major interests, each focusing on a shadow or surrogate issue of authority—was the voice of the managerial interest. This was a clearly dissenting voice, but it, too, was misheard, the depth of its dissent misunderstood by the other interests—and also by succeeding generations whose understanding of the era had been shaped by the majoritarians who dominated it. That is, later generations, perceiving the New Deal as a success, have understood its success in the terms through

which the majoritarian New Dealers themselves understood it—
which is to say through the majoritarian version of the myth. And
the majoritarians understood the managers to be the enemy. Or
rather, irresponsible managers were the enemy—those who were
abusing their positions of power and resisting reform. The others,
the good or progressive managers, were assumed to be as concerned with reform as anyone else, to be part of a broad consensus
behind Roosevelt's programs. Therefore, majoritarians heard all
managerial dissent as an expression of a wrongful and outdated
insistence on the part of "bad" managers on the prerogatives of
self-interest.

To a degree, this mythic perception of the business world, its
division into "bad" and "good" managers, did correspond to
reality. There were those who looked backward to an era of
unrestrained competition and opposed—vehemently—all forms
of governmental intervention, and there were those who saw the
need for enlightened restraint. But this last category, primarily
the ever-growing group of professional executives who ran the
nation's largest and most complex firms—the functionalists, the
believers in economic rationality and functional efficiency—by
no means supported the New Deal approach to restraint. On the
contrary, the functionalist managers, too, were opponents of the
New Deal and for reasons more deeply rooted, less likely to be
changed or controlled, than a simple refusal to look beyond a
narrow, shortsighted conception of self-interest. These reasons
were precisely the differences, the conflicts between the inherent
interest of even reform-minded managers and the interest of wage
earners and other economically weaker groups.

It was this level of dissent—the managerial claims stemming
from unchanging conflicts—that majoritarians did not hear, and
that later generations have not clearly heard. Of course, the
clarity of this message was muffled by the fact that managers, as
well as wage earners and localists, spoke the political language of
the myth. Thus they did not speak explicitly of interest and their
needs stemming from it, but of authority—the needs of all for
the placement of decision-making authority in the right hands.

The central issue for the forward-looking managers or functionalists was the same as that for majoritarians—the authority

of the federal government. And for functionalists this was a complicated issue. Unlike business interests still enamored of laissez-faire, functionalists did not oppose the extensive involvement of government in economic affairs—recall the battles of Charles Evans Hughes and his Progressive colleagues for the greater use of regulatory commissions early in the century. Later, with the growing complication of the economy after the First World War, a new generation of managers became convinced that the role of government had to be enlarged. But the functionalist conception of what that role should be differed drastically from the approach of majoritarians.

The key figure—philosopher and practitioner—of the new functionalist politics was Herbert Hoover. Like Hughes, Hoover was a latecomer to political life. He was a member of the first graduating class of Stanford University, a mining engineer who started with nothing but skills and determination and built a worldwide network of mining enterprises that made him a millionaire in his forties. His business headquarters was in London, and when war broke out in 1914, he was drawn into civilian relief operations, primarily in Belgium. This was his first public service, but he went on after the American entry into the war to become United States Food Administrator for Woodrow Wilson and then Secretary of Commerce under Presidents Harding and Coolidge. In 1928, he was himself elected President.

Brought up in a Quaker family in small towns of the Midwest and West, Hoover was a quiet, disciplined, methodical man who abhorred violence and loved reason. Both in business and in war, he had known the vast complication, conflict, and turbulence of his time and his entire public career was devoted to a search for deliverance from the evils causing such conditions.[24] His longing for a realm of order and peace appears graphically in an offhand remark in his memoirs about his mining experience. "Going below after many years of working with the surface people I always have again the same thrills, the same feeling of separation and safety from the meanness and handicaps of those on the top," he said. And he added that in medieval stories of gnomes and other underground people, such creatures always appear as good-humored and helpful, never malevolent.[25]

These remarks can also stand as a metaphor for his general political stance. While he felt keenly the forces of chaos and meanness, he believed that beneath the tangled surface of human affairs, there *were* principles of order—and these were the principles of functional efficiency.

As an engineer, Hoover had been actively involved in the early movement for scientific management, and he carried its principles explicitly into the political realm.[26] The problems Americans faced in the 1920s, Hoover thought, were a compound of normal human selfishness and greed and the opportunity to indulge such weakness that was available in the wealth and confusion of the modern corporate scene. In Hoover's view, businessmen were using the economy as if it were a grab bag, seeking short-term gain for themselves, regardless of the efficiency, or lack of it, with which they used resources. The cumulative effect of such practices was to reduce the productivity of the system as a whole. And insufficient productivity was the root of all economic trouble, he thought, from recession to conflict between labor and management. The problem with the American system, he insisted, was waste, and his program for deliverance was the elimination of waste—through principles of functional efficiency in business promoted by an active, helpful government.

In a typical speech as Secretary of Commerce developing this theme for a business audience, Hoover listed fifteen forms of unnecessary systemic waste. They included: boom and bust cycles; seasonal production; lack of standards of quality and grade of products within an industry; unnecessary multiplication of sizes and varieties of similar products; lack of uniformity in business documents producing misunderstanding as well as fraud; disorderly sales programs based on insufficient market information; and destructive competition by companies reducing capital because of lack of knowledge of their own trade. Hoover's message to the business community was that if waste were eliminated, the capital being expended on waste could go into making other products, thus raising the standard of living by lowering its costs.

The prescription that followed for saving resources from loss by needless inefficiency was a system Hoover called voluntarism or mutualism. It was a system of voluntary cooperation between government and business by which government would help business acquire complex information on industry-wide or even economy-wide conditions. With such information, individual companies could make decisions with intelligent regard for the broader context of their operations, and thus avoid wasting resources at their disposal. The agency for implementing this system was the Commerce Department, which, under Hoover's leadership, sponsored hundreds of conferences of various trades and industries to circulate the data necessary for business to undertake scientifically based self-reform.[27]

As with other tenets of functionalist belief, Hoover's systemic approach to public policy ran directly counter to localist attitudes toward the proper role of government in ensuring national economic welfare. As localists saw it, low farm prices, inadequate wages, and other sufferings of the economically weak were caused by deliberate machinations of groups that were illegitimately strong. Hoover was explicit in denying that the source of economic evil was so clear. He acknowledged that to amass and distribute information was not so dramatic or entertaining as "the discovery of wicked profiteers and leeches who are sucking out the blood of the nation." But, he insisted, it was necessary, whereas the search for evil in an easily isolable form was futile. The problem was waste, and waste could not be reached by the "Ten Commandments or by any legislative extension thereof," he said. "You cannot catch an economic force with a policeman."[28]

Hoover also denied that you could leave the corporate world to combat the intangible force of waste on its own, as the necessary defenses against it were too complicated for the private sector to organize without public help. Thus Hoover and functionalist managers generally were not opponents but champions of a government-business liaison. They actively sought to create bureaucracies capable of gathering information beyond the scope of most corporations to provide for themselves.

But, in the functionalist scheme, the government should not itself become an economic actor. Congress should not impose economic choices on corporations as a matter of public policy, because Congress acts, necessarily, at the behest of constituents and not on the basis of scientific analysis—a prospect that Hoover, like Hughes, found appalling. With Congress making decisions about economic matters, business would be subject to rules that were the result of "logrolling and politics," Hoover said, of bargaining based on power, and all hope of rational decision making would cease.[29]

This was the creed with which Hoover as President attempted to deal with the nation's economic collapse in 1929 and with which he opposed—vehemently—much of the New Deal after losing the presidency to Roosevelt in 1932. And it was his strong opposition to direct governmental intervention in the economy throughout the depression that won him the reputation as a champion of laissez-faire—a reputation that still obscures the complicated functionalist position he actually held. More important, however, the misunderstanding of Hoover's role as opponent of the New Deal obscures and confuses the position of the powerful interest—the nation's corporate managers—whose views Hoover shared and expressed.

Corporate managers do not oppose big government. They do not oppose economic planning or the involvement of the government in long-range economic planning. What they oppose is politics, the intrusion of political power in economic decisions or long-range planning. In the functionalist view, the role of government should be advisory. Experts in government should advise corporate managers concerning trends and conditions affecting the efficiency of business operations, but the responses of managers to such advice should be voluntary, not coerced.

This is the point that marks the crucial difference between functionalists and majoritarians on the issue of governmental authority—the difference that follows from the difference in their economic interests. The wage-earning constituency, possessing less economic power than managers, must use political power to protect itself in the process of setting the terms for work. And much of the Wilson-Roosevelt reform effort was aimed at building channels of political power usable by wage earners for just this purpose. But it is precisely the use of political power in the economic process that functionalists oppose, which means that they are opposing the intrusion of the power of wage earners in the control and disposition of capital. Each group, of course, sees its conception of the proper role of government as aimed at deliverance for all. But, in effect, their respective systems would capture the government for the protection of their respective interests.

Thus to see the New Deal as evidence of *lack* of intransigent conflict among interests in American politics is to look at the surface only. Beneath the surface the separate interests were there —not simply good and bad interests, but three groups with inherently different interests which pulled them, inevitably, in different directions. And it is the common misreading of the depth of these differences that has beguiled Americans of later generations into believing—mistakenly—that reform is mainly a matter of building consensus through skill in political maneuver, cleverness in patching together enough groups with enough votes to win elections and pass laws. What we need to see, beyond the immutability of interest, is that the major accomplishments of the New Deal were based mainly on the particular vision of one interest—the wage earners—and on a broad consensus built *within* that interest.

What, then, was the New Deal accomplishment? If majoritarians, like the other groups, were blocked by the myth of deliverance from probing to the root of the nation's problems, how significant were their reforms? Do the New Deal laws deserve their reputation as important landmarks in the American record of social justice? These are large questions but, in short, Roosevelt's reform drive did produce effective legislation where the problems it addressed did, in fact, derive from specific abuses. That is, the New Deal was effective where majoritarian assumptions of a removable evil corresponded with an actual evil that could be controlled by a balancing of power.

A panoply of New Deal laws exerted governmental power to control such evils as misrepresentation in the trading of securities, exploitation of marginal labor, banking practices unfair to farmers, and the refusal of employers to take responsibility for industrial accidents and unemployment. And the National Labor Relations Act, which legitimized collective bargaining by labor, was a classic exercise in general power balancing. That is, it sought to right the generally unbalanced relation between management and labor by enhancing the negotiating power of labor. Robert Wagner, the Democratic senator from New York who sponsored the legislation, explained its virtues on the Senate floor in exactly these terms.

The plight of labor, Wagner said, was the result of the aggregation of capital into units of ever greater size since the mid-nineteenth century, with no corresponding organization of labor. As a consequence, he argued, the percentage of manufacturing product paid out in wages had dropped from 51 percent in 1849 to 36 percent in 1933. The NIRA, with its requirement that management negotiate with labor, was a step in the right direction but did not go far enough because the NRA had no effective power of enforcement. Wagner's bill would give a new National Labor Relations Board its own enforcement powers to ensure that employers did not interfere in the unionization process and that they bargained in good faith with properly chosen unions.

The virtue of his bill, Wagner claimed, was that in dealing with labor disputes, it avoided "European" solutions such as compulsory arbitration or dictated settlements. Perfectly stating the terms of the myth of deliverance, he went on to declare that Americans "have cherished always the ideal of employers and workers meeting together with friendly and open minds in order that they may exchange views and arrive at solutions based not upon compulsion but upon mutual concessions and mutual benefit." But by the mid-1930s, they had come to see "the necessity of establishing by law the underlying conditions from which agreements might arise." What the government was doing in protecting the rights of labor to bargain collectively, he concluded, was establishing "rules of fair play."[30]

And the new rules *did* work to labor's advantage, as did the other New Deal laws dealing with specific harmful practices. And they worked precisely because they were not the product of a patched-up consensus among essentially divided groups. Rather, they were the product of an effective address by one large interest to the real problems suffered by that interest—or to some of them.

There were, however, problems that the majoritarians did not address, problems they did not see. These were problems stemming, not from particular remediable abuses, but from the deeper, endemic conflicts between the needs of wage earners and those of other interests—the conflicts that none of the interests could see because of the myth of deliverance. That is, majoritarians could deal with corporate abuse through power balancing but could not go beyond this concept, beyond the myth, to contemplate broader controls on corporate power through some form of deliberate economic planning for the purpose of gaining a more certain measure of fairness, of liberty, of equality for weaker groups.

This point—the inability of majoritarians even to contemplate a program of economic planning—is confused, paradoxically, by the long-standing assumption that the New Dealers *were* planners. Some of them called themselves planners and their political opponents often hurled the term at them as an accusation —especially in attacks on the first major New Deal program, the National Industrial Recovery Act of 1933.

To many at the time, the NIRA looked precisely like an outright exercise in socialist planning, a governmental takeover of the management of the economy. Certainly the requirement of the NIRA that each American industry adopt a code setting standards for labor contracts, pricing levels, and marketing practices seemed socialistic, especially as NRA staff would participate in drafting the codes and the final product had to be approved by the President. Thus it seemed that the New Deal designers *had* leapt beyond the myth into the realm of admitted conflict among interests and were restrained in this attempt only by edict of the Supreme Court.

The NIRA, however, in its actual design and function was anything but socialistic. On the contrary, it remained well within the tenets of the myth. The conception of the NIRA was rooted, in fact, in Herbert Hoover's assumption that much of the economic wreckage of the American corporate world had been self-imposed. The point of the codes was to set industry-wide standards on many matters—capital-destroying competition, for example—that Hoover had long tried to convince industries to adopt for themselves. The NIRA took the Hoover idea that government should *advise* industries to engage in rational long-term planning and *required* them to do so. Of course, it also required corporations to negotiate the codes with representatives from labor and from the NRA staff, which was not at all what Hoover had in mind. This was a bargaining process, not a search for efficiency. It utilized majoritarian techniques—discovering terms of fairness through balanced negotiating power—not functionalist techniques of expert analysis.

But even with the presence of NRA officials, the code-writing process was not an exercise in government planning, and could not be, for two powerful reasons. One was that the NRA had no policy-making division. The act did not provide for a staff to draw up codes or set carefully researched standards for codes. There was simply no source within the agency for the independent design of substantive policy to be imposed on the various industries. Rather, the act ordered that the industries themselves draw up their own codes.

Secondly, there was no strong enforcement mechanism in the NRA structure. The codes, once adopted, had the status of law and code violations were breaches of law, but the NRA had no authority to bring legal action against violators. Instead, the NRA dealt with grievances through regional boards made up mainly of local businessmen, who relied, for the most part, on investigation and conciliation to settle local differences. Thus here, too, the thrust of the act was not to impose government rules against business in an adversarial manner, but to require that business take responsibility for enforcing fair practice among its members.

The prevailing assumption in the design of the NRA and in its operation was that no government-defined, government-imposed policy was necessary because *naturally* fair terms for the operation of business would be uncovered if everyone involved sat down and tried in good faith to find them. And once found, they would be followed because all sides would benefit. There would always be unscrupulous managers who would try to cheat, but peer surveillance would be enough to control them because most managers would be motivated by the obvious benefits of the system to be willing to keep others in line. That is, in spite of the fanfare and the fury, the NRA was still a regulatory scheme for deliverance to honest private bargaining, not a revolutionary leap to national public planning.[31]

Thus, in spite of the radical reputation of what historians call the First New Deal, Roosevelt's majoritarians never challenged the precepts of the myth, they never based programs on the conception of immutable conflict among major economic groups. In fact, the very effectiveness, in their own way, of the programs succeeding the NIRA obscured the fact that there *were* deeper dilemmas that problem-solving legislation could not touch.

Of these issues, two were especially serious—both noticed and defined at the time but not in ways that could be addressed politically. One was the question of technological unemployment, which was discussed by Rexford Tugwell, an economist and early Roosevelt adviser whose hopes for actual economic planning under the New Deal were doomed to disappointment.

In a book published in 1933, Tugwell wrote that machinery was inexorably replacing labor in the production of goods and that this was good because "to achieve release from labor . . . is what the race has been blindly striving for always." But release from labor meant unemployment, and unemployment meant lack of income, because the distribution of income to workers was tied exclusively, and as Tugwell saw it, irrationally, to employment. The lesson that had to be learned, he said, was that "income has to be dissociated from jobs." This, he thought, was obvious, and only "our perverted theory of motivation has prevented its discovery."[32]

Tugwell's solution included governmental responsibility for the allocation of investment to ensure that investment decisions did not unnecessarily contribute to unemployment, and also government programs for unemployment insurance. The latter did become part of the New Deal initiative but as a limited and temporary expedient. The possibility that in any large and continuing sense the relation of management and labor might not be mutually beneficial, that management could serve itself by dispensing with labor on a large scale, was beyond the myth and thus beyond the bounds of political contemplation.

The other major dilemma left essentially untouched by the New Deal received fuller official attention and definition than the issue of technological unemployment. This was the issue, as Roosevelt stated it in a message to Congress in 1938, of the growing concentration of economic power. The President's message documented a vast increase in concentrated ownership or management of American industrial and financial resources. And this caused worry because it placed large segments of American business effectively beyond the power of the market, thus placing the average worker and consumer in situations of increasing disadvantage.

The nation, Roosevelt said, required "a realistic system of business regulation" that "has to reach more than consciously immoral acts." It must provide "practical controls over blind economic forces as well as over blindly selfish men." Outright selfishness, he said, is an easier problem to solve; it is harder "to deal with men . . . who are good citizens, but who cannot see the social and economic consequences of their actions in a modern, economically interdependent community." The message recommended increased anti-trust measures and also a study of the phenomenon of concentration.[33]

Congress approved the proposal and established the Temporary National Economic Committee, which spent three years on the commissioned study. It produced a 17,000-page record and numerous reports concluding that the American corporate world *was* highly concentrated and that the matter was one of the largest problems of the time. But the committee came up with no recommendations for action.[34] Partly, this was due to the imminence of war; by the early 1940s, the season for reform was over. But to an important extent, the inability of the committee to deal with the issue of economic concentration was due to the myth of deliverance.

Concentration of economic power—the control of an increasing proportion of resources by a decreasing number of corporations—is a problem that cannot be solved within the bounds of the myth. The localist solution—break up the concentration and return to an economy of small corporations—does not accord with the necessary scope and level of capitalization in industries using advanced technology. The functionalist solution—trust experts to run corporations of any size efficiently—ignores the likelihood that the most earnest experts will perceive problems in terms compatible with their own interests and will slight the claims of opposing interests, especially as the ruling standard is efficiency. It is efficient to displace human labor with machines, but the standard of efficiency offers no guidance for dealing with the human needs, and the claims to liberty and equality, of the unemployed. And the majoritarian solution—power balancing—is defeated by the magnification of capital through concentration. No degree of enhanced labor power could match that of the largest corporations, or rather their combined force.

A massive concentration in corporate power allows managers to set the terms of exchange with other interests—labor, agriculture, small business—themselves, and such terms are inevitably advantageous to managers and disadvantageous to the others. The only source of protection for the weaker interests in this situation is the government. But effective action by the government in protection of the economically weak would require wide recognition of the scope of the problem. The government would have to impose on corporations rules that denied managers the full discretion they claim over the use of capital, rules that denied managers the right to base decisions on efficiency alone where the human costs were too great, broad rules that would amount to some form of economic planning.

In other words, the government would be in the business of allocating costs and losses that arise out of the conflicting interests in the society, which means it would be operating beyond the myth. To break such a monumental impasse in American culture and politics was certainly beyond the capability of Roosevelt's Temporary National Economic Committee—hence the 17,000-page record with no recommendation for policy.

As the New Deal era ended, the problems faced by American labor and agriculture, and even small enterprise, were muted by war and an immense investment in war production. But the underlying problem of concentrated economic power and technological unemployment—and the conflicting stakes held by different groups of Americans in the handling of these problems

—remained to be dealt with by a later generation. Sadly, this generation would be burdened with economic and political limits even more bleak in their implications than those of the Great Depression—and burdened as well with the ever-present, ever-obfuscating myth.

IV

The American Mission: Three Versions, to 1945

The myth of deliverance shapes the way Americans understand conflict in world politics just as it shapes their perceptions of conflict at home. Built into the American view of the world is the assumption that conflict is no more inevitable in international life than it is within a nation. Or rather, we assume there are no international conflicts that could not be resolved positively for all sides—if leaders on all sides approached such solutions with goodwill and rationality. International exchange in itself could only be beneficial if allowed to flow naturally.

The mythic corollary is that violence between nations stems not from unresolvable conflict but from the intrusion into international exchange of some form of unnecessary, illegitimate power. Some party to the conflict must be pressing unreasonable claims, seeking unfair advantage, failing to exercise goodwill. Therefore, the very existence of destructive conflict is evidence of an illegitimate force, some form of evil, at work.

This assumption—that serious conflict is caused by an evil or illegitimate force—is, of course, sometimes true. It is difficult to characterize Nazi Germany, for example, in any other terms. And the experience of dealing with Nazi Germany, of defeating and removing a clearly evil force, strongly confirmed Americans in their mythic convictions about trouble and response in world affairs. But serious trouble, serious international conflict, is not always the result of illegitimacy. Sometimes trouble is produced by a clash of national interests, each of which is reasonable and justifiable. That is, nations seeking to protect the welfare of their own people may take actions, often in the economic sphere, that seriously threaten the interests of others. This is a form of international trouble—the most common and ultimately the most serious—that Americans, searching for a wrongdoer, do not see clearly.

That shapers of American foreign policy have persistently ignored or misunderstood the play of normal national interest in international politics is a well-known, much-analyzed phenomenon. Commentators attribute it variously to a naïveté peculiar to Americans, to an idealism rooted in the nation's founding, to the particular provincialism of American education, or to the wealth and physical isolation that has protected the United States from the constant experience of competition and strife common to most nations.

Then there is the explanation of hypocrisy—the charge that Americans refuse to admit conflicting national interests as a ground for trouble in the world and instead conduct a perpetual search for evil abroad as a cover for America's own national designs. In this view, Woodrow Wilson, for example, could only have been engaged in hypocritical moralizing when he called on Americans to fight in Europe "to make the world safe for democracy" when, in fact, American bankers and industrialists were reaping huge profits from the war. And since Wilson's day, similar suspicions have attached themselves to leaders from Franklin Roosevelt to Lyndon Johnson, Jimmy Carter, and Ronald Reagan—suspicions that American leaders do not act out of the idealism their words express but out of the cynical intention to extend American power behind a mask of moral principle.

But the most important, if invisible, force behind the foreign policies of these Presidents—more important than any element of cynicism, hypocrisy, naïveté, or geographical isolation—is the myth of deliverance from evil. American leaders do not perceive conflicts among the legitimate interests of nations as the source of serious international trouble because, according to the myth, conflicts of such seriousness do not exist. The legitimate interests of all nations are complementary, just as, in the mythic view, the fundamental interests of all groups within the nation are complementary. That is, in world politics as in domestic politics, the myth severely limits the range of problems we are able to see.

In world politics, however, the mythic reading of conflict results in even more serious misperceptions of events than at home. Within the nation, leaders must respond constantly to the press of facts, needs, and claims that may or may not fit mythic principles. The myth clouds the issues and thereby precludes effective responses to some problems, but domestic policies must still respond roughly to realities because of the constant presence and pressure of interested parties. In foreign affairs, the irreducible, intransigent facts behind events are distant, the actual needs and claims of the parties involved more removed than at home. Therefore the role of ideas, which means the role of the myth of deliverance, is larger in foreign than in domestic policy and the gulf between policy and reality is wider.

To an even greater extent than in domestic affairs, then, American responses to foreign affairs are fixed by the myth in a focus on wrongdoing. In crises, eruptions of violence and war, a narrow focus on identifying and defeating a villain becomes explicit. The American people "desire peace by the overcoming of evil by the defeat once for all of the sinister forces that interrupt peace and render it impossible," Woodrow Wilson said in 1917.[1] In less obvious ways, the control of wrongdoing dominates American foreign relations in normal times as well. Starting with the assumption that international conflict stems from wrongful uses of power by wayward nations, Americans see international order and stability as dependent on a trustworthy system for keeping such waywardness under control. What are needed are the right rules, which in turn depend on the right rule makers holding authority, and willingness on the part of most nations to observe the rules. The final assumption is that, with such rules in place, the natural complementarity of interests among nations will be released—taking form mainly in a free flow of beneficial exchange across national borders.

Defining the rules that would produce a beneficial order and bringing such a system to the world, convincing others to adopt it, is the generative principle behind all American approaches to foreign policy. It is, in the familiar term, the American mission in world politics—the mission to ensure international order both by combating evil in times of crisis and by putting in place a trustworthy system for controlling it in times of peace.

But what system, what rules, what rule makers will ensure peace? Again, as in domestic affairs, there are different answers to that question—those proposed by majoritarians, functionalists, and localists. That is, in responding to foreign conflicts as to those at home, each of the three groups has its own conception of what the source of trouble is, who or what the enemy is, and what system of rules and rule makers is best able to control that enemy. And in each case, the system for international deliverance each group proposes is a projection of the system it seeks to enact at home.

There is thus not one American mission, but three—and a continuing three-sided debate on foreign policy that parallels the continuing domestic debate. There is also the same possibility for coalitions on policy among groups, and the same tendency for the coalitions to erode because of the underlying differences among the parties.

These differences make it chronically difficult for the United States to follow any consistent approach to foreign problems. In practice, from the turn of the century to 1945, there were only two occasions—the points of entry into the two world wars— when there was sufficient agreement among the three groups on the presence of an enemy for the government to take clear-cut action. And in 1941 even that agreement and action were precipitated only by the Japanese attack on Pearl Harbor.

At no time in that period was there sufficient agreement among the groups, or even between any two of them, to serve as the basis for ongoing peacetime policy of any coherence. All three had strong positions on what such a policy should be—on the system that would deliver willing nations from war—but there was too little correspondence among them for any approach to be tried with full consistency.

The terms of the standoff among the three emerged in the long debate surrounding the First World War—debate as to whether the United States should fight in aid of England and France, and then, at the war's end, in the bitter debate in the Senate over terms of peace and peacekeeping. This was the first time that the United States was drawn into the larger questions of world affairs and the point at which each group first clearly formulated and enunciated what would become its characteristic version of the American mission—its particular plan for international deliverance.

Wilson's initial response to the war in 1914 was to declare American neutrality, and at the outset there was little disagreement with this policy. It appeared to all three groups that the United States should stay disengaged from the senseless, horribly destructive quarrel engulfing Europe. But neutrality, in the diplomacy of the time, was not simply a passive policy of disengagement. It was also a principle defining the rights and duties of nations with respect to international commerce in time of war. As such, it was a policy that carried at least the possibility of conflict between neutral nations trying to carry on international trade and warring nations interfering with it. And it was on this question of potential trouble arising out of American neutrality policy that differences among majoritarians, functionalists, and localists soon appeared.

Neutrality was a legal principle, part of the international law progressively elaborated throughout the nineteenth century by the trading nations of Europe and the Americas. In international law, belligerent nations—those at war—were forbidden to interfere with the trading activities of neutral nations, which meant, mainly, non-interference with shipping. Neutrals were bound, for their part, not to favor one side or the other through trade —forbidden, for example, to sell munitions to one belligerent and refuse to do so to another. It was a law designed to contain the effects of war by maintaining the maximum degree of normality, but beyond that it was a principle that affirmed the beneficence of trade. It affirmed the idea that exchanges linking widely distant markets in complex patterns of production and sale were good in themselves—good for all parties to them—and should be protected.

Wilson insisted on the importance of protecting the principle and the practice of open trade, or, in terms he and others often used, the principle of freedom of the seas. During the war, he frequently spoke of a future when the prosperity of all the world's people would be quickened by the movement of trade and insisted that even during wartime the principle of free movement, and the links that it made possible, must not be compromised.

The crux of the matter after 1914, however, was what the United States would do if the belligerents did not honor neutral rights—a likelihood, given the circumstances of the war. The circumstances were that England, with its superior surface fleet, was imposing a blockade (illegal in international law) on Germany, preventing food and supplies from getting through. Germany did not have the fleet to do the same but retaliated by mining the approaches to Irish and English ports and by using submarines to attack ships approaching these ports. By the old rules of sea warfare, an attacker was bound to "visit and search" a presumed enemy ship to determine whether it was armed or unarmed and whether it carried cargo and passengers from neutral countries. But submarines could not do this; they could not surface without making themselves vulnerable to attack. Therefore, as long as Germany relied on submarine warfare, neutral shipping approaching England was in jeopardy. Americans traveling on merchantmen were in constant peril, and whenever Americans died on a ship sunk by German submarines, the question of retaliation was raised. Should the Wilson government insist on neutral rights even to the point of fighting for them, or simply allow the belligerent nations to control the seas?

The issue came to a head in May 1915 when over a hundred Americans died in the sinking of the *Lusitania,* a British merchant ship torpedoed by a German submarine. Wilson had to decide, in protesting an incident of this magnitude, whether to continue the American insistence on full respect by Germany for neutral shipping rights or to retreat to a less contentious position.

Most of Wilson's advisers pressed for a rigorous protest. Secretary of State William Jennings Bryan passionately opposed it and argued instead that the government should warn Americans to stay off ships headed for the war zone. Strong diplomatic protest, Bryan feared, would not stop German attacks and it would force the United States eventually to back up its protest with armed action, drawing the country inevitably into war. And for Bryan—still the foremost leader of the nation's localist constituency—there was no conceivable reason for the United States to fight.

Bryan's position on the *Lusitania* protest was the culmination of a decade's crusade he had carried on—a crusade promoting a peace system squarely based on localist premises concerning conflict and its solution. Peace, Bryan believed, was the natural state of relations among people and would prevail if rule making in all countries were carried out by ordinary citizens organizing the affairs of their own communities at the local level. War was caused by the manipulative use of force by groups that had gained power—wrongfully—within a nation and were using power to advance their own special interests. This being the case, Bryan thought, conflict could be resolved and war avoided if, as crises arose, the obvious wrongdoing behind them were exposed to full public view—the same solution he advocated for management-labor disputes.

The system he devised for dealing with international crises was a variation of the fact-finding commissions he proposed for trouble at home. It worked through the mechanism of what he called "cooling-off treaties"—bilateral treaties by which nations would bind themselves to refer "all disputes of every nature whatsoever" that could not be settled diplomatically to a peace commission for impartial investigation. The commissions would be given one year for thorough study of a dispute, during which time the signatory nations, by the terms of the treaty between them, would not go to war. Bryan was confident that such investigation, if given a chance, would preclude serious conflict because the glare of publicity on wrongdoers would end their dangerous activities.[2]

In the years prior to the First World War, Bryan tirelessly

pressed his cooling-off treaties through peace groups, Chautauqua speeches, and a continuous barrage of articles in *The Commoner*. When Wilson offered Bryan the office of Secretary of State, Bryan accepted subject to two conditions: first, that he and his wife not be expected to serve alcohol at diplomatic functions, and second, that Wilson support the vigorous promulgation of cooling-off treaties. The signing of thirty such treaties was one of the great successes of Bryan's life, but the success was offset by his bitter disappointment over the failure of nations to use his principles in the crisis of 1914 to avert the horror of general war.

Bryan's first moment of disillusion occurred at the outset of the war, when an American offer to mediate the dispute was refused by all European parties. He could scarcely credit this refusal, according to his biographer, because of the depth of his belief that "men had grown in Christian brotherhood and become intellectually and morally incapable of undertaking naked militarism."[3] He assumed that the whole thing was a terrible mistake that all parties would naturally prefer to set straight. As he said later in the war, "A week's time for investigation would probably have prevented the present war. . . . A month's time would quite certainly have done so. A year's time would allow passion to subside and reason resume her sway, time for the separation of questions of honor from questions of fact." There are, he said flatly, no legitimate interests that are irreconcilable, and therefore "no disputes which must necessarily be settled by force."[4]

If Bryan was shaken by the European refusal to mediate, so was he appalled by the fact that Americans could even contemplate entering the war. He could see no honest reason for doing so. "If you will scratch through the veneer of those asking for preparedness," he said in a *Commoner* article, "you will find they want war." He urged, therefore, that "the masses, honestly desiring neutrality, should steadfastly oppose the schemes of those who have been infected with the war virus." The masses, that is, are honest and do not want war. Those who want war are dishonest schemers, hiding their true motives behind a protective veneer. The interests behind war are never the ordinary people, but "the munitions shylocks, the professional man-killers and the jingoes." The people must learn how to protect themselves "from ambitious monarchs, from greedy merchants and from the excitement of representatives who act without deliberation."[5]

There was only one way to achieve peace for Bryan—"a peace universal and perpetual"—and that was to put "the HEART of the world in control of the destinies of mankind." He never relinquished his belief that with truly popular, locally based government which affirmed the moral capacities of ordinary human beings, nations would no longer "descend to the brute level to fight out all difference 'with tooth and claw.' "[6]

Holding such strong convictions, Bryan was in agony as Wilson's Cabinet reached its decision on the need for a strong protest to Germany about the *Lusitania* and an insistence on respect for neutral rights in the future. As the decision approached, he could not sleep, lost weight, and looked ill. At the height of this emotional crisis, he apparently developed a fever and had difficulty walking. Then, after several days of tormented soul-searching, he resigned his office rather than acquiesce in a gesture he felt certain would lead to an unjustified war.

"Force represents the old system—the system that must pass away," he said, explaining his resignation. What must replace force, he went on, was a system of persuasion—"the system that has been growing, all too slowly . . . but growing for 1,900 years." And he urged again his belief that America's best contribution to a sane and decent future would be to stand aside, to remain an exemplar of the new system that would end war. "Some nation must lift the world out of the black night of war into the light of that day when 'swords shall be beaten into plowshares,' " he declared. "Why not make that honor ours?"[7]

For Bryan, then, the road to deliverance from the old system of force playing itself out in Europe was to stay away from it and to provide a new model for the future. He was absolutely certain that this was the best route because of his equal certainty that there were no necessary connections that had to be protected between the United States and other nations—none that was worth great risk or great cost.

Functionalists and majoritarians naturally saw the same picture differently. They, too, saw the war in Europe as the product of a corrupt system of power politics. They, too, sought a future marked by deliverance from corrupt power—a future in which the American model for the control of power would prevail. And they, too, wanted to avoid war. But for wage earners and capital managers—groups whose well-being was bound up with the health of an increasingly intricate industrial system—connections between the United States and other industrial nations could not be ignored. They saw the logic of industrialism linking enterprise not only nationwide but worldwide and saw a future that would be either decent or desperate depending on whether or not nations could be delivered from the power abuses that destroyed such links.

Functionalists, not surprisingly, had been in the forefront of efforts to regularize international commerce well before the war began, and to do so through channels not controlled by politicians. The focus of their efforts was the promotion of international law and international courts as the best means of resolving disputes among nations on objective, not political, terms. Around the turn of the century, when American fortunes, interests, and hopes became increasingly linked to those in other countries, international lawyers and progressive business leaders founded a number of organizations to advance the cause of peace and peaceful exchange through international law. Notable in this group were the multimillionaire Andrew Carnegie and Charles Evans Hughes's longtime mentor, Elihu Root, a New York lawyer, Secretary of State for Theodore Roosevelt, and later senator from New York. The efforts of such people produced the American Society of International Law in 1906, the American Society for the Judicial Settlement of International Disputes in 1910, and, in the same year, the World Peace Foundation and the Carnegie Endowment for International Peace, both of which promoted international law as part of a broader peace program.

The coming of war was only further evidence for functionalists that power must be replaced by law as the medium for international exchange. As Root declared in 1915, writing to business leader Charles Francis Adams, "We must have a court, that is certain; but if it is to be really a court and not a new form of arbitrary government by plot and counterplot, the court must have a law which it is bound to apply." And further, the law must be based on agreement as to "adequate rules of conduct" and backed up by "sanctions for its enforcement." To apply such sanctions there must be an "international peace force" run by "experts" employing "technical knowledge" of the law and offenses against it so that the system could preserve principle—so that it would not promote political ends through the use of power.[8]

That is, functionalists were advocating the same principles for ordering international affairs as those they pressed at home. The first principle is that economic exchange is vital for industrial economies, and should be organized by people who, by training and experience, understand the logic of their transactions. The major enemy in international affairs, in this view, is the nationalist, the politician or military leader who would use national power to seek special advantage over other countries, thus disrupting the logical efficiency of functional relations. The solution —the mythic solution—is the replacement of governments based on power manipulation with governments based on the functionalist model that entrusts authority to those who use knowledge and reason, not power, as the ground for decisions and action.

But how did principle apply to practice? What did functionalists think the United States should do about the war convulsing Europe—specifically about the German refusal to honor neutral shipping rights? Without question, they believed in keeping channels of international trade open by warning Germany that the United States would not accept the sinking of merchant ships and the loss of American lives. And they further advocated backing up that warning with the immediate construction of warships. Germany would not dare to bring a strongly armed America into the war, Charles Evans Hughes argued throughout the 1916 presidential campaign. He insisted that a display of strength would allow the United States to stand apart while still preserving the legal system of rights and duties necessary for a healthy future. And he criticized Wilson for being too soft, for not making it clear that the United States would not tolerate violations of neutral rights.[9]

Hughes had been on the Supreme Court in 1915 when the *Lusitania* sinking forced each group to clarify its position on the war and therefore had not been a functionalist spokesman at that moment. But a new voice articulating the beliefs of the managerial interest did speak at that time. Herbert Hoover, in one of the first political stands he ever took, urged President Wilson to send a strong protest to Germany and a warning against future attacks. Hoover spoke from his vantage point as organizer of relief supplies for Belgium, as an American close to the scene of war. American protest would be important, Hoover thought, in its effect on the German government, but equally important in keeping in check the emotions of Americans.

If Germany continued to sink ships and kill Americans and the United States did nothing, Hoover warned Wilson, "it could arouse a flood of feeling on the part of our countrymen such as manifested itself at the time of the Spanish War and which could not be controlled by the sane minds at the head of the Government."[10] That is, Hoover was hoping to avoid war by restraining what he saw as two sources of equally dangerous irresponsibility —the leaders of Germany, who were imbued with an ethic of power and would respond only to displays or threats of power, *and* the American populace, who, like all unsophisticated people, were likely to react to world events emotionally.

The differences between functionalists and localists on this point could not be more clear. Where Bryan, the localist, trusted only the common people and counted on them to restrain "the excitement of representatives who act without deliberation," Hoover and functionalists generally took precisely the opposite tack—to minimize the influence on decisions of the excitement they expected from ordinary people. They wanted to enlarge the decision-making discretion of "the sane minds" of those whose knowledge and responsibility allowed them to assess circumstances carefully and respond in a principled way. And, of course, the underlying principle functionalists sought to apply in international relations was the maintenance of links among traders around the world and the promotion of openness among nations to the practice of such linkages.

This was a majoritarian principle as well—Wilson's major principle. "American citizens act within their indisputable rights in taking their ships and traveling wherever their legitimate business calls them upon the high seas," the American note to the German government declared after the sinking of the *Lusitania*.[11] But Wilson's view of American linkages to the rest of the world was not just a matter of legal right. Unlike Bryan and the localists, he saw international interdependence as a matter of economic and political fact. "The United States was once in enjoyment of what we used to call splendid isolation," he said at the end of the 1916 presidential campaign, but now "from across the Atlantic and from across the Pacific, we feel to the quick the influences which are affecting ourselves."

Making the lesson yet clearer, he pointed out that the United States used to seek capital abroad, but now "we have become, not the debtors, but the creditors of the world, and the part that other nations used to play in promoting industries, which extended as wide as the world itself, we are playing. . . . We can determine to a large extent who is to be financed and who is not to be financed." For this reason, he concluded, the United States could no longer be "provincial and isolated and unconnected with the great forces of the world, for now we are in the great drift of humanity which is to determine the politics of every country in the world."[12]

Wilson's point was that American economic power had grown so large that whatever the United States did would influence events elsewhere—whether it acted or did not act, invested or did not invest. Therefore, for Wilson, it was crucially important that the United States act on principles conducive to a good, peaceful life for Americans and for all others—in mythic terms, principles of deliverance from evil. And the central principle, "the *sine qua non* of peace, equality, and cooperation" was the freedom of the seas, the "free, constant, unthreatened intercourse of nations."[13]

As Bryan predicted, however, the pursuit of principle produced war. Stiff protests to Germany during the summer of 1915 were followed in April 1916 by an American threat to break off diplomatic relations if neutral rights were further violated. In May, Germany announced restrictions on its submarine warfare and this policy continued through the end of the year. In January 1917, however, German military leaders declared a resumption of unrestricted submarine attack, having decided that cutting off all shipping to England would defeat the Allies before the United States could effectively mobilize to respond militarily. In February, the United States broke diplomatic relations. In March, German submarines sank several American ships without warning. On April 2, Wilson asked Congress for a declaration of war against Germany, and on April 6, Congress declared war, almost unanimously.

It was the essential correspondence in outlook between majoritarians and functionalists that laid the basis for American entry into the war. That is, these two groups both saw as a positive value for all countries a system of open international relations allowing maximum levels of trade and other exchange. They both saw the violation of neutral rights by Germany as a wrongful use of national power threatening an open system of relations. And, by 1917, leaders in both groups had begun to fear that a victorious Germany, still governed by a military aristocracy, would thwart an open order far into the future.

Localists did not share this interest in fostering an open world order through active engagement in international dealings, let alone through war, and there was some localist dissent to Wilson's conclusions that the United States must fight. But by 1917, their dissent was muted because by then so many ships had been sunk and so many American lives lost that German submarine attacks had taken on the character of attacks on the United States —which even localists could not tolerate.

Thus all three groups agreed finally that Germany was an enemy and should be defeated. But this did not mean that the three had reached fundamental agreement on what exactly they were fighting, what the evil was that Germany represented. The localist differences from the other two were clear; majoritarian and functionalist differences from each other were less so.

For functionalists, the enemy in general was nationalism, the commitment by national leaders to promote national interests through the use of power. Germany, a nation in which the military strongly influenced policy, was a particularly dangerous enemy because it practiced a more virulent version of power politics than most nations, but in the functionalist view, national political leaders everywhere were prone to exert power, not reason, in their international affairs.

Majoritarians, on the other hand, saw Germany, not as a nation somewhat worse and more dangerous than most, but as a total perversion of what a nation should and *could* be. Wilson, in leading the nation into war, characterized the conflict in terms of power abuse general enough to express the convictions of all three groups. But the logic and implications of his messages about the war, to Congress and to the people, were distinctly majoritarian. What was wrong with Germany, for Wilson, was that the power of its government was detached from control by the majority of its people.

In his April 2 speech asking Congress for a declaration of war, Wilson said that "the menace to . . . peace and freedom lies in the existence of autocratic governments backed by organized force which is controlled wholly by their will, not the will of the people."[14] Later that year he emphasized the illegitimacy of the German government, removed as it was from the will of the German people, by referring to it as "this intolerable Thing." The United States was fighting, he said, "this intolerable Thing of which the masters of Germany have shown us the ugly face, this menace of combined intrigue and force which we now see so clearly as the German power, a Thing without conscience or honor or capacity for covenanted peace." He concluded that "this Thing" must be defeated so that the Allies could construct the terms for a just peace with the real spokesmen for the German people.[15]

The ultimate enemy, Wilson told Americans, was not Germany but rather the remaining hold on Europe of ancient aristocracies generally. "The past and the present are in deadly grapple," he declared in a Fourth of July speech in 1918. And the past was manifested by ruling groups who pursued "selfish ambitions," through "governments clothed with the strange trappings and primitive authority of an age that is altogether alien and hostile to our own."[16]

Thus where functionalists saw the enemy as the power-wielding nation no matter who ran it, majoritarians saw it as the nation captured and run by selfish and irresponsible minorities, serving special instead of general interests. At the point of American entry into the war, this distinction was not important; Germany was an enemy on both grounds, threatening to both groups. But after the war, in efforts to arrive at terms for peace, the differences between the two surfaced, cracking the wartime coalition wide open and precluding the possibility of postwar cooperation.

Wilson set the terms of the postwar debate with the peace proposals he outlined even before the United States entered the war. His plan for peace was the work of a political theorist; it was general, systemic, logical in the relation of all of its parts. And as his conception of what had gone wrong rested on majoritarian premises, so did his solution for putting things right.

In the majoritarian version of the myth of deliverance, nations whose power was safely harnessed by popular control could organize among their own people rules of fairness that would naturally extend to relations with people of other nations—if such relations were not blocked by power abuse on the part of other countries. But the nation-state, with strong democratic institutions, was the key because in majoritarian belief, the only way that illegitimate power *could* be controlled was through national institutions. If the political tools of a nation were firmly in the hands of the majority, then powerful minorities—political or economic—could be kept from using the nation for their own special interests. And a world of nations so organized would naturally remain in peaceful balance because natural links—economic exchange most importantly—could be pursued to the benefit of all. These premises formed the basis for Wilson's general scheme for peace incorporated in his famous Fourteen Points and in his elaboration of the Fourteenth Point—his call for "a general association of nations" to keep the peace.

A first and basic step toward peace through democracy for Wilson was national self-government. All national groups held subject to other nations had to be released to organize themselves. Nine of Wilson's Fourteen Points applied this principle—later called the principle of self-determination—to specific areas of Europe, mainly to areas of Eastern Europe long controlled by Austria, Russia, or Turkey. Even more important, however, was the League of Nations, the "general association" written into the Versailles peace treaty to provide a means by which nations could cooperate to keep peace in the future. The League was to work through joint decisions by its members to subject any wrong-doing nation to collective diplomatic or economic pressure, or—where such measures failed—to collective military action to stop wrongful uses of power.

In Wilson's conception of the League—and it was principally his design—the force of majorities would come to bear on questions of international order through the League Council. Under Article 10 of the League Covenant, the Council, made up of delegates from the major nations of the world, would decide when the wrongful behavior of a particular country had become threatening enough to require counteraction by the League. As most of the major nations, including the United States, were democracies, their voting on the League Council—Wilson presumed—would have to reflect the general interest of their people. That is, democratically elected officials could not make secret deals for the benefit of powerful groups and special interests as in the old days of secret diplomacy.

As Wilson also presumed that the general interests of the people of all nations were compatible, he was sure that League decisions based on such interests would necessarily promote peace. Thus pressure from national majorities, channeled through their governments to the League Council, would be the effective mechanism for enforcing a just peace, the effective agent of deliverance.

Outlining his idea for such a league in his 1917 speech asking Congress for a declaration of war, Wilson said the United States should seek "a partnership of democratic nations" committed to the control of abusive power. "It must be a league of honor, a partnership of opinion," he said. And such a partnership would guarantee peace because the aggressive schemes that are possible when power is controlled by "a narrow and privileged class" are "happily impossible where public opinion commands and insists upon full information concerning all the nation's affairs."

*   *   *

After the war, Wilson went to France to negotiate the peace and returned home early in 1919, buoyed by the ecstatic response of crowds wherever he went in Europe. Disembarking in New York, he told Americans that "the great pulse and heart of the world" were behind the Covenant. The people had come to understand, he said, "that if there is right in the world, if there is justice . . . there is no reason why nations should be divided in support of justice."[17] And he submitted the peace treaty including the League Covenant to the Senate, asking for its speedy ratification. This, of course, did not happen. Instead, the proposed treaty, and particularly the League, met the outraged opposition of both functionalists and localists, for whom—for different reasons—Wilson's majoritarian premises were anathema.

Charles Evans Hughes declared the League, as Wilson conceived it, "a grave mistake" as soon as the terms of the Covenant were made public in March 1919. Stating the position that would be consistently followed by functionalist Republicans through the entire League debate, he declared his sympathy for a league whose purpose would be "to provide international arrangements for conferences, for the judicial settlement of disputes, for conciliation and for cooperation"—but not "the attempted compulsion of an inflexible rule."[18]

The "inflexible rule" that Hughes and other functionalists objected to in Wilson's design was Article 10, the provision for collective enforcement of the peace directed by the League Council. Without that offensive article, functionalists supported the League for the same reasons they supported the development of other international institutions—to create channels facilitating the international linkages they sought. In fact, a number of prominent functionalists, including William Howard Taft, Theodore Roosevelt, financier Bernard Baruch, Herbert Hoover, and Wilson's archenemy in the League debate, Senator Henry Cabot Lodge of Massachusetts, were founders or backers of the League to Enforce Peace, a group formed in 1915 to promote a postwar peace system based on an institution formalizing international cooperation.

The problem with Article 10 for its functionalist detractors was precisely its virtue for Wilson—that it placed decisions over

war and peace in a council of *political* leaders necessarily responsive to the interests of popular majorities. Wilson counted on
popular pressure to keep politics honest and principled, but functionalists feared the opposite result. In their view, the ordinary
citizenry—as Hoover said to Wilson at the time of the *Lusitania*
question—was emotional, excitable, and therefore more likely to
be stirred to fight for foolish reasons than to hold political leaders
in check.

Hughes, commenting on this point as Secretary of State
several years later, said that the impulse to self-aggrandizement
and violence is in "the very woof and warp of human nature,"
the result of "insistent human will, inflexible in its purposes."
Thus "war is not an abnormality" but an ever-present danger in
international dealings, especially "when the smoldering fires of
old grievances have been fanned into a flame by a passionate sense
of irremediable injury, or the imagination of peoples is dominated by apprehension of present danger to national safety, or by
what is believed to be an assault upon national honor."[19]

And in the immediate aftermath of the 1914–18 war, grievances were far from subdued. Herbert Hoover repeatedly urged
on Wilson the advice that the principles for peaceful order Wilson outlined in his Fourteen Points and in the League Covenant
were wholly out of keeping with the nationalistic aspirations of
all European governments. Lloyd George, Hoover said, operated
on one principle alone—expediency in pressing the United King-
dom's interests. And Clemenceau was a man whose "soul contained to his dying day all the bitterness of the sufferings of
the French people" and who was convinced by bitter experience
that "force always triumphed over abstract justice." European
nations were still committed to the Old World system of power,
Hoover believed, and thus the United States should not be tied
in the League Council to judgments on war and peace made by
Europeans.[20]

What functionalists sought in 1919 was ratification of the
League Covenant but with the American commitment to Article
10 made subject to a reservation stating that any League decision
to use force would not be binding on the United States without
congressional approval. This group did not champion congres-

sional authority generally, and their purpose in seeking such a reservation was not to increase the scope of congressional decision making in foreign affairs. Rather, led by Senator Henry Cabot Lodge, they fought for the reservation to constrain the political authority of the President—and his ability to act quickly. Congress, although responsive to voters, was unlikely to engage the nation in international politics through the League because the many constituencies pressuring Congress would be divided in their demands. The President, however, taking a reading of general opinion and interest, might very well lead the nation— foolishly—into war.

The effect of Lodge's reservation, therefore, would be to constrict the influence of national majorities on questions of foreign policy by constricting the power over foreign policy of national political leaders. And its general effect would be to keep the United States unengaged in League politics while still engaged in the non-political processes that were part of the Covenant—various processes for the peaceful settlement of disputes.

In other words, Hughes and functionalists generally opposed international political engagement, but favored international arrangements in which disputes would be turned over to judges, conciliators, and diplomats. They wanted decisions kept out of the hands of political leaders and entrusted to men of reason, knowledge, and experience—the experts whose training and discipline allowed them to overcome the pulls of selfish interest and the impulses to violence that place international relations in constant peril of conflict and war.

Localists were hard pressed on the issue of the League. They were not internationalists. They did not believe in the need for integrating American policies with those of other nations and further assumed that advocates of extensive commitment abroad were pressing special interests under cover of a pretended national interest. The real national interest, for localists, lay in organizing a society in which all important commitments were made at the local level. This did not mean that localists thought that an ongoing foreign policy could literally be made by the people themselves, but rather that there was no *need* for foreign policy except for self-defense.

Given these predilections, localists were generally against American membership in the League. But they had difficulty maintaining this position because they were divided between the two political parties, and the leadership in both parties was strongly committed to some form of League—the Democrats to Wilson's conception, the Republicans to Wilson's League with their reservation to Article 10.

In the end, most localists voted with their parties. Those who were Democrats backed Wilson, as they were urged to do by William Jennings Bryan—in spite of his own strong objections to the provision in Article 10 for collective military action. Bryan was willing to accept Article 10 because he thought it would never be used, given the capacity of the League to act as a grandly inclusive agency for cooling off, for conciliation. That is, Bryan saw the League as the institutionalization of his own long-held answer to international conflict. Republican localists had an easier time following their leadership because, as believers in congressional as opposed to presidential authority, they welcomed the functionalist reservation to Article 10. Fearing foreign entanglement, they trusted Congress to keep the United States disengaged from world affairs in situations where the President might not.

But if most localists followed party leadership, not all did. Fifteen senators followed their convictions and refused to support the League in any form. These were the Irreconcilables, as they were called. They came from both parties, but ten of the fifteen came from the localist heartland in the West, Southwest, and South, or from semi-localist regions of the Midwest and the West Coast.

The most articulate, most passionate voice among the irreconcilable opponents of the League was that of the localist leader from Idaho, William Borah, and he feared foreign entanglement even if the Republican reservation was accepted. In a major Senate speech on November 19, 1919, Borah called for the rejection of the League because it would rob the American people of essential control over their own lives. The transfer of power over war and peace to an international council would be a major threat to true democracy, he said, and a formal provision for congressional review of decisions to go to war would not protect democracy because Congress could not control the vote of the American representative on the League Council. What if the American member, following instructions from the President, voted with a Council majority to send troops to a threatened country? Borah asked. When the President submitted that decision to Congress, what choice would Congress have "except the bare technical right to refuse which as a moral proposition it will not dare to exercise"?

Democracy, Borah insisted, does not depend on forms and technical rights but on "a continuing trust in the moral purposes of the average man and woman." In transferring power to the executive and beyond to an international body, "you will have soon destroyed the atmosphere . . . of confidence in the self-governing capacities of the masses, in which alone a democracy may thrive." The only guaranty of peace, he concluded, is "the guaranty which comes of the control of the war-making power by the people."[21]

The issue for Borah, as for Wilson and Lodge, Hughes, Root, Hoover et al., was finally one of authority—"control of the war-making power." And again, for Borah, control should be placed in the people, not the people as a whole or in vast majorities, as Wilson wanted, but in the people individually. He wanted, Borah said, a "free untrammeled Nation," a nation free "to determine for itself and in its own way where duty lies and where wisdom calls"—and a nation where such determinations were those of the people. "There is not a supreme council possible of creation . . . equal in wisdom, in conscience, and humanitarianism to the wisdom and conscience and humanitarianism of the hundred million free and independent liberty-loving souls to whom the living God has intrusted the keeping of this Nation," he declared.[22]

Wilson needed a two-thirds majority in the Senate for ratifying the League Covenant, a number he could easily have obtained if he had accepted the functionalist reservation and gained the reservationist votes, or if he had persuaded functionalist leaders to accept his position. But both sides were adamant, as were those irreconcilably opposed to any League.

To many, the major issues in the Senate debate—attaching or

not attaching a Republican reservation to Article 10—seemed absurd. In this view, the requirement that Congress vote on any commitment by the United States to join in military action sponsored by the League was a meaningless technicality, because Congress already had authority under the Constitution over declarations of war. The reservation merely restated the Constitution, which made it seem equally foolish for the Republicans to insist on it and for Wilson to stake the whole League battle on it. And as the ostensible issue seemed of little real consequence, many commentators have assumed that the real issues lay elsewhere—for example, in badly mistaken tactical judgment on Wilson's part, or personal animosity between Lodge and Wilson, or in attempts by both sides to discredit the other with a view to the 1920 presidential election.

All of these matters were undoubtedly implicated in the League fight, but at a deeper level, the ostensible issue—the reservation to Article 10—*was* the real one, or rather it was the political form taken by the real issue: the deep commitment by each of the three groups to different versions of the American mission. Each, starting with the mythic premise that conflict among nations was *not* inevitable, proffered different solutions for international violence and war. As with domestic policy, the solutions for all three were procedural—finding a trustworthy system of rule making. And, of course, each group looked to a different rule maker, the one consistent with its own interest and outlook.

Wilson insisted on the authority of the President to make basic decisions about American foreign policy because the President was responsible to national majorities and would be held by them to decisions reflecting the general interest of the people. Functionalists, horrified by the prospect of foreign policy tied to popular opinion, sought to block the influence of the people on foreign affairs by blocking the authority of the President and increasing the role of professional diplomats and other conciliators. Localists wanted to block both the politicians and the professionals—in fact, anyone likely to pursue an active policy of engagement with other countries for the promotion of trade or anything else. Keeping authority over foreign policy in Congress

was therefore an imperative for localists, the best means of blocking the internationalist impulses of the other two groups.

Thus the differences over Article 10 were real and deep.
Wilson tried to break the impasse in the League debate by
reaching over the heads of the quarreling senators, as he had done
during the Underwood tariff debate, and going directly to the
people. In early September 1919, he set off on a train tour of the
country to explain personally the logic of his peace system to
the public, asking voters to instruct their senators to support a
League which would be moved in its decisions by the interests
of the whole people, not special interest.

He spoke day after day, in city after city, insisting that a
league enforcing international justice would not draw the nation
into war. Rather, it would prevent war by discouraging would-
be aggressors from the start. It would be, as he had said earlier,
not an entangling alliance, but a means "to disentangle the peoples of the world from those combinations in which they seek
their own separate and private interests and unite the people of
the world to preserve the peace . . . upon a basis of common right
and justice."[23] The tour had gone on for three grueling weeks
when on September 25, after speaking in Pueblo, Colorado,
Wilson collapsed and several days later suffered a debilitating
stroke.

When the Covenant came before the Senate in November,
no compromise had been reached. There were two large blocs—
Wilsonians and reservationists—neither of which had two-thirds
of the votes. Then there were the fifteen Irreconcilables—localists, essentially—who would not join either group. Thus the
possibility of American membership in the League of Nations was
defeated because the major interests in the United States—in
agreement on the defeat of Germany in war—could not agree on
the design of general policies for peacetime. More to the point,
the two groups interested in active international engagement—
majoritarians and functionalists—could not agree on terms for
peace, and thus the localists controlled the result by default.

This essential equation—lack of agreement between majoritarians and functionalists on approaches to world affairs and
the consequent control of foreign policy by localists—continued

throughout the interwar period. A Republican coalition of functionalists and localists held the presidency and Congress throughout the 1920s, and a Democratic team of majoritarians and
localists did the same through the 1930s. Within both coalitions,
there was tension over foreign policy, but neither the functionalists nor the majoritarians chose to fight their localist partners very
hard on foreign issues. Both, in effect, relinquished foreign policy
to localists in return for support on domestic questions.

The localists had an advantage in this bargaining relation
because most matters in foreign affairs, especially those concerning treaties, lay—constitutionally—in the province of the Senate.
And with two senators from every state, the localist-agrarian
regions had far greater weight (42 votes from 21 states[24]) than
their proportion of the national population warranted. Preemi-
nent among localist senators and highly influential in foreign
policy throughout the period—as in the League debate—was
William Borah. He was chairman of the Senate Foreign Relations Committee under the Republicans and ranking minority
member under the Democrats. And from this vantage point, he
firmly squelched any initiative, functionalist or majoritarian, that
threatened to engage the United States in serious commitments
to others.

First and most important, Borah and the localists kept at bay
any remaining possibility of United States membership in the
League of Nations, in the face of some continuing pressure from
functionalists to reopen the League question on the basis of the
Lodge reservation. In fact, during the presidential election campaign of 1920, Charles Evans Hughes, Herbert Hoover, and Elihu
Root, among other prominent professionals and businessmen,
formed a Committee of 31 to urge the election of the Republican
Warren Harding on the grounds that a Republican would best
ensure American membership in the League on proper terms.
Harding, on his election, appointed Hughes Secretary of State,
but listened to Borah on the issue of the League and refused even
to resubmit the Covenant to the Senate.

The embarrassed Hughes considered resigning but stayed to
press what he could of the functionalist cause. In his first year in
office he organized a successful naval disarmament conference in

Washington—although its success was due in important part to Borah's backing. Reducing the military power available to national political leaders suited both functionalist and localist purposes. A more strictly functionalist mission for Hughes was to reorganize the foreign service corps of the State Department on a professional basis. "The notion that a wide-awake, average American can do anything is flattering to the American pride, but costs the government dearly," he told the Chamber of Commerce in 1922. And in 1924 Congress passed the Rogers Act, providing for regularized training, assignment, and promotion for foreign service officers.[25]

Hughes employed functionalist techniques also in solving, for a time at least, the problem of collecting war debts owed the United States by England and France. The problem was that payment to the United States depended on receipt by the debtor nations of war reparations owed to them by Germany. But Germany could not pay, because its economy was in collapse. Political attempts to settle this round of trouble had been fruitless. Hughes's response was to call in the financial experts. "If statesmen cannot agree," he said, "why should they not invite men . . . of such prestige, experience and honor that their agreement upon the amount to be paid, and upon a financial plan for making out the payments, would be accepted throughout the world as the most authoritative expression obtainable?" The result in 1924 was the Dawes Commission and a financial plan that worked fairly well until it collapsed under the pressure of world depression after 1930.[26]

Another functionalist cause, once American membership in the League was completely foreclosed, was American participation in the League's Permanent Court of International Justice, which operated under its own treaty. Proponents of international law managed to get the Permanent Court treaty submitted to the Senate for ratification twice, first in 1926 and again in 1935. Both times Borah led the opposition, mainly from localist regions, in moves that effectively blocked the possibility of the United States joining the Court.

In spite of their belief in international law, however, the nation's managers—the businessmen, lawyers, engineers, and other professionals who sought international linkages ordered by reason, not politics—did not confine their search for world order to the construction of leagues and courts and other international agencies. They were also concerned with enlarging the influence of professionals generally on the internal process of foreign policy making. The most notable effort along this line was the formation in 1921 of the Council on Foreign Relations.

A Council publication describing the genesis of the group marks its beginning in 1918 in discussions among expert advisers at the Paris Peace Conference who were disturbed by what they saw there. They were especially unsettled by the degree to which political pressures displaced the counsels of the "diplomats, generals, admirals, financiers, lawyers, and technical experts" who were there to make their knowledge available to the negotiators. Concerned to prevent "such a state of things in the future," a number of the American advisers at Paris formed the Council to conduct a "continuous conference on international questions affecting the United States, by bringing together experts on statecraft, finance, industry, education and science." The "continuous conference" took the form of study groups to which public officials were invited so that they could learn from experts who have "direct access to the facts which affect foreign policy—or ought to affect it."

Another Council concern was to develop a pool of leaders for the future in foreign affairs. For this purpose, the Council sought groups of "outstanding young men from Columbia, Harvard, Princeton and Yale Universities—seniors, graduate students and young instructors" to meet in short conferences with Council members "who had had or were having a direct part in the evolution and application of American policy."[27]

The Council also engaged in public education on international affairs through articles in its journal, *Foreign Affairs,* its yearly survey of American foreign policy, *The United States in World Affairs,* and books on particular subjects growing out of study projects. Its publications were not aimed, however, as were those of some internationalist groups, at a wide public audience. Rather, they addressed an educated and sophisticated readership whose functions in various fields involved them in worldwide dealings and whose influence on foreign affairs the Council sought to foster.

In the government, however, even with Charles Evans Hughes as Secretary of State, functionalists did not have the power to move very far toward their goal of active, professionally ordered interdependence among nations. Allied with the localists, they could go only as far as the common interest of the two groups extended. In practice, the functionalist-localist alliance could block the engagement of the United States in *political* relations abroad on the Wilsonian model, but it could not supply solid ground for international engagement on any other terms.

The localist search for political detachment from world conflict reached its high point in the 1930s as increasing tensions in Europe and the threat of war raised again the issues Wilson had faced—questions about what the American connections to Europe were; which, if any, were vital; and what the United States should do to maintain and protect them.

The localist response to the renewal of European trouble stemming from the expansionist policies of fascist states was the formulation and passage of the Neutrality Acts, beginning in 1935. This legislation was inspired, in its timing and its form, by reports from a Special Senate Committee on Investigation of the Munitions Industry. Chaired by Gerald Nye, a Republican from North Dakota, the committee documented extravagant profit taking by the arms industry during the 1914–18 war. These findings lent wide credence to the conception that munitions makers were the invidious interest behind war—a direct extension of the localist conviction that trusts, monopolies, and a minority of dishonest, irresponsible, plundering businessmen were the cause of social inequities at home. The committee concluded that American financiers, munitions makers, and other corporations that did business with the belligerents were the real interests behind Wilson's decision to enter the war and its only beneficiaries.

This had been Bryan's message to the country twenty years earlier, and the Senate, having adopted Bryan's views about the forces stirring war, turned also—in the Neutrality Acts—to his solutions. The purpose of the 1935 act, renewed by successive

Congresses through the 1930s, was to block every use of the presumed avenues to war. Pressed enthusiastically by Borah and his fellow localists, the laws forbade credit to belligerents, the sale to belligerents of arms or implements of war, and the shipping of American goods or the passage of American citizens on belligerent ships. The assumption was that if there were no American monetary stake in Europe, there would be no reason for the United States to fight in Europe should war erupt again.

The localists were not alone in their suspicions about big business or in their desire to keep out of the quarrels of Europe. There was wide sympathy in the wage-earning constituency for both views. But majoritarians, or certainly their leaders, did not share the localist assumption that the *only* important ties to Europe were the questionable connections of the profiteers. Franklin Roosevelt preached the message, more and more insistently through the 1930s, that Americans were indissolubly linked to Europe and the rest of the world by ties that should be multiplied, not broken.

Roosevelt was exasperated with Nye and Borah and other promoters of neutrality legislation. They imagine, he said, "that if the civilization of Europe is about to destroy itself through internal strife, it might just as well go ahead and do it and that the United States can stand idly by."[28] His own view was that within a generation technological change "will so narrow the oceans separating us from the Old World, that our customs and our actions are necessarily involved with hers, whether we like it or not." Further, air transportation will make the entire world "a unit," so that "no interruption of it anywhere can fail, in the future, to disrupt economic life everywhere."[29]

In 1937, with the tensions in Europe worsening and many Americans more anxious than ever to steer clear of them, Roosevelt stressed again the inescapable linkages between the United States and the rest of the world. "There is a solidarity and interdependence about the modern world both technically and morally," he declared, and then spun out a metaphor of illness and contagion to describe the forces threatening that healthy condition. "It seems to be unfortunately true that the epidemic of world lawlessness is spreading," he said, and when this occurs with physical disease, local authorities impose "a quarantine of the patients in order to protect the health of the community against the spread of the disease." The same was true of politics, he concluded, warning that "war is a contagion [that] can engulf states and peoples remote from the original scene of hostilities."[30]

Two years later, announcing the German invasion of Poland, he abandoned metaphor to declare outright that "when peace has been broken anywhere, peace in all countries everywhere is in danger," and "passionately though we may desire detachment, we are forced to realize that every word that comes through the air, every ship that sails the sea, every battle that is fought does affect the American future."[31] The following year, with France defeated, the threat, as Roosevelt described it, was clearer and more immediate than ever. "If Great Britain goes down, the Axis Powers will control the continents of Europe, Asia, Africa, Australia and the high seas—and they will be in a position to bring enormous military and naval resources against this hemisphere. It is no exaggeration to say that all of us in the Americas would be living at the point of a gun—a gun loaded with explosive bullets, economic as well as military."[32]

Elaborating on the economic danger, he said that German dominance of Europe would put American laborers in competition with workers held in virtual enslavement, at wage levels set by the state. "The whole fabric of working life as we know it —business, manufacturing, mining, agriculture—all would be mangled and crippled under such a system," he declared.[33]

Roosevelt's political aim in the later 1930s was to loosen the restrictions of the Neutrality Acts sufficiently to allow England and France to buy arms in the United States, financed by American banks if need be. Roosevelt's logic was that arming England and France would deter Germany from attacking them or their allies, and such deterrence was the best means of keeping the United States out of another war. Functionalists, while wholly in agreement with Roosevelt on the fact and the virtue of interdependence, were divided on his strategy of keeping the peace through a balance of military power. Some thought it was the best option available; others were too mistrustful of exertions of power by politicians to back his views.

And the localists remained adamantly against amending the neutrality policy. The major fight on the issue occurred in 1939 over the fourth Neutrality Act, which Roosevelt proposed to amend so that England and France could at least buy arms even if the purchases could not be financed by American banks or carried to Europe on American ships. Roosevelt sought to gain Borah's support for the amendment at a famous White House meeting in July. At that meeting, Secretary of State Cordell Hull stressed the point that war seemed imminent but that American arms sales to England and France would give Germany pause. Borah, however, dismissed Hull's premise, saying he doubted that war was close. The angry Hull then invited Borah to read State Department cables from embassies in Europe reporting signs of war, but Borah loftily refused. He said he had his own sources of information carefully built up over the years and they led him to different conclusions. Borah was, completely characteristically, refusing to trust the experts, but in this case the experts were right.[34]

Germany attacked Poland in September, and in November, against still strong localist opposition, a shaken Congress agreed to cash-and-carry arms sales to friendly countries. Several months after the amendment of the neutrality policy, Borah suffered a cerebral hemorrhage and died, and the two events marked the end of an era. The actual change in policy accomplished by the 1939 Neutrality Act was small, but it was only the first of a succession of steps—a draft law, the destroyer deal, lend-lease, convoy protection for British ships—by which a majoritarian President reversed the localist policy of detachment from the fate of Europe.

What had happened, slowly and with little political clarity over a period of several years, was that majoritarians and functionalists once more became alarmed at the threat to an open world order posed by the possible defeat of the European democracies—the countries that prized at least the hope of such an order. There was great uncertainty in both groups about what degree of German expansion the democracies could withstand and how the United States should respond to particular moves by Germany. But neither managers nor wage earners could take the position that the United States had *no* stake in the conflict shaping up in Europe. And after 1939, the conviction grew for both that at some point the United States would have to act, and possibly fight, to protect a future in which beneficial linkages among nations remained possible.

The dilemma of what to do and when was settled, not by the achievement of clarity and consensus at home, but by the Japanese attack on Pearl Harbor—although that event in itself was partly the result of the common commitment by functionalists and majoritarians to international openness. That is, neither the Republican functionalists of the 1920s nor the Democratic majoritarians of the 1930s wanted to relinquish the possibility of open exchange with China and the East. Both therefore insisted on American trading rights in the face of widening Japanese hegemony in the Pacific, and both maintained bases and warships at Pacific outposts to back up those rights—policies that ulti- mately resulted in the Japanese attack on the base at Pearl Harbor.

In short, neither majoritarians nor functionalists wanted war, but neither could accept the posture advocated by the localists, which was to keep American arms, ships, cargoes, and even credit well away from any trouble abroad and to live with any outcome of the foreign conflict. The coming of the Second World War thus marked the coming together of majoritarians and functional- ists in a common effort to protect common interests. And after the Second World War they remained in coalition, as they had not done after the First. The localist predominance in foreign policy was thereby foreclosed and an American commitment to an internationalist foreign policy assured.

But if an international commitment was assured in general, what its specific terms would be, how the differences between majoritarians and functionalists would be contained in a common policy, was less than clear. It was also not clear who would define new terms for policy. By the time the war ended in August 1945, Roosevelt was dead. The Vice-President who succeeded him in office was a former senator from Missouri with no established position as a national leader. No localist leader of Borah's stature had replaced him. And with Herbert Hoover still associated in the public mind with the Great Depression, the managerial interest lacked respected national leadership to argue the functionalist cause.

A new generation, then, would define policy in a political arena that had greatly changed, at home and abroad. But new leaders making policy in vastly changed conditions would still do so within the confines of the myth of deliverance. The hold of the myth had not changed, nor had the different visions of the world held by majoritarians, functionalists, and localists. The programs of the three would change in response to changed conditions, but their essential differences would remain intact —and would remain a continuing source of contention and confusion.

V

Mission to the World, after 1945:
Seeming Consensus

Harry Truman, describing in his *Memoirs* his first few days in
office after Franklin Roosevelt's death, recounts going for the
first time to "the super-secret Map Room" in the White House
—a place he had learned of only a few months before when the
President was leaving for the Yalta Conference. Roosevelt had
told Vice-President Truman to use the Map Room if he had any
urgent messages to send, but it was for "only absolutely urgent
messages," to be kept "as brief as possible in order not to tie up
communications."

Roosevelt had set up the room early in the war as a constantly operating, world-reaching communications center, and he
went to it every morning for briefings. Truman was awed. "It
was lined with a map of the world and maps on larger scales of
Europe and Asia, on which were outlined the locations of all
major military forces . . . Detailed maps showed the battle lines
everywhere, and from the center of the room it was possible to
see at a glance the whole military situation. There had been
nothing like it in the First World War. This was the first global
war that had ever been fought with fronts on every ocean and
every continent . . ."[1]

The Map Room signified that the American mission had expanded. And the possibility for the United States to carry its mission "on every ocean and every continent" had grown as well. The President could stand in the Map Room and survey the state of battle everywhere, the forces lined up on each side of every front. Further, he could send communications from Washington almost instantly to any point around the world.

This vision of the world within American reach, encapsulated within the White House itself, was Truman's introduction to the postwar era, and it rapidly became a vision familiar to Americans generally. The United States was not only part of a wider world but its center—suddenly the most powerful nation in the world. In Europe and the East, other powerful nations—battlegrounds in the war—had been physically and financially devastated. They, as well as weaker countries, were dependent on the United States for help in reconstituting their national lives. And it was within the power of the United States to supply that help. American leaders could survey the world from Washington, as Truman had done in the Map Room, and decide what help to send abroad and on what terms.

Wilson had seen the United States both as the model for a new kind of nationhood—non-contentious, non-jealous, non-militaristic, rooted in democracy—and as a leader in moving other nations toward this goal. Resistance both in Europe and at home had thwarted Wilson's hopes for offering such leadership. But in 1945, American primacy in world affairs was a fact, as was its potential for giving shape to the national and international institutions that had to replace the disorder left by war. Many Americans in the postwar years shared a sense of limitless possibility for American influence, a sense that, with American leadership, deliverance for people everywhere from an old order of chronic conflict was now actually at hand.

This spirit is perfectly captured in *The Fifteen Weeks* by Joseph Jones. A State Department officer, Jones participated through the spring of 1947 in the discussions that produced the first postwar commitment of the United States to serious engagement in Europe—the policy of aid to Greece and Turkey. "The Fifteen Weeks was one of the rare times in history when shackles fall away from the mind, the spirit and the will, allowing them to soar free . . . to discover new standards of what is responsible, of what is promising, and of what is possible," he wrote. With this freedom of mind, there were virtually no limits to what the United States could do "to help build around the world . . . the economic, social, political and military conditions that protect freedom and diminish the danger of war." The only limits, Jones concluded, were "what we think we can accomplish and what we think it is necessary to accomplish at any given time."[2]

Jones's ebullience reflected not only a new sense of American power in world affairs but also the new political alignment within the United States that made active involvement abroad possible. The United States had entered the war against Germany and Japan with growing certainty among both majoritarians and functionalists that it was wrong for the United States to stand detached from the major problems of the world—the maintenance of democracy in countries under siege by totalitarian states, the protection of world trade against national blockages and restrictions, the threat of violence generally.

During the war, the joint commitment to internationalism solidified. Roosevelt authorized a working group in the State Department to begin planning for the kind of postwar international cooperation that had eluded Wilson. To avoid the political divisions Wilson had encountered, the administration deliberately included in the planning process people representing a variety of views—from functionalist believers in technocratic control of international affairs to labor leaders who believed in the efficacy of voter control of all important national commitments.

By 1944, planning for postwar stability extended to conferences among the Allied nations, with the result that charters for the United Nations, the International Court of Justice, the International Monetary Fund, and the International Bank for Reconstruction and Development were drafted and, by the war's end, internationally accepted. And in the United States, the new political consensus for internationalism produced Senate approval of the new organizations by overwhelming votes and without the long and troubled debate that greeted Wilson's proposed League in 1919.

Some of the old questions did arise—the Article 10 issue among them. Like Wilson's Covenant, the United Nations Charter did *not* provide for congressional review of American involvement in any use of military force by the United Nations. But where this issue had defeated Wilson, Roosevelt turned away criticism with a metaphor. He compared the United Nations to a police force which often has to act quickly and decisively. A policeman would not be effective, Roosevelt said, if he saw someone break into a house but could not arrest the person without calling a town meeting to authorize an arrest warrant. "If we do not catch the international felon when we have our hands on him," he warned, "if we let him get away with his loot because the town council has not passed an ordinance authorizing his arrest, then we are not doing our share to prevent another world war."[3]

There were only two votes (one from North Dakota, one from Minnesota) cast against the Charter when it was submitted to the Senate for ratification in July 1945. The Second World War had taught functionalists—and many localists—that the danger of *not* acting against an aggressor state could be worse than the danger of excessive presidential authority. Thus the nation entered the postwar era with broad consensus behind a general internationalist commitment to prevent a recurrence of aggression such as Nazi Germany's, and to move nations away from habits of economic and political nationalism disruptive of healthy cross-national exchange—in short, to deliver the Old World from its destructive habits of national competition, conflict, and war.

After 1945, however, the focus of internationalist policy shifted from the construction of institutions and channels for heightened cooperation to defense against a specific enemy threatening the new international design. The Soviet Union, allied with the Western democracies in a common battle against Germany and Japan, did not share the West's postwar goals of protecting democracy and fostering international trade by private corporations. The Russian aim was to protect its boundaries and its governing system, but, beyond self-protection, the goal of Soviet leaders was to foster communist, not democratic, systems in other states—and a worldwide collectivist economy. That is, the Soviet Union, as a totalitarian nation with an international mission directly opposed to that of the United States, posed the same threat to Western goals as Nazi Germany had done.

The conflict between the Soviet Union and the West—the United States allied to the nations of Western Europe—produced or heightened a succession of crises: Soviet control and communization of the Polish government, then that of Czechoslovakia; sharp disagreement on terms for the postwar governance of Germany; civil war in Greece between communist and Western-oriented factions; Soviet-supported efforts by large Communist parties and unions in France and Italy to gain political power in those countries. Promoting democracy and an open international order, then, quickly came to mean countering the Soviet threat to those goals, especially in Europe. And the consensus for internationalism within the United States came to be a consensus against the extension of Soviet power and influence.

The politics of consensus took practical form in a quickly established practice of bipartisanship on foreign policy questions, which meant consultation and cooperation between Democratic and Republican leaders in dealing with important foreign problems. Out of this process, led on the Republican side by Senator Arthur Vandenberg of Michigan, the Truman administration won from Congress a succession of programs aimed at containing the new enemy to American goals.

First, in 1947, was a program of aid to Greece and Turkey, both too weak to withstand alone their internal communist movements aided by neighboring communist states—an actual threat in Greece, potential in Turkey. In 1948, Congress passed the European Recovery Program, or Marshall Plan, providing massive aid to European countries suffering war damage, shortage of food, depleted capital resources, and, in conditions of domestic strain, the growth of internal communist movements. In 1949, the North Atlantic Treaty Organization (NATO) was formed to construct between the United States and European countries a coordinated military defense against the Soviet Union. Contributions to this effort from the United States included, after 1950, the ongoing presence of American troops in Europe.

The only strong opposition to the new politics of internationalism by consensus came from a group of intransigent localists —the new irreconcilables, from traditional localist territory in the West, Southwest, South, and rural areas of the Midwest. In the Senate, such opposition amounted to one to two dozen dissenting votes on any particular program committing American power and resources abroad—although the enduring threat of wider localist dissent had always to be taken into account, as discussed later. Otherwise the most heated debates over foreign policy—such as those of the 1952 presidential campaign—centered on the question whether the United States was doing *enough* internationally, whether it was taking a tough enough stand against the communist enemy.

This being the case—that cross-party agreement on foreign policy was broad and strong dissent limited—why call postwar bipartisanship only a "seeming" consensus? Where were the differences, other than those that surfaced in election years as quarrels over tactics? The answer is that differences over foreign policy lay where they always had throughout the century, in deep differences among majoritarians, functionalists, and localists over their essential purposes and expectations.

The common aims of the three groups, especially that of restraining Soviet influence in Europe and elsewhere, obscured the divisions among them. But while majoritarians and functionalists—and to some extent localists—regarded expansive Soviet totalitarianism as an enemy, each group saw it as an enemy to *its own conception* of a just order. Each of the three saw the Soviet system as impeding the international agent of deliverance *it* sought to empower as the most trustworthy controller of conflict. That is, they had a common enemy to be rid of, but they held different conceptions of the world order that should follow its disappearance.

These differences, while not destructive of consensus behind particular programs, set up strains and confusions over particular American goals and priorities. Policy had to be cast broadly enough to avoid areas of disagreement—stressing, therefore, the common aim of anti-communism—and this degree of generality could not match the degree of complication actually present in foreign problems. Then, depending on which group was the primary partner in the coalition—majoritarians to 1952, functionalists from 1953 to 1960—the emphasis of programs shifted. And these shifts, all presented within the same anti-communist framework, heightened confusion—not only at home but among other nations, whether friends, neutrals, or rivals.

Worse, however, was the fact that policy had to be cast and explained in negative terms only, because an enemy was all that the three groups had in common. A coherent basis for constructive policy was impossible because each group sought to construct different systems. Each held on to its separate vision and worked toward it, interpreting problems and arguing for solutions within its own conception of deliverance. That is, they all spoke the same language of anti-communism, but each attached its own meaning to the words. There were thus three different voices speaking at once, sounding much the same, but in fact profoundly different.

What, then, were the three groups seeking in the postwar years and how, specifically, did they differ in this quest?

There is no mystery about majoritarian belief in this period. It was a straight extension of Wilsonianism. Its basic premise was the premise of the myth—that the potential for wrongly used power could not be eliminated from the world but it could be controlled. And for the majoritarians of 1945 and thereafter, as for Wilson, the way to control the abuse of power was through democracy, through the empowerment of majorities, nation by nation. With power literally in the people, powerful minorities —from landowning or corporate elites to military cliques— could be kept from using governmental authority to serve their own ends.

Franklin Roosevelt, throughout the 1930s, drew the connection between the abuse of governmental power and lack of democratic controls on officialdom. He saw both the German and Japanese governments in the same way that Wilson had seen that of Imperial Germany—as regimes run by fanatics bent on domination, both inside the nation and abroad, by force. The cause of war, he said in 1940, lay in a pernicious "philosophy of force" and the availability of new and terrible machines of war to the users of force—"infinitely small groups of individuals who rule without a single one of the democratic sanctions that we have known."[4]

And in his last State of the Union message to Congress before his death in 1945, Roosevelt again linked international peace with the democratic control of power, with governing systems in which power is harnessed to the service of the people generally, not simply a ruling few. "We cannot deny that power is a factor in world politics any more than we can deny its existence as a factor in national politics," Roosevelt said. "But in a democratic world, as in a democratic nation, power must be linked with responsibility and obliged to defend and justify itself within the framework of the general good."[5]

The first step toward building a world of democracies was maintaining peace and economic stability and, for the majoritarians of 1945, this task was to be carried out by the United Nations. Following the logic of Wilson's design, the major nations of the world were to take joint responsibility for putting down attempts by any nation to control others by force. That is, a majoritarian end—a world of strong democracies—was to be fostered by majoritarian means—the enforcement of peace through the political judgment and military power of the world's great nations. These were, for the most part, democracies, and their judgments would, in majoritarian theory, be kept honest and sensible by the voting power of their own people.

The system depended, of course, on the Soviet Union's finding it in its interest to cooperate with the democracies in their peacekeeping judgments, which, it was soon apparent, was not to be the case. No agreement between East and West proved possible as to what disputes in the world required United Nations intervention and to what end. Roosevelt's majoritarian successors, therefore, were left with a Wilsonian commitment to use national power to control threats of power abuse abroad, but without the international structure Wilson had imagined would be the means for carrying out that responsibility. It was in response to this dilemma that the Truman administration formulated the programs, beginning with aid to Greece and Turkey in 1947, that were to protect international peace and stability mainly through American power, or the joint power of the United States and the democracies of Western Europe.

But if the form of the Truman programs departed from the Wilsonian design, the underlying assumption relating majority rule and the control of illegitimate power, majority rule and peace, were unchanged. Truman drew these connections explicitly in his message to Congress requesting aid for Greece and Turkey. The purpose of the aid, Truman said, was to help build conditions that would make possible a way of life "based upon the will of the majority, and . . . distinguished by free constitutions, representative government, free elections, guarantees of individual liberty, freedom of speech and religion, and freedom from political oppression." The United States should actively help other people, Truman urged, to avoid a "way of life based upon the will of a minority forcibly imposed upon the majority" through such means as "terror and oppression, a controlled press and radio, fixed elections, and the suppression of personal freedoms."[6]

In 1949, Truman extended the logic of aiding countries threatened directly by communist military pressure to a concept of aid to countries whose movement toward democracy was stymied, not by communist disruption, but by poverty—mainly the countries of the non-industrialized world. What was needed to remove this blockage to progress was a flow of capital from the developed nations to the underdeveloped—but on terms that would not stifle majority rule. For majoritarians this meant, among other things, capital transfers from governments, and primarily from the exceedingly wealthy United States. Private investment was important but not alone sufficient, both because it would not move into risky places and because its power in weak, developing economies created too much potential for abuse.

The policy proposed to fulfill this newly defined responsibility was the Point Four program, so called because it was the fourth of four principles Truman outlined as guides to foreign policy in his inaugural address in January 1949. A program of "technical, scientific and managerial" assistance, Point Four was designed to provide underdeveloped countries, "stirred and awakened" to the potential for industrial development, the aid needed for "a firm economic base for the democratic aspirations of their citizens."[7]

In following the majoritarian tradition of using the nation to build strong nations elsewhere, Truman stood ready to use national military power as well, in the face of military moves by other countries. Thus when the Soviet Union cut off road and rail access to West Berlin in 1948—a violation of occupation agreements and an action which, if unchallenged, would have resulted in Soviet control of all of Berlin—the Truman administration maintained access by means of a military airlift until the blockade was lifted.

More important, in 1950, when North Korea, whose communist government was supported by the Soviet Union, invaded South Korea, an American-supported state, Truman instantly ordered an American military response to what was a clear-cut act of territorial aggression. He was also able to honor the Wilsonian vision of *collective* response to aggression by gaining United Nations approval and sponsorship of the action. This was possible because the Soviet Union was boycotting the United Nations at the time and was not there to veto the move.

The response to aggression in Korea was the occasion for Truman's putting into practice one other important majoritarian principle as well—executive as opposed to congressional decision making on foreign policy. Decisions on crises abroad had to be made in the interests of the *whole* people, Wilson had taught, and therefore had to be made by the official representing the whole people. Such decisions could not be submitted routinely to Congress, where they would be subject to the push and pull of particular constituencies. Roosevelt had affirmed this point in his "international felon" metaphor, and Truman, faced with the news of war in Korea, consulted with congressional leaders but deliberately decided *not* to submit the question of response to Congress. He insisted on acting as a *national* leader, taking the decision on the basis of principle, not local politics.[8]

Thus, in fashioning the general postwar commitment of the

United States to active responsibility for international order and opposition to communism as the enemy to that order, Truman followed distinctly majoritarian lines in the emphasis and form of his policies—the empowerment of majorities as an international goal, the need for national executive initiative and leadership, the implicit trust in the democratic nation as the agent of international deliverance, trust that the use of American power would be the means for delivering others from conflict caused by illegitimate power.

Functionalists, sharing the general internationalist aims of the majoritarians, faced the difficulty after 1945 of coming to terms with majoritarian means. In 1919, the managerial constituency had refused to accept the Wilsonian League system—or at least its Article 10 provision for forceful action—precisely because such action rested on national political judgments about the handling of conflict. Then, in 1945, this constituency joined enthusiastically in ratifying the United Nations Charter in spite of its provision for a decision-making process similar to that of Article 10. And furthermore, the managers backed Truman's programs for the resistance of communism in Europe even though such policies brought national power into play *more* directly than did the United Nations system. This was a radical change for functionalists and the basis for the radical change in the American stance internationally from the years following the First World War to the period following the Second World War. That is, the majoritarians had not changed in any essential way, so that the new consensus and new stance depended on the functionalists accepting majoritarian policies.

But if this alteration of the historic functionalist position made broad agreement on postwar foreign policy possible, it also set up a relation with built-in conflicts in premises and purposes —and therefore built-in incoherencies in policy. The problem was that functionalists entered the coalition with a double set of purposes. They agreed on the goal of active interdependence for the United States and on the need for some kind of forceful resistance by the United States to enemies threatening an interdependent international system. But they retained their earlier principles about how such a system should work once it was possible to build it, and on who should run it once it was built. While majoritarians sought a world order based on political cooperation among strong democratic nations, functionalists wanted to build an international network of beneficent exchange organized, not by political leaders, but by professionals.

Thus, the nation's managers lent their support to the Truman programs but not out of newfound trust in the use of national political and military power. Rather, they saw such policies as a necessary expedient, given the appearance on the scene of a dangerous enemy. And the expedient required a suspension, or postponement, of their ultimate goals. But for functionalists, it did *not* require, or result in, the abandonment of those goals. Accepting, supporting, and, in office, practicing national militancy in foreign policy, functionalists tried simultaneously to promote their own opposite agenda.

In general, functionalists retained their vision of a world in which national boundaries and national politics would recede and the functional linkages, the logical relations of trade and other exchange, would prevail. This view had formed part of the challenge addressed to Franklin Roosevelt in the presidential campaign of 1940 by his Republican opponent, Wendell Willkie, a businessman with strong functionalist enthusiasms. Then, during the war, Willkie published a popular treatise called *One World*, which stated graphically the anti-national, anti-political outlook held by many of his managerial colleagues. The message of the book was that "peace must be planned on a world basis," meaning "quite literally that it must embrace the earth." Emphasizing this point, Willkie went on to describe the view of the earth from the air, a perspective open to increasing numbers of people in the 1930s and 1940s. "Continents and oceans are plainly only parts of a whole, seen, as I have seen them, from the air," he said. That is, the air traveler could see natural barriers and boundaries on the earth below—mountains, rivers, oceans—but could not discern the political boundaries that majoritarians saw as all-important. It was this non-political world map that functionalists insisted was the proper basis for social organization and for peace.[9]

The functionalist agenda was worked out in greater detail in several lengthy studies conducted during the war, with recommendations for postwar order. The most ambitious was the War and Peace Studies project of the Council on Foreign Relations. In 1939, just weeks after the German invasion of Poland, the Council, originally formed to build up a private reservoir of knowledge on foreign affairs, offered to the State Department the resources of its study groups to gather and analyze information on foreign problems facing the United States. The offer was accepted, and from 1939 to 1945, Council members produced 682 documents on questions ranging from highly technical matters concerning war production to general political aims for a postwar world.

The political convictions of the group surface in the reports on longer-range political and economic questions, and the central focus of these reports is on the need to construct systems displacing politicians and empowering experts. "Postwar Agreements on Commercial Policy," for example, advocated national tariff policies based, not on considerations of national self-protection, but on "the most effective utilization of the world's resources"—as assessed by experts. Alvin Hansen's report on "International Monetary and Financial Programs" also turned to experts to define coordinated monetary policies for the member states of a postwar international organization.

"Some Problems of International Policy," prepared by Grayson Kirk and others, discussed principles for a postwar international organization. The basic principle advocated in the report was agreement by all countries to reduce drastically their national armed power and to rely for protection against others on an international police force. Such a force, using mainly air power, would be directed by "some central control independent of individual national states." Thus the nation-states of the world were to be delivered from their historic condition of conflict and insecurity through the benevolent guardianship of an international air force.[10]

Another functionalist design for the postwar world was that of the Commission to Study the Bases for a Just and Durable Peace, a group sponsored by the Federal Council of Churches and headed by John Foster Dulles. A "Statement of Guiding Principle," adopted by the Commission and approved by the Council's National Study Conference in 1942, marked out an uncompromising anti-national, anti-political stance.

Principle 1 proclaimed that "moral law, not less than physical law, undergirds our world," and Principle 4 that "cooperation and mutual concern, implicit in the moral order . . . calls for a true community of nations" and that the old order of "irresponsible, competing and unrestrained national sovereignties" must give way to "a higher and more inclusive authority." Principle 5 stated that because natural resources are not evenly distributed around the earth, they should not be regarded as a tool of national advantage but as wealth held in trust for the general interest of all, and thus subject to some form of regulation by an international organization. Principle 8 declared that "military establishments should be internationally controlled," and Principle 10 called for changes in United States national policy to allow American engagement in such matters as "international control of tariffs, limitation of armaments, participation in world government."[11]

Dulles himself further proposed to the Commission that a postwar international organization should function through "an executive organ made up of outstanding personalities who would be solemnly pledged to place the peace and welfare of humanity as a whole above the advantage of any particular nation, race or class"—the disinterested trustees of social welfare whom functionalists ultimately turn to as public decision makers.

Dulles himself, in the development of his thought and his career, perfectly personified the dilemma of postwar functionalists—bearing deep commitments to the diminishment of national political power, but finding it necessary to join in the enhancement and increased use of American power nonetheless. An important Republican adviser on foreign policy after 1945, and Secretary of State under Eisenhower from 1953 to 1959, Dulles played a central role in shaping that problematic transition.

In the prewar years, Dulles can only be described as the quintessential functionalist. Born in 1888, he was the son of a Presbyterian pastor and grandson of John Watson Foster, a prominent Republican leader who was for a short time Secretary of

State under Benjamin Harrison. Both male mentors stood, some-times embattled, as apostles of reason in their respective profes-sions. Dulles's father, Allen Macy Dulles, fought for the modernist cause in church councils against fundamentalists seek-ing to remove from their pulpits Presbyterian ministers who refused to teach the Bible as literal truth. John Watson Foster was a serious and active proponent of peace causes. A founding mem-ber of the Carnegie Institute for International Peace, he took his grandson, then a student at Princeton, to the Second Hague Peace Conference in 1907—a heady affair whose participants were full of confidence in the efficacy of arbitration and the laws of war to reduce contention and violence in international affairs.

The young Dulles adopted both the family concern about the large social and moral issues of the day and its predilection to seek solutions through institutional structures grounded in reason. He became a lawyer, entered practice with the New York firm of Sullivan and Cromwell, then during the First World War was commissioned an army captain and served on the War Trade Board as assistant to Vance McCormick. At the war's end he went with McCormick to the Paris Peace Conference as an expert adviser on economic matters, only to be co-opted by Bernard Baruch as counsel for the American delegation to the Commis-sion on Reparations. With Baruch, Dulles was an advocate of reason and moderation in planning peace terms with Germany, and he was convinced throughout the interwar period that the punitive terms finally incorporated into the Treaty of Versailles were the cause of Germany's subsequent aggressive behavior.

Dulles's main role in the 1920s and 1930s was that of an increasingly skilled and experienced lawyer whose clients were primarily large corporations dealing in the complication of inter-national trade at a time of economic uncertainty and then all too certain depression. However, his early sense of connection to large social and political questions never left him, becoming instead more acute as international tensions heightened in the 1930s.

In 1939 Dulles published a book, *War, Peace and Change,* an ambitious effort setting out a theory of international relations that ran directly counter to the growing sentiment within the

Roosevelt administration in favor of some form of collective Western effort against the growing threat of German expansionism in Europe. Dulles was not in favor of American aid to England and France at this time, or even opposition to Germany, and his book explained why.

The cause of war throughout history, he wrote, was the suppression of a social force he called dynamism and its pressure for change. By dynamism, Dulles meant the eruption of economic creativity that occurs within different societies at different times, setting in motion new ideas, interests, and needs, seeking expression in new institutions, new patterns of relations among various social groups. If suppressed by older institutions protecting themselves against change, he thought, dynamic forces necessarily seek outlets by any means available, including war. Dulles saw both the First World War and the gathering forces of what would be the Second in these terms.

The institutions most at odds with social dynamism in the twentieth century and thus most resistant to change, for Dulles, were nation-states, and continuing war was inevitable as long as nations operated to place irrational constraints on new economic and social patterns. In an open international order, however, an order in which people, goods, ideas, credit, information, and all other tokens of human exchange could move freely, the incidence of war would be reduced because dynamic forces could find constructive, creative expression.

Dulles's theory located as the great obstacle to development of international openness the tendency of people to personify nations, their own and others, and to invest them with qualities of good and evil, making it difficult for nations seeking change to be understood as anything but "nation-villains." His prescription for peace was a change in mental habits which would allow people everywhere "to subordinate and dilute the personification of one's own nation" and thus to reduce the psychological impact of the "boundary barrier." He saw American federalism as the prime example of the successful erasure of boundaries as demarcations of sovereignty and the Civil War as truly a war to end wars because, by ending the Southern secession, it resisted the right of indiscriminate sovereignty.[12]

During the Second World War, Dulles devoted himself to the peace project of the Federal Council of Churches, already discussed, still seeking ways to "depersonalize" or depoliticize international relations. It was not simply an intellectual task. He organized church campaigns throughout the country to build popular support for postwar international organization and worked actively with Republican leaders, urging the commitment to internationalism that was still resisted by localist elements in the party. He became the chief foreign policy adviser to Thomas Dewey in his presidential campaigns of 1944 and 1948, and served as the Republican member of several bipartisan delegations to international conferences at the war's end. From 1946 to 1948 he also served as a delegate to the United Nations, where he worked on the drafting of the Declaration of Human Rights and the Genocide Convention.

How, then, and when, did Dulles turn from this lifelong, wholehearted crusade against nationalism to acceptance of American engagement in national power politics as a necessary means of dealing with the Soviet Union?

Dulles did not come to this radical reversal overnight. Immediately after the war, he recognized that the Soviet Union was committed to oppose the open international order the West sought and to press instead the extension of its own system. This meant, he said in a 1946 series of articles in *Life,* that the West must make clear to the Soviet Union its intention to resist Soviet expansion and must build its capacity to do so. At the same time, however, he saw hope for progress toward functionalist goals. He thought that progress would be possible, in spite of Soviet hostility, because it would be in the interest of the Soviet Union as of the United States to avoid using force to seek change.

Thus within the councils of the Republican Party, Dulles sought, where possible, lines of accommodation with Soviet interests. As late as 1948 he backed the suggestion of Ernest Bevin that Marshall Plan aid be offered to the Soviet Union and other communist states and was, reportedly, shocked when the Russians refused to accept it.[13]

By 1950, after repeated Soviet rejection of all tenders of Western cooperation, Dulles had become deeply pessimistic about relations between East and West and in 1950 published a book called *War or Peace,* in which he depicted the Soviet government unqualifiedly as an enemy. It had become clear, he wrote, that the United States and the West faced the threat of ineradicable hostility from the "fanatical Soviet Communist Party" that wields "despotic political power in Russia" and— what is worse—commands "the blind obedience of the hard core of loyal Communist Party members everywhere in the world." The communist leaders "believe it right to use fraud, terrorism, and violence, and any other means that will promote their ends," the key goal being to promote class revolution either violently or insidiously, depending on local circumstances.[14] Thus what Dulles saw in Soviet leadership was a degree of intransigence that went beyond the shortsighted promotion of national interest usually to be expected in officials of nation-states.

Traditional nationalist behavior—its resistance to dynamic change—was bad enough because it placed narrow, self-interested goals in the way of new economic forces that would serve the common interests of people in numerous nations. But even with this serious impediment, an international system made up of nation-states could still allow some degree of progressive change through the patient efforts of professional elites in all countries working to build more rational forms of exchange. The Soviet system, however, if actually based on a theory of class conflict, would not permit even slow steps toward international accommodation because its ideology denied that any grounds for mutually beneficial relations existed except where the capitalist system had been abolished.

Dulles was not alone in his postwar shift of views toward committed anti-communism. Other functionalists were reaching the same conclusions by the end of the decade after the same initial hope that in spite of vast differences and suspicions, the United States and the Soviet Union could define a broad enough common ground for workable relations. The 1946–47 annual report of the Council on Foreign Relations noted that a group examining Soviet foreign policy had projected a two-year study of several questions it had to that point not been able to answer. One was: "Is Russia's uncompromising attitude largely determined by a desire for security or is this merely a pose?" And another: "Is Soviet foreign policy determined by a fixed and immutable doctrine—that Communism cannot be safe in one country while capitalism remains in others—or may Russia still realize that security can be attained through cooperation with capitalist countries better than through constant friction?"

The report on the project the following year, 1947–48, stated that at the beginning many members of the group thought that the problem between the United States and the Soviet Union was "Russian suspicion and fear of the Western powers" and that Russian fear would be reduced "by a reasonable American policy." Others thought that such an approach would amount to dangerous appeasement. After a year's study, however, the group as a whole, while still favoring American policy that was "fair and reasonable rather than provocative," had concluded that "expansion and revolution seem inherent in Soviet doctrine" and that the United States would thus have to meet such pressure with firm resistance—with force, if necessary.[15]

This tone continued in Council publications throughout the 1950s and early 1960s, although, as was the case with Dulles, the shift in the Council's stance toward the Soviet threat took several years to solidify.[16] At first, the lawyers, business leaders, financiers —the capital managers making up the Council membership generally—approached the Russian question as realists in the uses of power, expecting the Soviet Union to press interests, especially in Eastern Europe, that were opposed to American interests, and to press them hard. But the managers also assumed that, while politicians postured in public view, reasonable men on both sides, working quietly behind the scenes, could locate the real problems between the two powers and negotiate reasonable solutions with practical advantages for both.

When this did not happen, when at conference after conference Soviet leaders insisted on impossible demands, when they refused to explore the mutually beneficial solutions functionalists knew were there, the conclusion was inescapable that the Soviet position *was,* in the words of the Council study project, only a pose. The demands could not be sincere because no effort was being made to find reasonable grounds for settlement. Therefore the Soviet leaders must be bent on a crusade of unreason shaped by their ideology and must be stopped.

Thus, reluctantly, John Foster Dulles and functionalists generally came to accept the necessity to retain in the postwar world all of the tools of national power they had hoped to banish in international relations. Moreover, Dulles, as Secretary of State, brandished these tools so ferociously that their use is peculiarly associated with his name.

He conducted a diplomacy employing the threat of war (brinkmanship) to counter communist pressures, especially in Asia; he supported the buildup of an American military machine capable of massive nuclear retaliation against any Soviet aggression. He approved covert military operations that removed left-leaning governments in Iran in 1953 and Guatemala in 1954. He condemned as immoral the choice of Third World governments to remain neutral as between the United States and the Soviet Union. And he built alliances against communist aggression, patterned after NATO: in Asia, the Southeast Asia Treaty Organization (SEATO), and in the Middle East, the Central Treaty Organization (CENTO).

It was within the context of SEATO that the United States in 1954, after the defeat of the French Army in Vietnam, committed itself to support the newly created government of South Vietnam, to contain the area held by the communist force that had defeated the French and gained control of the North.

This record suggests that prior functionalist commitments to a world ordered by reason, not by power, had disappeared without a trace, that there was no essential distinction between functionalist and majoritarian outlooks on the world in the era after the Second World War. But the functionalist position was more complicated than that. It was a position retaining the old vision intact, while embracing the new resort to power only as a means of preserving the possibility for building an order on reason in the future.

The outline of this order was clearly defined—again—by the Council on Foreign Relations in a 1959 report, *Basic Aims of United States Foreign Policy*, prepared for the Senate Committee on Foreign Relations. "A new world is in the making," the report declared, out of the desire of people everywhere for liberation from old bondages, political and economic, and this meant that the United States could not pursue foreign policies "conceived and carried out purely as national policies of the United States." Rather, Americans must search for "an international order in which the freedom of nations is recognized as interdependent and for which policies must be jointly undertaken by various nations of the free world."[17]

These policies, the "basic aims" the United States *should* be pursuing, included further development of the United Nations; support for the institutions of European and Atlantic unity, not only NATO but the European Common Market and the other instruments for the diminution of national divisions in Europe; greater use of the International Court of Justice; arms control; transfers of development capital to the underdeveloped world— not nation to nation, as in Truman's majoritarian scheme, but through international institutions; regional, not national, planning for economic development in the underdeveloped world; and education, the promotion of liberal and technical education worldwide to create the pool of knowledge and competence necessary to the rational ordering of international life.[18]

But what difference did this dual vision of the functionalists make for foreign policy as long as one side of it put them in firm coalition with majoritarians in the exercise of American national power worldwide? During the 1940s and 1950s, the major problem produced by the divergence between majoritarian and functionalist conceptions of international relations was the *lack* of clear purpose and clear strategy beyond the immediate postwar imperative of protecting Western Europe from Soviet power. When England and the European democracies had regained their strength and the power balance in Europe was stabilized, what then?

Differences between the two groups began to take shape in the 1950s. Functionalists, whose views dominated foreign policy in the Dulles State Department, sought to use national power in a generalized way *only* to keep the channels of international exchange open. This meant, most importantly, preventing the spread of communist systems to important areas of the world. For this purpose, they favored a military stance that would deter any direct expansionist moves by the Soviet Union—the strategy of nuclear deterrence—and a capacity for small-scale military action to prevent communist groups from coming to power where they threatened to do so. This purpose was well served, in functionalist terms, by the Central Intelligence Agency under the direction in the 1950s of Allen Dulles, brother of John Foster and a longtime, active member of the Council on Foreign Relations. The CIA could conduct quick, surgical operations against communist or other regimes threatening the goal of international openness, and do it without fanfare or extensive political involvement—essentially policing operations.

But beyond the functions of deterrence and policing, the managerial constituency had no use for American national power politically directed. That is, they saw national power as necessary to keeping the lines of international exchange clear, but they believed that further movement toward a rationally ordered world should be left to the organizing capacities of professionals —either in private corporations or in international institutions. It should not be the province of nations and their politicians— even Americans—to design the order that would follow the elimination or control of international communism.

Majoritarians, on the other hand, convinced that a decent order in the future depended on healthy political systems within each nation, were far more inclined than functionalists to be concerned with political conditions and social reform in troubled countries. This was the basis for Truman's Point 4 proposal in 1949 and the urgings of Democratic Senators throughout the 1950s that the United States supply more economic as opposed to military aid to poorer countries for their long-term economic development and ultimately their development of democratic institutions. But under the Eisenhower administration, funding for such purposes was negligible. Functionalists did not believe in long-term development through national political channels.

The fate of economic aid was not a deeply divisive question in the postwar years, however; nor were there any other issues that produced serious battles between functionalists and majoritarians. Rather, the negative focus on containing communism kept the two groups operating on ground they held in common. But the differences were there and ready to surface at any point where the anti-communist imperative became unclear.

Unlike the functionalists, the localists had clear and dramatic differences with the majoritarian formulation of foreign policy in the postwar years, and for a clear reason. Unlike the functionalists, localists had not changed their essential position on international relations out of the experience of the Second World War. They were anti-internationalist before the war and remained anti-internationalist after the war. That is, they did not share with majoritarians and functionalists the conviction that any force threatening an open system of international exchange was thereby automatically a threat or an enemy to the United States.

For localists, after 1945 as before, an enemy was a country deliberately and maliciously pursuing policies that directly threatened the security of the United States. Thus localists joined the postwar consensus on foreign policy only when they could be convinced that the Soviet Union *was* such an enemy. And this was not easy for majoritarians and functionalists to demonstrate when localists did *not* accept the premise that the fate of the United States was inextricably bound up with the fate of countries far from America's borders and immediate concerns.

Senator Leverett Saltonstall, a functionalist Republican from Massachusetts, attempted to convey this lesson in the 1947 debate over aid to Greece and Turkey by employing a metaphor. If the United States remained detached from the tensions besetting postwar Europe, Saltonstall said, the danger of violence in areas threatened by communist pressure would increase. And the resulting disorder could sweep the United States into war again, helplessly—like "being swept over Niagara Falls." This scenario, however, was unconvincing to the localist Democrat Edwin Johnson of Colorado. Johnson rejected Saltonstall's image of inseparable links between the United States and Europe by retorting that he was certain "so long as I stay away from Niagara Falls, that I shall not be swept over it."[19]

In the same debate, Senator George Malone, Republican from Nevada, pressed Arthur Vandenberg, the moving spirit of Republican bipartisanship, to clarify the danger he foresaw if the

Truman program was not passed. Did the United States expect Russia to invade Greece or only to try to take control of the Greek government through civil war? If the latter, and if American aid did not succeed in maintaining the Greek government in power, would the United States be at war with the Soviet Union? Under what circumstances, in Greece or elsewhere, would the United States actually go to war?

Expressing similar concern, Senator Henry Dworshak, Republican of Idaho, demanded information that would clarify whether the Soviet Union was a friend or an enemy. It did not make sense, he said, to send Lend-Lease aid to Russia two years after the end of the war and at the same time to send money to another country to protect it against Russia. What the Senate needed from the State Department, Dworshak insisted, was information that would answer the question whether or not Russia was a nation the United States could collaborate with peacefully. He also wanted information as to how the State Department intended to determine whether Russia was a friendly or a hostile power.[20]

The following year, when the Marshall Plan for massive development loans to Europe was before the Senate, Malone again insisted that the Senate had insufficient information about the nature of the threat the administration perceived. He complained that "no one knows, least of all the American people and the United States Senate, what nations the State Department and the President of the United States feel it necessary for us to protect . . . and no one has even named the areas or the nations." He said that the Marshall Plan was defended as a way to "stop Russia," but, he asked, "Stop Russia where? And what will we do if we do not stop Russia at the designated place?"[21]

Most senators from localist regions ended up following their party leaders in bipartisan support for these measures, but a steady minority—anywhere from twelve to twenty-four senators—voted against all of the Truman programs for aid to Europe, including the establishment of NATO, and 80 to 90 percent of these opposition votes came from localist territory—the states of the South, West, and Southwest and the semi-localist Midwest.

More important than their opposition votes, however, was

the *spirit* of localist resistance to the determined internationalism of majoritarians and functionalists. It was an angry and suspicious spirit generating accusations of hidden motives and hidden wrongdoing—at its worst, wholesale accusations that traitorous communists were infiltrated throughout the American government. This spirit of suspicion contributed powerfully to the emotional anti-communism that afflicted much of the country in the postwar period and that made candid public analysis of any foreign policy issue, for a time, virtually impossible.

Why did this occur? What was there in the localist tradition that lent itself to the ugliness of mind and tone that colored American politics in the postwar years—particularly on questions of foreign policy? The root of the problem was the premise localists applied to world affairs—the radical difference between their premise and that of the other groups. Starting with the assumption that authority properly belonged at the local level, and the further assumption that the economy should—and could —be organized so that local decision making was a *practical* system, they resisted claims that an ever more complicated economy required *national* coordination. And they resisted, as even more outrageous, claims that it required *international* coordination or protection.

Administration officials argued that American aid to Europe under the Marshall Plan would benefit the United States because of the interdependence of the American and European economies. They claimed that strength in Europe would make the United States stronger. Rejecting this claim, localists saw aid going abroad as a *loss* of American resources, a "giveaway," or money poured down "a rathole."

In localist belief, honest trade and other exchange across national borders should be possible without elaborate governmental arrangements; there was no *need* for links between the United States and other nations to be contrived, financed, and expensively protected. And yet a bipartisan coalition was pushing through Congress program after program setting up extensive linkages around the world. Why? The answer for localists— given no explanation that made sense to them on the surface of things—was to assume that the explanation lay under the surface.

What must be going on, they assumed, was a sellout of American interests on the part of groups that had got hold of some corner on governmental power and were serving interests of their own.

In the immediate postwar years, localist suspicions about the source of self-serving power abuse took the familiar form that they had for earlier localists—the assumption that the executive branch was arrogating to itself control over choices that were properly the province of Congress. This suspicion was implicit in the localist demands, pressed by Malone and Dworshak and others, for more information on the actual nature of the Soviet threat. The line from inexplicable policy to complaints about insufficient information to suspicions of executive wrongdoing was a natural one for localists to follow because they had long recognized and opposed executive secrecy as an insidious technique for increasing executive power. It was an issue on which Borah, as a member of the Senate Foreign Relations Committee, had been relentless. He had frequently sought his own information directly from foreign leaders, as in the last major battle he fought—on the fourth Neutrality Act, discussed earlier.

But as the succession of programs proposed by the Truman administration was approved one after the other by both the Senate and the House of Representatives, it became clear that whatever self-serving force was at work was not confined to the executive branch. It had spread all over Washington, into Congress and out into the country as well. By the late 1940s, localists had come to identify the force behind policies that defied all good sense as the hidden but deliberate influence of communists in various parts of the federal government—a conspiracy of communists to subvert the true interests of the society from the inside.

The acceptance of communist conspiracy as an explanation for the postwar course of foreign policy in particular was strongly reinforced by what came to be called the loss of China to the communists in 1949, a catastrophe many anti-communists thought the Truman administration could have done more to prevent. Then, in 1950, localist sensibilities were further outraged by Truman's reaction to the invasion of South Korea by troops from communist-controlled North Korea. That Truman committed American forces to defend South Korea without asking congressional authorization was bad enough from the localist point of view. But his seeking and receiving authorization for military action from the United Nations was insupportable. With these events, the search for communists in government began in earnest.

In February 1950, Senator Joseph McCarthy, Republican of Wisconsin, had come to sudden prominence with a speech in Wheeling, West Virginia, announcing, among other things, that he had knowledge as of that moment of fifty-seven card-carrying communists in the Department of State. In September 1950, Congress passed, over President Truman's veto, the Subversive Activities Control Act, declaring in its preamble that "the Communist organization in the United States, pursuing its stated objectives, the recent successes of Communist methods in other countries, and the nature and control of the world Communist movement itself, present a clear and present danger to the security of the United States . . ."[22]

The act required the registration of communist organizations, barred members of such organizations from appointment to positions in the federal government, barred them also from receiving passports, as well as requiring that any material from communist organizations communicated by mail, radio, or TV carry identification of its communist origin. A few months after the passage of the 1950 anti-subversive law, the Senate Judiciary Committee formed a new Subcommittee on Internal Security to oversee enforcement of the law and to conduct continuing investigations of communism in the United States. Such investigations became the forum for some of the most furious accusations against officials during the entire period.

In the course of Senate hearings in August 1950 on the confirmation of General George Marshall as Secretary of Defense, Senator William E. Jenner, Republican of Indiana, had called Marshall a willing dupe, "eager to play the role of a front man for traitors." He went on to call Secretary of State Dean Acheson a "Communist-appeasing, Communist-protecting betrayer of America," and President Truman a director of a "criminal crowd of traitors and Communist appeasers who . . . are still selling Americans down the river."[23]

Marshall provoked particular localist outrage both because of his sponsorship of the "giveaway" European Recovery Program, or Marshall Plan, and because, as the President's special emissary to China in 1946 and Secretary of State from 1947 to 1949, he was held specially responsible for the American failure to prevent the takeover of China by the communists. The full crescendo of localist outrage, however, occurred when Truman and, again, Marshall—this time as Secretary of Defense—recalled General Douglas MacArthur in April 1951 from his command of the United Nations forces in Korea.

At issue was MacArthur's refusal to follow administration directives that ran counter to tactics he favored, tactics designed not only to unify Korea under non-communist control but to carry the war beyond Korea to China. The objective in Korea, as defined by the United Nations Security Council, was "to repel the armed attack [by forces from North Korea] and to restore international peace and security in the area."[24] The Security Council left ambiguous the question whether the military effort should be limited to expelling North Korean troops from South Korea or extended to the defeat of North Korea in its own territory.

Truman's advisers were divided on the question of limiting or extending the war, opting finally to extend it and to seek a complete military defeat of North Korea, but only if it could be accomplished without Soviet or Chinese military intervention. Thus when Chinese troops did enter the war in force in November 1950, as American units pushed toward the Manchurian border, Truman ordered MacArthur to respond with strictly limited defensive tactics—not to attack Chinese territory, not to provoke a wider Chinese effort. MacArthur resisted these restrictions in various ways, including the dispatch of messages to members of Congress advocating increased pressure on China for the purpose of undermining its communist government. After several months and a number of attempts to restrain MacArthur's political role, Truman relieved him of his command.

MacArthur returned to a hero's welcome in the United States —the warrior who sought to defeat the enemy but was stopped by timorous politicians. For localists in Congress, however,

MacArthur had been victimized, not by the ineptness of political leaders, but by a traitorous pro-communist design. Senator Jenner charged that MacArthur was taken out at the instigation of Secretaries Marshall and Acheson (he referred to Acheson this time as "head of the pro-Soviet bloc in the State Department") just when MacArthur was on the point of aiding a Nationalist Chinese attack on Mao Tse-tung's government that would drive the communists out of power. "I say powerful people in the administration did not want MacArthur to win," Jenner declared. "When he dared to win, and then dared to say that, if he were given the minimum of military authority, he could doom Red China to the risk of imminent military collapse they decided he must go."[25]

Localists were not, of course, alone in their attacks on the loyalty of public officials. McCarthy himself, although from the semi-localist Midwest, did not exhibit a pattern of localist interest and voting behavior as a general rule, nor did Senator Robert Taft of Ohio, the Republican leader whose encouragement and support lent weight to McCarthy's efforts. These and other anti-communist enthusiasts found a variety of interests served by the issue, not the least of which were wide personal publicity in some cases and the weakening of the incumbent Democrats prior to the 1952 election in others. Localists, however—Democrats and Republicans alike—were among the most persistent, coherent, and vigilant workers in the anti-communist crusade. It was Democratic Senator Pat McCarran of Nevada who proposed and promoted the 1950 Subversive Activities Control Act—it was called the McCarran Act—and the Senate Internal Security Subcommittee was made up, at its inception in 1951 and in subsequent years, almost entirely of senators from the old Bryan states or the Midwest.

Communist conspiracy offered explanations on several different levels for the defiance of reason that for localists characterized the postwar world. Most directly, it explained why government officials were suddenly proposing and backing policies localists regarded as obviously harmful to American interests. Some officials, it was assumed, were themselves communists who had insinuated themselves into positions of power, but the danger of communist conspirators in government was not limited to their own contributions to policy making. According to Senator Jenner, for years either chairman or ranking Republican on the Internal Security Subcommittee, the more insidious power of communists in government was their ability to manipulate others in subtle ways. This they did, Jenner said, "by praise and fear, and by creating a climate of opinion, by an elegant form of brainwashing" through which innocent officials were persuaded to adopt policies "they would never have chosen in the free air."[26]

In this view, the hidden communists, protected by impeccable credentials and reputations, undermined true American interests through seemingly innocent proposals and arguments, through positions that taken alone seemed reasonable, but added together formed a preconceived plan to subvert American democracy. To illustrate the conspiratorial danger, Jenner was fond of telling a story about an ordinary workingman in Nazi Germany in the 1930s. An employee of a baby carriage factory, this man could not himself buy a carriage for his own expected child and therefore contrived over time to steal all the parts of a carriage from the factory to assemble at home. However, when he finally put them together he found he had, not a baby carriage, but a machine gun.[27]

In addition to explaining the behavior of public officials, the theory of subversion through subtle indirection helped to explain also why the people as a whole seemed to approve, or at least accept, the new official directions in both foreign and domestic policy. That is, in both areas, postwar policies were harming the best interests of the people, in the localist view, by shifting an increasing range of responsibility from the local to the national level, and yet the people elected and reelected officials who stood for such policies. The failure of the people to understand their own interest was partly attributable, according to Jenner and fellow investigators, to the influence of communists in those institutions and professions important to the molding of public attitudes—through the "elegant form of brainwashing" Jenner was concerned about. Thus the congressional committees sought communists not only in government office but also in schools, universities, and, most spectacularly, in Hollywood, in their attempts to root out and deliver the nation from hidden manipulators of the public mind.

The postwar localist conviction that communist subversion had become the most serious enemy of the Republic did not entirely displace their sense of threat from older enemies as well. Rather, well into the 1950s, both old and new conceptions of danger coexisted in the localist outlook, a state of mind expressed in all its anger and frustration in the long debate over the Bricker Amendment in 1954. The amendment, proposed by Senator John Bricker, Republican of Ohio, would have modified the treaty power as defined in the Constitution with two ends in view. One was to curb the power of the President by making executive agreements subject to regulation by Congress. The other was to curb the power of Washington—the combined power of the President, Congress, and Supreme Court—by giving the states, in effect, a veto over treaties affecting questions normally subject to state, as opposed to federal, law.

The attack on executive agreements was a leaf out of the old localist book, a general attack against secrecy and chicanery in the executive branch. The more general localist concern, however, was the potential for displacement of wide areas of state law by foreign agreements, which, under the Constitution, require only the approval of the President and two-thirds of the Senate to take effect. They feared especially that the postwar enthusiasm for the United Nations, at least in its role of conscience for the world, might result in the United States' acceptance of various agreements defining universal standards for social policy—agreements such as the Covenants on Human Rights and Political Rights and the Genocide Convention—both special projects of John Foster Dulles.

The Bricker Amendment was designed to block any possibility that national treaties might nullify state laws. The amendment provided that treaties inconsistent with American law—including state law—could have no effect until the American law was changed by whatever jurisdiction had authority under the Constitution over the particular subject matter. As Bricker explained it, if the United States ratified a treaty establishing a uniform divorce law, for example, its provisions could take effect in the United States only through state law. That is, the treaty would have no effect in a state whose divorce law varied from the treaty unless the state passed a new law conforming to the treaty provisions.[28]

For the South, the main concern was to protect local race segregation laws from federal interference, and southern leaders backed the Bricker Amendment wholeheartedly as much-needed protection of the claims of states' rights. Senator Walter George of Georgia defined the heart of the southern position as the conception "that States had rights in the larger field of personal relationships which grow up in the States and which affect all their people, all their businesses, all their schools, and all their churches." And he added that human liberty generally would be lost "whenever such rights are abandoned, . . . when one looks alone to a central government in Washington." Freedom depends on keeping decisions about basic human relations at the local level, in the hands of people "who are responsive to local opinion, and who can hear petitions for redress of grievances and correction of wrongs."[29]

The new enemy, then, was not only the presidency or the executive branch but promoters of the alien idea that social standards should be defined at the national or, worse yet, international level. Bricker insisted that the greatest opponents of his amendment were the advocates of world government, people who regarded national sovereignty as outmoded and dangerous and who "yearn for the domination of a supranational government." The purpose of the amendment, he said, was to close the "loophole in our Constitution . . . through which could come a tyrannical world government and a Marxist covenant on human rights."[30]

The Senate finally reached its decision on the Bricker Amendment in February 1954. The vote was 60–31, only one vote short of the two-thirds majority necessary for Senate approval of a constitutional amendment, and those voting in favor included nearly all of the localists. Only four senators from states in the localist heartland voted against—Fulbright of Arkansas, Hill of Alabama, Hayden of Arizona, and Monroney of Oklahoma.

The primary enemy for localists in the postwar years, therefore, was not communism abroad but communism at home—the
explanation they found for the otherwise inexplicable drive by
the leaders of both parties to link the fortunes of the United States
with those of other countries. The devastating result of this focus
on an internal enemy—apart from the ruined careers of many
accused of communist sympathies—was distraction from the real
events and conflicts of the outside world. Calm, clear public
discussion, for example, of the relation of China under its new
communist government to other countries of the Far East, including Vietnam, the strains of impending decolonization in
Africa, or the seeds of desperate trouble in the Middle East, not
to mention Latin America, simply did not occur.

The further result of the localist stance on foreign policy was
the tendency of leaders in both the Truman and the Eisenhower
administrations to present their foreign policies in localist terms
in order to win over some, at least, of the localist votes. That
is, in asking for aid to Greece and Turkey in 1947, or South
Vietnam in 1954, or the Middle East in 1958, administration
officials would paint a lurid picture of Soviet threats to those
areas as part of a worldwide plan of subversion, the ultimate
object of which was the takeover of the United States.

Truman's Secretary of State, Dean Acheson, seeking to persuade localists that the communist threat to Greece and Turkey
was in fact a threat to the United States, borrowed FDR's metaphor of contagion to dramatize the connection. "Like apples in
a barrel, infected by one rotten one," he said, "the corruption of
Greece would infect Iran and all to the east. It would also carry
infection to Africa, through Asia Minor and Egypt, and to
Europe through Italy and France, already threatened by the
strongest domestic Communist parties in Western Europe."[31] By
the 1950s, the metaphor applied to Vietnam and the Far East had
changed to the faster-acting "falling dominoes."

This form of appeal for localist support, by concentrating
public discussion generally on an enemy depicted as malicious
and conspiratorial, further reduced the possibility of attention to
the complication of issues in distant areas. And yet the localists
could not be ignored politically. Especially in the Senate, there

were too many of them, as the close vote on the Bricker Amendment powerfully illustrated.

Localists contributed most directly to foreign policy, however, through their part in the functionalist-localist coalition that was the governing coalition under Eisenhower in the 1950s. In matters of foreign policy, the primary effect of the coalition was to curb the majoritarian initiative that had shaped policy, with functionalist support, throughout the Truman years.

The same coalition—functionalists and localists—had cooperated after the First World War also to curb Wilson's majoritarian design, although then its purpose was to keep the United States completely detached from political conflicts elsewhere. In the 1950s, the purpose was less radical, as functionalists had, in the meantime, become converts to collective security and thus supported the United Nations as well as the other programs, such as the Marshall Plan and NATO, making American commitments to the security of Western Europe. But functionalists as well as localists resisted policies beyond those designed for the defense of Europe, that would engage the United States in intricate, expensive, long-term involvement in the internal problems of other nations.

More specifically, both opposed the majoritarian inclination to involve the United States in the building of economic and political institutions of democracy abroad. The localists did not think the internal structures of other countries were of any concern to the United States. Functionalists *did* see the importance of compatible institutions in other countries—otherwise an international order of free-flowing exchange could not work—but they did not think that such institutions should be built by national governments, including the American government. Rather, the functionalist agents for building social order abroad, as at home, were private corporations and non-political public agencies—both run by experts, people who understood and respected the functional logic of the problems they dealt with.

Thus, with functionalists and localists agreed on what the nation should *not* do, majoritarian activism abroad was brought to a halt under Eisenhower, as it had been in the 1920s. And, as in the 1920s also, there was no positive vision to replace it, no ground shared by the coalition partners for a constructive policy abroad. Their only other area of agreement was on matters of defense, on the need to maintain strong defenses against the Soviet Union. The primary product, therefore, of the functionalist-localist coalition in the 1950s was the construction of a nuclear arsenal as the primary instrument of American foreign relations —the instrument behind Dulles's threats of massive retaliation.

Paradoxically, Dwight Eisenhower, the President who presided over this construction, left office in 1961 with a warning to the nation of its dangers. Eisenhower's own views were a blend of localist and functionalist attitudes—the outlook of a young man from a small town in Kansas blended with the experience of a professional army officer—but this commentary was clearly rooted in the classical localist tradition.

In a dramatic farewell speech, Eisenhower dwelled on the threat to Americans of the new weight of the military within their society. He pointed out that prior to the Second World War the United States had no arms industry or standing army but that by 1960 the nation's annual spending on military security was greater than the net income of all corporations in the United States combined. The dangers for national policy that he saw in this situation precisely reflected old localist concerns. One was the potential for the subjection of the government to "unwarranted influence, whether sought or unsought, by the military-industrial complex." This was a force, he said, with potential for "the disastrous use of misplaced power."

The other concern Eisenhower defined was a force produced by the combination of military needs and a technological revolution that made scientific research fabulously complicated and expensive. The scale of expense, he said, had forced scientists in universities to become dependent on the federal government to fund their research, and new, close ties were developing between the government and universities as a result. The problem Eisenhower saw in this was the danger "that public policy would itself become the captive of a scientific-technological elite."

The tone of Eisenhower's warning was calmer than the earlier localist warnings of William Jennings Bryan against the "merchants of death" and the "professional man-killers," but the concern about the "misplaced power" of special interests undermining the general public interest, and the loss of power to an "elite" uncontrollable by the ordinary citizen, was the same as Bryan's—as were the spirit and the words of Eisenhower's closing prayer that "all peoples will come to live together in a peace guaranteed by the binding force of mutual respect and love."[32]

Eisenhower's address was an open manifestation of the deep differences that lay beneath the postwar practice of bipartisanship in foreign policy. Under the seeming consensus, the separate visions and purposes of majoritarians, functionalists, and localists remained strong, and the amalgamation of these views in the period from 1945 to 1960 had implanted deep confusions in the relations of the United States internationally. The deepest confusion, however, stemmed, as always, from the promise of the myth of deliverance that informed the outlook of all three.

Because of the promise of the myth, all three groups approached international politics with the conviction that serious conflict among nations was not necessary, that it was the result of abuse of power, and that this abuse could be located and controlled. It was with this common belief and with their separate convictions as to where the abuse came from and how it should be controlled that Americans entered the yet more complicated world of the 1960s, and soon found themselves, at desperate odds, in Vietnam.

VI

Deliverance from Poverty: Failure of the Majoritarian Promise

When majoritarians, led by John F. Kennedy, recaptured the White House in 1960, foreign policy was not the first matter on their agenda. And certainly few coming into office with the new administration had given any prior thought to such problems as American policy in Vietnam. Rather, the focus of Kennedy's campaign had been on the opening up of "New Frontiers" at home.

Majoritarian forces had been gathering since the end of the Second World War to extend the protections constructed by the New Deal for wage earners—to further redress the imbalance of economic power within the nation. Harry Truman had placed a long list of social needs before Congress, from full employment to adequate housing, health care, and education, and he had proposed also protections against racial discrimination in public institutions and places and in private employment. Very few of Truman's programs were passed, however, and during the Eisenhower administration from 1953 to 1961, the executive as well as the legislative branch stood opposed to majoritarian social initiatives.

Kennedy's election, then, released long-pent-up demands in

a new moment of social activism, a chance, as Kennedy had proclaimed throughout his campaign, "to get this country moving again." It was a tragically brief moment for Kennedy, assassinated during his third year in office, but the momentum of reform was picked up and accelerated by his successor, Lyndon Johnson. The result was the legendary explosion of legislation in 1964, 1965, and 1966—the programs launched in what Johnson declared to be a war on poverty, its eradication once and for all from America—and the further construction, beyond the New Deal, of a just society, the Great Society as Johnson called it.

Unlike the New Deal, however, the New Frontier/Great Society does not stand as a permanent monument to American social progress. Important accomplishments do remain—notably the restraints in the Civil Rights Act of 1964 against racial segregation and discrimination, and the protections of Medicare/Medicaid programs for the elderly and the poor. But most of the anti-poverty programs, the agencies clustered under the umbrella of the Office of Economic Opportunity, were dismantled within a decade—attacked, discredited, reversed, defunded by subsequent administrations and Congresses. Furthermore, majoritarian contenders for the presidency—Hubert Humphrey in 1968 and George McGovern in 1972—who bore the message that the Great Society should still be built and essentially as Presidents Kennedy and Johnson had tried to build it, were defeated. And so was Edward Kennedy in his effort to win the Democratic nomination for President in 1980, explicitly portraying himself as the carrier of his brother's legacy of reform.

Why did this happen? Why did programs long demanded by a wage-earning constituency come to be so widely regarded as failures, and so soon? As a group, wage earners in the 1960s were better off than their parents had been in the 1930s, but they were still insecurely employed, still less healthy than those at higher income levels, less well schooled, with important choices concerning work, housing, child care, and education still greatly constricted by limited income. And yet attitudes within this constituency for programs that promised greater opportunity, greater protections against privation and its costs, changed from wide enthusiasm to wide disillusion within a few years. Why?

The general reason was that the *promise* of the programs quickly faded. While certain programs worked well and particular constituencies benefited, the promise of greater security and greater justice for the whole was not redeemed. The hopes aroused in the early 1960s had been betrayed by the end. But again, why? What accounts for the vast differences between promise and result in the 1960s, particularly when compared with the earlier accomplishments of the New Deal?

Contributing to any historical development are many reasons, an intertwining of given and accidental conditions that contribute to a final result. But the core reason, the primary condition for the failure of the Great Society, was that the nation's economic and social troubles, by the 1960s, were larger and more complicated than political leaders thought they were. That is, looking at the nation's troubles as Americans always had, through the myth of deliverance, the leaders of the 1960s saw only a scattering of problems—problems that could be defined in terms for which solutions could be readily found, problems that were fixable. The full scope of economic trouble in particular—its roots and structure—was screened out of their vision, and by the 1960s, the scale of the actual problems at hand was such that piecemeal solutions could have little effect. Of course, there had been a real gap in the 1930s between the scope of the nation's problems and what Americans could see of them. But by the 1960s, the discrepancy was larger because the problems were larger, and there was even less possibility that partial solutions could have a positive effect.

Another critical difference between the two reform eras was that a different coalition of interests was at work, which meant that different versions of the myth with different identifications of the enemy lay behind the two reform programs.

In the 1930s, majoritarians and localists formed a coalition to place restraints each needed on the power of the corporate world. And the coalition produced effective results because it identified and addressed—in however limited a way—the real source of trouble the coalition parties faced. That is, New Deal programs were based on the accurate premise that managers had excessive power over the terms of exchange between the corporate world

and weaker economic groups, and the programs, in various specific ways, reduced that power. The results achieved—greater
fairness for wage earners and farmers primarily—were less far-
reaching than the two groups expected from their mythic reading
of what was wrong, but the benefits of the New Deal for these
two large constituencies were, nonetheless, substantial.

In the 1960s, however, majoritarians were working, not with
localists, but with functionalists, in a cooperative effort to
strengthen the economy generally as well as the position of
certain weaker groups within it. And in this case, the myth had
a doubly damaging effect. Not only did it blind both groups to
the full scale of the nation's problems, but it deceived both as to
the actual possibilities of cooperation between them. That is, the
mythic denial of serious conflict among different economic interests led majoritarians and functionalists in the 1960s to assume that
their common purposes were wider than in fact they were. More
specifically, majoritarians, looking at the troubles of the time
through the myth, failed to see the gulf, the conflict, between
their own real interests—the continuing common interests of the
wage-earning constituency as a whole—and those of the functionalist managers. Consequently, the programs produced by the
majoritarian-functionalist coalition were *not* based on wholly
accurate premises as to the source of the problems addressed and,
for that reason, could not be broadly and lastingly effective.

A shifting in alliances on domestic issues became apparent immediately after the end of the Second World War. Truman's
classic majoritarian approach was to continue the New Deal
traditions, to extend still further the power of the national government to help those in the society without sufficient power to
protect themselves—helping "the average man who has no pull
in Washington," as he put it.[1] His proposals, which he called the
Fair Deal, sought particularly to redress unbalanced economic
power in areas beyond the workplace but still vitally important
to the economic position and general well-being of wage earners.

Truman's program included a federal employment act making full employment a goal and a responsibility of the federal

government; a national health insurance system to be made part of the social security program established under Roosevelt; various programs of federal aid to education; and a program of federal aid for the construction of housing. In addition, he submitted proposals directly addressing the problem of racial discrimination—a fair employment practices law guaranteeing equal employment opportunity regardless of race, religion, or color, and a broad civil rights program attacking official policies of racial segregation that existed mainly in the Deep South—the old Confederacy.

Truman's "fair-dealing" or power-balancing approach to reform was as significant for what it was not as for what it was. In the congressional elections of 1946 and his own presidential campaign in 1948, he identified as the major problem of the society the increasing concentration of economic power, but he did not advocate the nationalization of that power, taking it away from private managerial responsibility altogether. Various socialist and communist groups urged just such solutions in the years immediately following the war, raising the question whether American wage earners, having suffered a depression and a war, would contemplate radical change. Would they approve a politics that leapt beyond the bounds of the myth to an assumption of intractable class differences and to legislation following from that assumption? It was soon clear that they would not.

The rejection of socialist-communist solutions and the affirmation of majoritarianism among wage earners occurred within various groups, but most dramatically within the unions. Fierce struggles took place between communists and non-communists for leadership within many CIO unions, including the United Auto Workers, the Transport Workers Union, the United Electrical Workers, the Mine, Mill and Smelter Workers Union, the Longshoremen's Union, and among the leaders of the CIO central organization, but by 1950 the non-communists were in firm control.

Wage earners further affirmed a majoritarian outlook in their strong support for Truman in the election of 1948—and in their lack of support for Henry Wallace, running for President as a Progressive and calling for a radical reduction in the power of

private capital in the society. Wallace's message, while not defini-
tively socialist, was still not squarely based on the mythic assumption of complementarity among economic interests, and thus it
could not engage broad public enthusiasm.

In spite of wage earner backing, however, Truman's Fair
Deal was doomed to failure in Congress. Except for the Full
Employment Act of 1946—which provided only for federal
monitoring of the economy, not provision of jobs—and a Housing Act in 1949, the legislation met adamant opposition from a
majority composed of two groups. One was the functionalist
interest, which offered the same objections it had made to New
Deal legislation—generally that the private economy would supply social needs more fairly and efficiently than the federal government could. The other opponents, however, were Roosevelt's
old allies, the localists.

What had happened was that the common interest underlying the old alliance had dissolved. That is, during the New
Freedom and New Deal years, the farmers and entrepreneurs of
rural states and the workers of industrial states alike had sought
controls on monopoly and unfair trade practices and such measures as public regulation of utilities, the banking system, and
stock exchanges. When, by the end of the 1930s, these protections
and others specifically designed for farmers—notably parity pricing—were in place, the localist agenda, insofar as national legislation went, was virtually complete. Thus, while wage earners still
had a long list of unfinished business, localists had no incentive
to continue their prior cooperation. On the contrary, they had
strong reasons not to.

Truman's Fair Deal proposals all required rules, standards,
and expenditures applicable nationwide, precisely that form of
federal invasiveness that threatened the localist interest and
offended localist political beliefs. As a result, a majority of localists in Congress—a majority previously allied with wage earners
against managers—formed a de facto alliance with managers
against the legislative demands of wage earners. This is not to say
that all legislators from all localist regions joined forces to oppose
all labor and social legislation, but rather that a consistent majority of them did and on most issues.

To look at the Senate, where the localist constituency is strong, with 42 potential votes from the 21 states with predominantly rural economies, 21 to 30 localist votes were consistently cast after 1945 against proposals for increased federal responsibility in social and economic areas—or in favor of measures cutting back such responsibility. Localists—generally southern Democrats joined with western and southwestern Democrats and Republicans—contributed a crucial 26 votes toward overriding President Truman's veto of the anti-labor Taft-Hartley bill in 1947; 29 of the 33 votes that kept the Senate from passing on a strong Fair Employment Practices bill in 1950; 25 of the 56 votes defeating the establishment of nationwide standards for unemployment compensation in 1954.

On domestic questions, therefore, the identification by localists of threats to social well-being—meaning, for them, threats to local autonomy—shifted in the postwar years from big business to big government and their tactics for deliverance shifted correspondingly. While they retained some mistrust of the power and interests of large corporations, they were prepared to cooperate with the managerial interest as far as their common purposes would carry them to fight the newer enemy of invasive federal power. This shift in alliance was solidified with the election in 1952 of Dwight Eisenhower, whose administration represented the joint interests of functionalist and localist constituencies. During Eisenhower's two terms, initiatives involving federal government protection of the nation's workers were virtually shelved under a reigning philosophy of private—or local—responsibility for economic and social health.

In spite of this common ground, however, there were important differences between localists and managers in their views of the role the federal government *should* play in national economic and social matters. And by the end of the 1950s these differences had produced enough disaffection to open the way for another shift in political alliance—a shift in functionalist support away from policies of federal quietism, backed by localists, to policies of activism pressed by a new generation of majoritarians. This shift did not signal a change in basic belief on the part of functionalists. Rather, it reflected a greater emphasis on the activist elements of their continuing belief in voluntarism—the theory which prescribes, as Herbert Hoover formulated it, a non-coercive but still active role for government in economic affairs.

The growing acceptance of greater governmental activism on the part of functionalists had begun during and soon after the Second World War, as the managerial interest began to take stock of changes in the rapidly expanding, vastly complicated American economy. And Herbert Hoover himself played an important part in shaping this direction of functionalist thought in his role as chairman of two successive Presidential Commissions on the Reorganization of the Executive Branch—the first set up under Truman in 1947, the second under Eisenhower in 1953.

For many Republicans who supported the formation of the commissions, reorganization meant cutting out a number of New Deal programs. Not surprisingly, they assumed that Hoover, a vehement critic of much of the New Deal, thought in the same terms, but he did not. On the contrary, Hoover, as always, saw a large and active federal government as a clear necessity given the complexities of an industrial economy. His concern, as always, was to keep government limited to a cooperative, not a coercive, role and to protect its operation from the wasteful distortions imposed by special interest on governmental functions.

The first Hoover Commission concentrated on the problem of assuring honesty, rationality, and responsibility in the processes of administration, and it recommended a variety of managerial techniques to accomplish this result: grouping agencies with related functions into single departments and concentrating authority in department heads rather than allowing a scattering of fiefdoms accessible to special interest; standardizing the internal organization of all departments; and organizing budgets on the basis of function to allow administrators and legislators to evaluate expenditures in relation to actual functional performance.

The second Hoover Commission continued this quest for functional efficiency, but its purpose was expanded to evaluate the substance of programs as well, with the aim of abolishing services, activities, and functions not necessary to the efficient conduct of government and those "non-essential" programs "which are competitive with private enterprise." This was a radical-sounding charge, but it did not produce radical results. The Commission did no more with it than to recommend the abolition of government power installations, some lending programs, and a variety of small-scale enterprises performing normal business functions, such as Defense Department bakeries, meat-cutting and clothing plants, and laundries.

For all of their expressed outrage with the spirit and some of the programs of the New Deal, the fact was that Hoover and his fellow functionalists had, in the postwar government, essentially what they wanted. As Hoover had insisted in the prewar years, government had to play an active role in maintaining an economic framework within which the private sector could plan its business rationally. In the conditions of a complicated postwar economy, government needed expanded authority to perform that role and that is what the New Deal structure provided.

The Securities and Exchange Commission, the National Labor Relations Board, and the Agricultural Adjustment Administration, along with the earlier Federal Reserve Board, could protect against a recurrence of national depression by careful monitoring of credit supplies and stock sales, by maintaining the purchasing power of workers, by protecting farmers, especially vulnerable to economic downturns, from a degree of weakness that could undermine other economic sectors. Further, by working through these agencies and others, the federal government could assure sufficient bank credit and provide sufficient information and support for research to aid in the expansion of the economy.

In the decades following the period of postwar adjustment, functionalists came not only to accept much of the New Deal, as Hoover had, but to contemplate new governmental functions as well—new dimensions to the earlier concept of voluntarism. No single figure of Hoover's stature has served to articulate this further development of voluntarist thought, but management organizations studying the country's domestic problems have done so—and in considerable depth.

A particularly active group has been the Committee for Economic Development (CED), founded in 1942 "to use objective research to determine private and public policies which will promote economic growth and stability in a free society."[2] Its membership, which overlaps considerably that of the Council on Foreign Relations, is drawn primarily from large, often internationally operating corporations such as the John Hancock Company, Scott Paper, Bankers Trust, Federated Department Stores, General Electric, and Sears, Roebuck. Its mode of operation, like the Council's, is to form study groups to address a wide range of policy questions, although, unlike the Council, the CED publishes reports setting out the findings of each group and recommendations that represent the position of the organization as such.

The studies of the CED typically deal with large, long-range problems—inflation, recession, financing better public schools, improving management in government, metropolitan transit, a cleaner environment, financing national housing needs, or modernizing state government. And the resulting reports, characteristic of the functionalist approach to public policy, present answers to the issues they address in the form of comprehensive systems, placing a range of interconnected factors into logical, rational patterns of efficiency.

The basic assumption running through all of the CED studies is that the systematizing of most functions in the society is best carried out privately, but with recognition on the part of the managers in the private sector of the complication of their task. The reports carry the repeated message that managers must engage in long-term planning within their firms. They must deliberately coordinate data on a wide array of interlocking factors— including the impact of business decisions on general economic and social health—in order to carry out their particular functions efficiently in an era of advanced industrialism. A 1971 CED report, *The Social Responsibilities of Business Corporations,* put it that in earlier times the coordination of all the various interests and needs in the economy was supposed to be accomplished by the "invisible hand" of the market, but now "it is the *visible hand* [their emphasis] that is supposed to achieve the same result."[3]

The further insistent message of the reports is that some functions, some social responsibilities, defy private resources and systems and require governmental involvement. On this question, the concern of the CED has been both to identify the functions —increasing over the years—for which some governmental responsibility is necessary and to outline the principles that define what the government should do, and *not* do, in carrying out that responsibility. And the primary principle for the CED, as it was for Hoover, is that the relation between government and the private sector, as both address the modern mix of economic and social problems, should be cooperative.

The title of a typical report, *Jobs for the Hard-to-Employ: New Directions for a Public-Private Partnership,*[4] signals its message. There is strong emphasis on the importance of government support for the collection and dissemination to business of useful information on the problem of chronic unemployment as well as a recommendation for the further development of public-private "jobs corporations." These would, in effect, use a percentage of welfare funds to subsidize the training and employment of the hard-to-employ by private firms.

Similarly, a 1965 report, *Guiding Metropolitan Growth,* stressed the necessity for private-public cooperation in long-range planning for metropolitan development—and further insisted that such planning should be based on expert evaluation of the economic base of an area. To add yet another functionalist note, "economic base" was to be defined, not in terms of city or suburban boundaries, but in terms of the interlocking functional needs and resources of an area—transportation, education, labor supply, water supply, waste disposal, pollution control. To accomplish needed planning thoroughly and rationally, "local business leaders should participate more actively with local officials and other groups in setting goals for their community and guiding metropolitan affairs."[5] The writers of the report acknowledge that many businessmen do not involve themselves in local affairs because they assume that local politicians are not seriously interested in long-range rational plans, but, the report concludes, it is increasingly common to find communities run, not by politicians and their friends, but by professionally trained civil servants with whom businessmen can work in wide areas of common purpose and understanding.

In other words, the report, perfectly expressive of functionalist belief, carries the implicit assumption that there is no difference, or should be none, between the roles of government and business, at least in the realm of social planning. Government, of course, has roles, such as law enforcement, not shared by the private sector, but when it comes to analyzing the needs of people in a huge, highly advanced, highly complicated society, and doing the planning necessary to resolve the conflicting interests arising out of such complication, then—for functionalists—there is no distinction between business and government. There is only professionalism, the objective, rational analysis of data by people with technical knowledge of the problems in question and professional commitment to addressing problems disinterestedly.

The key to successful cooperation between business and government in social planning, for the CED as for earlier functionalists, is to keep politics—meaning the use of power to promote particular rather than general interests—out of government and to enhance within government itself the role of professionals. *Making Congress More Effective,* a 1971 CED report, recommends that Congress strengthen its committees "by recruitment of highly qualified specialists—physical scientists, engineers, environmentalists, physicians, economists, and other social scientists, nutritionists, mathematicians, management experts, and others" —so that "every committee would have access to the best technical and analytical service."[6]

A 1979 report, *Redefining Government's Role in the Market System,* summed up the CED recommendations for the form governmental intervention in economic problems should take where it was necessary. First, and least intrusive, the government should try to solve the problem at hand through the dissemination of useful information. Failing that, it should use incentives and penalties to induce desired behavior in the private sector but should not impose its own specific rules. Or, if greater direction is needed, it could set specific goals for companies or industries dealing with a particular problem, but it should leave the private managers involved free to decide how best to meet the goals. The managerial voice of the CED thus sounds a consistent anti-governmental or anti-political warning, but still it does not call for a system of laissez-faire. Rather, it calls for experts and more experts—a call that assumes the need for complicated and ambitious action on economic issues, including extensive action by government—as long as government operates as an agency, not of power, but of reason.

As advocates of complex social action and cooperators with the national government, functionalists depart radically from the more straightforward anti-governmentalism of the localists. It is hard to imagine localist leaders in Congress or in their communities subscribing to *any* of the analyses advanced by the CED—which is to say by a wide cross section of the nation's corporate managers. The two groups did occupy overlapping ground—where the localist mistrust of political action led to the common conclusion that no national political action was warranted in a particular area. But still, by the end of the 1950s, there was growing discomfort within the Eisenhower coalition, fed by a variety of problems.

The economy was in recession after 1958, and the administration had no clear strategy for dealing with it, or rather its strategy, reflecting the common ground of the coalition, was to take no action. Eisenhower's primary economic aim had been to balance the federal budget, or at least reduce deficits, not to use government to pace economic growth. And the rate of national economic expansion in the 1950s was, in fact, low, producing among functionalists a restiveness not felt by localists.

A more sharply divisive issue, looming ever larger through the 1950s, was civil rights. An organized civil rights movement to end legal segregation in the southern states had grown throughout the decade, spurred by the 1954 Supreme Court decision in *Brown* v. *Board of Education*. In that case, the Court decided that the southern policy of maintaining separate schools for white and black children violated the Fourteenth Amendment requirement that states provide their people equal protection of the laws. This issue placed national law and state law in direct conflict, and the conflict placed Eisenhower's functionalist-localist coalition under direct pressure over the question of the role the federal government would play in enforcing the Court's decision. That question was answered in 1957 when Eisenhower sent federal troops to Little Rock, Arkansas, to protect black students entering Little Rock Central High School in the face of resistance by local officials. Nationalist or functionalist Republicans had won out over localists within the councils of Republican leadership, but not without producing added internal strain.

Another event of 1957, the launching of two Russian space satellites in advance of any such American accomplishment, shocked the country and simultaneously put pressure on another issue dividing localists and functionalists—the issue of federal aid to education. Many localists wanted local control of education more than they wanted federal money, but functionalists, seeing into the space age and perceiving the need for better scientific and technical training for Americans, were willing to back federal spending toward that end.

Majoritarians, of course, had been calling for federal aid to education since Truman's day and thus, in 1958, happily joined in passing the National Defense Education Act, which provided millions of dollars for scholarships, teacher training, and laboratory equipment. Again, the issue marked the straining of sympathies between localists and functionalists, but further, it presaged the potential for common ground on new issues between majoritarians and functionalists.

None of these issues brought a complete breakdown in political cooperation between localists and functionalists, and certainly not an abrupt shift to a functionalist-majoritarian coalition. But by the end of the decade there were a number of areas in which functionalists saw the need for greater national attention, direction, and leadership than were possible in coalition with localists. Many were ready at least to contemplate a new approach, a new emphasis in national government.

This was the point of entry on the national political scene of John F. Kennedy, who virtually embodied the joint interests of majoritarian wage earners and functionalist managers. An Irish Catholic Democrat from Massachusetts, he carried intact the political tradition of industrial wage earners—that is, the commitment to power balancing by the federal government. And he underscored this commitment throughout his campaign for the presidency in 1960 with frequent references to the political lineage of Wilson, Roosevelt, and Truman behind him. But he was also the son of a wealthy businessman. He and his brothers had been educated at prestigious New England prep schools and at Ivy League universities, the breeding grounds of the nation's professional elite—its lawyers, professors, scientists, and business executives. If Kennedy's grandparents had known intimately the world of powerless laborers, he knew, out of his own experience, the world of professional power and expertise. And his appeal for active, purposeful direction, his call to "get this country moving again," touched needs in both worlds.

Kennedy's election, then, marked a further shift toward a political alliance of majoritarians and functionalists for the construction of some kind of national response to national economic and social needs. But the shift was still not dramatic or even explicit in any immediate sense. It did not produce a quick amalgam of majoritarian and functionalist views in programmatic form or a wholesale delivery of functionalist (mainly northern and West Coast Republican) votes in Congress for the new President's domestic initiatives. Rather, there was a more subtle shifting of attitudes, a process that took several years to affect legislation.

Kennedy's primary appeal, clear in the ideas he stressed in his campaign, was majoritarian. Foremost was enthusiastic belief in the active use of the national government as an agent for movement and change. "The theme of this campaign is going to be action," Kennedy declared in September 1960, "action here at home to keep pace with the growing needs of an expanding country, and action abroad to meet the challenge of our adversaries."[7] And accompanying the call for action was an affirmation of power balancing as its fundamental rationale. "President Truman used to say that there are 14 million Americans who have sufficient resources to be able to protect their interests and it is the function of the President of the United States to protect the interests of the other 150 million," Kennedy said, making explicit his appeal to the economically powerless majority.[8]

Like Roosevelt, he emphasized the connected interests of the economically weak across the country, concerned as majoritarians must always be with building and maintaining the cohesiveness of their national constituency. Speaking in South Dakota, Kennedy said, "My people in Massachusetts cannot manufacture textiles or sell fish or make television sets and sell them to the Middle West unless you have the income to buy them. And you cannot prosper on the farms unless our cities move ahead." Then in words directly recalling Roosevelt's, he added, "I think the necessity for us is to recognize that we are not 50 separate states; we are not 6 different regions of the United States. We are one country with one great problem, and this is to insure the prosperity of our people and their security . . ."[9]

Finally, following his majoritarian predecessors from Wilson on, Kennedy stressed throughout his campaign the necessity for the President—as opposed to Congress—to lead in shaping policy responsive to national needs. "If the President does not set . . . standards, if he does not set our national goals, then a Senator from California, or the Governor of California, or a Congressman . . . cannot do it. Only the President speaks for the people," he said. And further, "the President of the United States must actively use the powers of leadership in pursuit of well-defined goals" to be effective as an agent for change.[10]

On taking office, Kennedy put the principle of presidential leadership into immediate practice through the Rooseveltian strategy of increasing the size of the presidential office, its staff and functions. Ironically, by Kennedy's time, the permanent bureaucracy in the Cabinet departments—the legacy of earlier majoritarians—had become a serious block to presidential activism. The departments, though headed by officers appointed by and loyal to the President, had developed over the years interests and constituencies of their own and an accumulation of commitments and policy preferences that were sometimes at odds with those of the White House.

Kennedy resisted the power of the bureaucracy by using an enlarged presidential staff to intervene in bureaucratic procedures. He replaced many established departmental committees with ad hoc task forces which included delegates from the White House charged with pressing the presidential viewpoint. And, to maximize presidential leverage, he insisted on reports from such task forces at early stages, before positions and recommendations had fully formed. Within months his activist staff began to produce a variety of foreign and domestic proposals.[11]

In spite of these firmly majoritarian emphases, however, the Kennedy administration was hospitable to functionalist interests as well. Functionalists, long opponents of serious policy making by politicians, had, for that reason, been opponents of a strong presidency. Their trusted arm of government was the non-political, independent agency or commission or the judiciary. But Kennedy's executive branch was attractive to the professional-managerial constituency because he deliberately turned to the professionals, the experts, for help in formulating solutions for the nation's problems.

This was not a new conception for Kennedy. He had discussed what he saw as the necessity for the involvement in public life of people with special knowledge in a commencement address at Harvard University as early as 1956. Speaking as a senator, he had asked his academic listeners to regard the search for truth as extending naturally to public issues, and he asked further that they offer their expertise, not simply as critics, but as contributors to public understanding of difficult issues. The politician may be too close to issues or too engaged in seeking public approval to see problems as a whole, Kennedy said, and scholars could supply needed knowledge and objectivity. "I do not say that our political and public life should be turned over to experts who ignore public opinion," he concluded, but rather that there should be "greater cooperation and understanding between politicians and intellectuals."[12]

In office, he acted on that principle by calling to Washington a small army of experts to serve on presidential task forces and study groups. There were economists, development specialists, sociologists and psychologists concerned with juvenile delinquency, city planners, administrators of health care and schools, space scientists, and authorities on race relations, as well as people who knew politics—elected officials, organizers, and advisers.

The mix of politicians and experts in Kennedy's Washington offered promise at the outset to both groups. To functionalists, it corresponded closely to the prescription for cooperation between political and professional realms they had long advocated. To majoritarians, the authority lent by experts to the analysis of nationwide problems and the design of nationwide solutions gave weight to executive proposals and increased the chance of their being taken seriously by Republicans—functionalist, if not localist Republicans—in Congress.

But hidden in this burst of activity, and in the near-euphoric sense of new possibilities suddenly opened up by a young President who *sought* change, were the old differences between the two groups. Once solutions were devised, majoritarians would *legislate* them into effect. That is, they would use political processes to impose changes needed by weaker groups dealing with the strong. For functionalists, however, change affecting private institutions should be voluntary—guided and facilitated by government, but not coerced.

This difference emerged dramatically within months of Kennedy's taking office in a battle the new President waged with the steel industry. Soon after his inauguration in 1961, Kennedy had put the principle of cooperation between public and private sectors into actual practice by opening discussions with the steel companies and the Steelworkers Union over wage and price levels. Specifically, the administration wanted to ensure that the next union contract, due in 1962, would be signed without a long strike, such as had occurred under Eisenhower in 1959. The government sought to persuade labor not to make wage demands in excess of increased productivity and to persuade the companies not to raise prices if labor stayed within the suggested guidelines. Labor did restrain its demands and the parties signed a contract in March 1962 without a strike. Then, on April 10, United States Steel raised its prices, followed within a day by most of the other companies.

Kennedy was outraged, and determined to force the steel companies to rescind the increase. The immediate problem was how to do it. As President, he had no authority to set prices for private companies. The administration had been engaging in *voluntary* cooperation among government, business, and labor, and the companies' agreement not to raise prices was voluntary, creating a moral, not a legal, obligation. But Kennedy regarded the agreement as binding, whether or not it had been reached voluntarily, and he set about enforcing it with whatever presidential power he could muster.

He called a press conference on April 11 and excoriated the companies for their "wholly unjustifiable and irresponsible defiance of the public interest." The Attorney General, Robert Kennedy, announced a grand jury investigation into possible collusion in violation of anti-trust laws by the companies that raised prices within a day of each other. The Secretary of Defense, Robert McNamara, announced a shift in the procurement of steel by the military, where possible, to the few companies that had not raised prices. Within a few days, under the pressure of this barrage, Bethlehem Steel rescinded its price increase, followed by United States Steel and finally all of the others.[13]

Kennedy's tactics were thus effective in the short run, but they left unresolved the differences between the companies and the government, the professionals and the politicians, as to where authority over matters of national economic policy *should* be. Kennedy, having embarked on a cooperative process only to be confronted by a breach of cooperation, had reacted out of a majoritarian impulse—a turn to political power and a firm use of executive authority—to restrain what he saw as an abuse of power by business. For the managers, on the other hand, Kennedy's reaction was an intrusion of political power into an issue—the level of prices—that was properly determined by functional considerations alone, and properly assessed only by the managers whose direct responsibility it was.

In spite of the battle over big steel, the alliance of majoritarians and functionalists in the Kennedy administration did not collapse. The commitment to expertise, and to cooperative as opposed to coercive uses of government in addressing the nation's larger problems, persisted through Kennedy's short tenure. In fact, not long after the dramatic clash with steel executives, the President affirmed and elaborated his views on cooperation as a principle of government in a commencement speech at Yale.

The United States was suffering, Kennedy said—with obvious reference to the recent battle—from a myth left over from the 1930s, which was that government was the enemy of business. In the meantime, however, the countries of Europe had discovered the reality that modern economic health required the cooperation of business, government, and labor. Cooperation was necessary because modern economies were exceedingly complicated and the actions of each major element affected the others profoundly. Tax levels, interest rates, the strength of the dollar in world markets, world commodity prices, automation and its effects on the employment of unskilled workers—all of these were issues affecting, and affected by, all three major actors in the economy. And then there was the problem of "barriers which separate substantial minorities of our citizens from access to education and employment on equal terms with the rest." In sum, Kennedy said, the question was: "How . . . can we make our free economy work at full capacity—that is, provide adequate profits for enterprise, adequate wages for labor, adequate utilization of plant, and opportunity for all?"

That it *could* be done, that the major problems and conflicts he discussed could be resolved on terms good for all, Kennedy apparently did not doubt. On the contrary, the point of his speech was that answers could be found, as he thought they had been in Europe, through cooperation among managers, government, and labor in "the practical management of a modern economy" and in "more basic discussion of the sophisticated and technical questions involved in keeping a great economic machinery moving ahead."[14] The lesson Kennedy had learned from big steel was not that cooperation would not work, but that business had not learned to cooperate.

There was little, however, in the domestic initiatives taken before Kennedy's death to further this sought-for collaboration. The legislation he submitted to Congress was essentially an updated version of the Truman program—majoritarian proposals for national health insurance, more aid to education, a housing program, and a civil rights bill striking at continuing forms of racial segregation and discrimination in the South. And except for aid to education, Kennedy's bills suffered the same fate as Truman's—defeat at the hands of localists and unconvinced functionalists in Congress.

Ironically, the fruits of Kennedy's attempts to build a joint wage earner–manager constituency behind social action came after his death, through the efforts of the succeeding Vice-President, Lyndon Johnson. The irony lies in the fact that there could be no politician or official less attuned by political belief to functionalist principles or by background and temperament to the professional-managerial establishment espousing them than Johnson.

Born in rural Texas, Johnson lived from earliest childhood in a region where strong localist values prevailed. He grew up among families—his own included—frequently on the edge of hardship, among people who prized toughness, strength, and endurance as opposed to cultivation and knowledge, at least for men. Accepting this tradition of hard work and self-reliance, Johnson added to it, as a young man making a career in politics, the majoritarian principles of the New Deal. As a congressman, he won federal aid for an irrigation project that transformed the economic potential for farmers of his region from a lifelong prospect of gritty survival to the possibility of decent prosperity. Thereafter this story, in his telling, became virtually a parable, showing the necessity for national action to enhance the power of the economically weak, to afford them opportunity from which they would otherwise be excluded.

Thus Johnson's early political values—a merger of localism and majoritarianism—placed him far from any functionalist political stance, and the distance was increased still further by his lifetime career as a politician. A congressman, then a senator, then Majority Leader of the Senate before his election to the vice-presidency in 1960, he was a confirmed believer in the use of political power to bring about change—a power broker by profession. In short, there was nothing in his background, career, or concept of politics that made him a likely bridge between majoritarian and functionalist interests. Yet it was under his presidency that the social designs constructed by Kennedy's experts won approval from Congress—with strong support from managerial as well as wage-earning constituencies.

Most spectacular was the passage in 1964 of the Civil Rights Act and the omnibus Economic Opportunity Act. The Johnson program for economic opportunity—which he sent to Congress in a message entitled "Nationwide War on the Sources of Poverty"—included a work-training program for underprivileged youth and also a more ambitious Job Corps, which established urban centers where young people could live while learning new skills or gaining work experience. It provided federal money for Community Action Programs—projects designed by local groups to provide some sort of service or plan for change responsive to particular local situations. Other parts of the program provided credit for small business—rural and urban—and for the training of volunteers (Volunteers in Service to America, or VISTA) to work in a variety of local anti-poverty projects. There were also programs for vocational education and retraining for workers unemployed due to technological change.

The Civil Rights Act, the strongest legislation ever passed by Congress on the issue of race discrimination, provided for the enforcement of voting rights by federal suits in federal courts, forbade discrimination in public accommodations such as restaurants and hotels, required the desegregation of state and local public facilities, provided federal aid for public school desegregation, forbade discrimination in any program receiving federal aid, and forbade race discrimination in employment practices by private as well as public employers.

This last section was Truman's Fair Employment Practices proposal, although still without strong teeth. The Civil Rights Act set up the Equal Employment Opportunities Commission to investigate complaints of discrimination in private employment, but the Commission had powers of investigation and recommendation only; it did not have the authority to issue cease and desist orders against offending employers.

In 1965, Johnson won two more parts of the majoritarian agenda. One was the Medicare Act, establishing compulsory hospital insurance for the aged—operating, as President Truman had first proposed, under the social security system. Johnson, in recognition of the political lineage of the legislation, went to Independence, Missouri, to sign the bill in Truman's presence. The second victory was a package of major housing legislation. Following a proposal first made in 1961 by President Kennedy,

Congress established a new executive department—Housing and Urban Development (HUD)—with Cabinet status, and it passed also an omnibus housing bill aimed especially at urban housing problems. Most notably, it provided rent supplements for low-income families and federal funding for the construction of housing for both low- and moderate-income groups and for the elderly.

And there were several additions to the war on poverty in 1965. Project Head Start funded preschool education for the children of poverty to offset the learning disadvantages they often faced in the early years of elementary school. Upward Bound did the same thing for poor and badly educated adolescents, with the aim of helping them acquire the skills and learning necessary to prepare for college.

What explains Johnson's extraordinary success with legislation generated in the Kennedy years but which Kennedy could not get approved? To a significant degree, the answer lies in the skill with which Johnson practiced the majoritarian principle of executive leadership. Doris Kearns, an aide and later a biographer of Johnson, wrote that his dealings with Congress were so active and intricate that the relation amounted to something like a parliamentary system—that is, a system in which the executive Cabinet and the legislative majority worked as one, not as separate powers. As a longtime member of Congress, Johnson knew legislative procedure, both formal and informal, and he knew, at a level of deep political intimacy, all of the important legislators. He was also a man of prodigious energy and used all his assets lavishly, including the prestige and patronage he could dispense from the White House.[15]

The primary targets of all this effort were Johnson's fellow localists who had been opposing majoritarian social proposals since 1945 and who were especially important in the Senate, where Arkansas or Utah has as much voting weight as New York. Thus, where a number of Kennedy's bills were stopped by localist resistance in Senate committees, Johnson pushed the legislation out of committees onto the Senate floor. And there he was able to hold localist opposition on most bills down to slightly less than half of the potential 42 votes. Even on civil rights, there were only 22 negative votes from the localist regions and 18 of those were from the nine states of the Deep South. Johnson had won 14 Democrats and 6 Republicans from the West and Southwest to offset the unanimous southern opposition.

But Johnson's great triumph in the passage of the Civil Rights Act was in splitting the coalition of Republicans and southern Democrats that had in the past prevented the Senate from voting on civil rights legislation at all by the stratagem of protecting southern filibusters. A two-thirds vote was needed to close debate, thus forcing an end to a filibuster, or—to put it the other way around—one-third plus one of the Senate votes (34 with all of the senators voting) could defeat a motion to end debate. This meant that the 18 southern Democrats needed only 16 allies to protect a filibuster and thus block unwanted legislation, and they could usually find such allies among Republicans who were opposed in general to national governmental action. In 1964, however, Johnson's intensive lobbying won nearly unanimous Republican support for ending the southern filibuster on civil rights and placing the bill before the Senate as a whole, which passed it by an overwhelming margin of 73–27.

But civil rights apart, Johnson's powerful leadership tells only part of the story of support behind the Great Society. Important also was the marked shift in general political alliances that had taken place since the reform era of the 1930s—a shift that produced a new source of support Johnson could draw on. And this was important because Johnson's success in minimizing the opposition of localists did not mean he could count on them for the kind of positive support they had given the New Deal. For example, out of the possible 42 localist votes in the Senate, there were 30 cast in favor of Roosevelt's National Industrial Recovery Act in 1933 and 29 in favor of the National Labor Relations Act in 1935, but only 19 in favor of Johnson's Economic Opportunity Act in 1964 and 20 in favor of Medicare in 1965. At the same time, however, the political stance of liberal or functionalist Republicans—in the Senate, Republicans from the industrial states of the Northeast and the West Coast—was shifting in the other direction.

In 1933, 9 majoritarian Democrats from the combined

Northeast and West Coast regions voted for the NIRA and none voted against, while 10 Republicans from the same regions voted against and none for. In 1964 and 1965, Democrats from these areas again voted nearly unanimously for the reforms proposed by a Democratic President—but this time so did the Republicans. There were still a total of 10 and they divided 8 to 2 in favor of the Economic Opportunity Act and 9 to 1 in favor of Medicare. And in this voting, unlike the voting on the Civil Rights Act, Republicans from other regions did *not* support the President. On the Economic Opportunity Act, there were only 2 other Republican votes in favor, and on Medicare, only 4. That is, Republicans from localist or semi-localist areas did not like the role Johnson's legislation was defining for the federal government. But Republicans from industrial areas were strongly positive.

The significance of support for the Great Society from northeastern and West Coast Republicans went beyond the 8 or 9 votes they cast on majoritarian initiatives in the Senate. Those votes represented large business-oriented constituencies in areas of the country where much of the nation's corporate leadership was concentrated—the areas and constituencies from which Roosevelt had received intense opposition thirty years before. What the switch in these votes meant was that important segments of the managerial world had come to accept the need for a far greater degree of governmental responsibility for the national welfare than such groups had a generation before.

Kennedy, welcoming professional consultants to Washington, had given impetus toward a merger of this changed managerial view with the long-standing concerns of majoritarians. And Johnson had successfully translated this new merger of interests into legislation both groups could accept. The formula consisted generally of a legislative design serving majoritarian purposes—enhancing the economic power of weaker groups in the society—but at the same time respecting or following functionalist principles on means.

Most important, for functionalists, there was nothing in the Great Society programs that placed the government in a seriously invasive or coercive position with respect to the private economy. Medicare, for example, was confined to the elderly and the poor, whereas Truman's national health insurance plan—bitterly opposed by the medical profession—would have covered everyone. And, as mentioned earlier, the section of the Civil Rights Act prohibiting racial discrimination by private employers did little more than set a standard; the act did not include a strong enforcement mechanism for that section.

Other legislation—the anti-poverty programs primarily—incorporated functionalist principles and modes of operation in positive form. Such programs, ranging from drug counseling to the construction of housing, were funded by the federal government, but much of the responsibility for running them was delegated to professionals in the various problem areas, on a contract basis. That is, the government would award a contract for the provision of specific services to a city-planning firm or a team of psychologists or nutritionists or specialists in preschool education and such firms or groups would run programs providing the designated services.

This was precisely the approach that the CED had recommended when a problem fell outside the ability of the private economy to solve and required government subsidy. The virtue of such a system for functionalists is that government funds contracted to professionals are, presumably, expended on the basis of professional judgments. The undesirable alternative, in this view, is to have programs run directly by government agencies, which—as Herbert Hoover long ago warned—are chronically subject to political pressure and are likely to expend funds on the basis of power and patronage.

Thus the Great Society programs set in motion extensive activity sought by majoritarians—activity starting in Washington and running from there to cities and towns, schools, universities, hospitals, prisons, and a variety of other institutions across the country. But still the activity took forms that did not offend the managerial constituency that had formerly opposed federal interventionism. On the surface it appeared that the two most powerful of the three major political groups of the nation—the two that shared an interest in fostering the health of industrial systems—had found common political ground from which to deal with common social and economic problems. It was a formidable coalition—wage earners and managers combined—and one that would seem to ensure the success of any venture it backed. But the Great Society venture did not last. Incredibly, given the enthusiasm with which it began, its sources of support soon collapsed.

Five or six years after the exuberant start of the Great Society, large parts of it were abandoned, and within ten years, only Medicare and parts of the civil rights and education programs remained intact. What had happened was that large numbers of wage earners—the primary constituency behind the reforms in the first place—had turned against the programs. Furthermore, their withdrawal of support was not simply a quiet matter of waning enthusiasm. It was angry. The tone of subsequent political campaigns in which the renewal of the Great Society was an issue —George McGovern's campaign for the presidency in 1972, for example—made clear that for the old majoritarian constituency the promise of the Great Society had been betrayed.

What, then, was the promise and what was the betrayal? The promise of the Civil Rights Act—broader than any other in the nation's history, reaching beyond public institutions into the private sector—was an end to racial discrimination. The promise of the anti-poverty programs—the war on poverty to be conducted by the Office of Economic Opportunity—was literally an end to poverty. The combined civil rights and OEO efforts would, in Johnson's words, "strike down all the barriers" and open up "new exits from poverty," thus delivering the society once and for all from the conditions condemning millions of Americans to lives of insecurity, disadvantage, or worse, of helpless degradation.

To wage earners throughout the country, Johnson's rhetoric and the programs it described seemed to be extensions of the New Deal—exertions of the power of the federal government to enhance the power of wage earners in their economic dealings with the overwhelmingly powerful world of corporations. It was a mark of this belief that organized labor provided full, consistent lobbying in Congress and in congressional districts behind Johnson's bills as they made their still difficult way through the House and Senate. And it was a mark of the rapid disaffection of wage earners that McGovern, calling in 1972 for a reinvigoration of the entire anti-poverty effort, became the first Democratic candidate *not* to be endorsed by the AFL-CIO since its founding in 1955.

The problem was that beneath the general aims and rhetoric of the Johnson initiatives, there were deep distinctions between the New Deal and the Great Society. The most important was the assumption pervading the 1960s legislation that the largest part of the wage-earning interest was already well provided for, that only pockets of poverty and special hardship remained for majoritarians to remove. Thus, unlike the New Deal, the focus of the Great Society was on the special needs of special groups —American blacks, Indians, Spanish-speaking minorities, Asian Americans—not on the needs of the wage-earning constituency as a whole. That is, the focus was on minorities, not the wage-earning majority, when the majority, too, in fact was suffering.

As Andrew Levison points out in *The Working Class Majority,* the majority of the nation's workers were beginning to feel by the 1970s the adverse effects of large-scale economic change over which they were powerless. Unionized, highly paid manufacturing jobs were increasingly displaced by automation, by the export of jobs to newly industrializing countries, and by plant closings due either to such investment or to competition from other industrialized nations. The only jobs available for many workers were in the growing service sector—that is, in menial, low-paying service such as pumping gas, serving food, or doing janitorial or clerical work.

Thus, Levison concludes, with the dwindling of well-paid factory work, the gulf in salary levels and power between the managerial class and the working class was increasing, but the Presidents or presidential candidates representing the wage-earning constituency did not address this economic problem. Rather, they continued to define American economic trouble in terms of deprivation suffered by minorities, especially blacks. "The myth that class no longer existed was in full flower," Levison said, "and liberals looked to blacks as a kind of 'last frontier' of domestic social injustice. . . . Thus, none of the social programs of the great society period were aimed at championing the new and growing social and economic grievances of all working people. Instead they were focussed entirely on blacks or the very poor."[16]

Another critical distinction between the New Deal and the Great Society—ultimately the most enraging for wage earners— was the placement of the burden of paying for the benefits produced by the new governmental programs. The New Deal programs, backed by a majoritarian-localist coalition, shifted power or resources from the corporate world to the wage earners in need of them. That is, the National Labor Relations Act shifted bargaining power from corporations to workers through the mechanism of collective bargaining. The Social Security Act shifted resources from corporations to workers by requiring that corporations pay part of the premiums for workers' unemployment and retirement insurance. And the Fair Labor Standards Act did the same by requiring that corporations pay a government-set minimum wage.

The Great Society programs, on the other hand, were funded by federal taxes, which meant that they were funded in important part by the wage-earning, tax-paying majority—whose own incomes were far from generous or even secure. Even more onerous for many wage earners were the social costs they were forced to bear for some of the anti-poverty programs—such as the disruption of already beleaguered northern city school systems by federally mandated desegregation, or the displacement of white ethnic government employees by members of minority groups to meet affirmative action criteria. In short, it was clear that the cost of benefits provided to disadvantaged minorities was being borne in large part by the wage-earning majorities.

This political fact and its consequences for the Great Society are clearly visible in the design and fate of the Community Action Program (CAP) organized within the Office of Economic Opportunity. As noted above, the Community Action Program made federal money available at the local level to fund programs which local Community Action Boards organized. The local boards were made up of people representing various groups within a particular community—generally a neighborhood or section of a city. Supporters of the program saw it as the ultimate form of direct action, bringing money and power directly to the people. But the beneficiaries of the program were not "the people" in the majoritarian sense of the term.

In fact, the term "community" in the CAP context usually meant the opposite of the majority; effectively it meant inner-city racial and ethnic minorities whose impact on city councils, school boards, and state legislatures had been too slight to command local attention and benefit through normal political processes. The tactic of the Community Action Program, therefore, was to work around local majorities, to reach minorities with funds they could control. But the money came from taxes, and the tax-paying wage earners making up the majority bitterly resented the CAP process.[17]

Put in terms of the myth of deliverance, the New Deal had defined the evil, or enemy blocking a fair distribution of income in the society, as the disparity of power and rewards between corporations and workers. That is, the enemy of the poor was the overpowerful corporation. The implication of many Great Society programs, however, was that the enemy of the poor minorities was the wage-earning majority holding political power and not using it for the benefit of minorities. Once this implication became clear and its effects began to be felt, the majority turned against the programs and the majoritarian leadership that had produced them. To wage earners who since Roosevelt's time had looked to the federal government for protection of their interests, the proponents of anti-poverty programs had betrayed the majoritarian trust and those who, like McGovern, insisted on continuing the programs, were met with anger and rejection. In fact, the whole concept of federal government protection had become suspect, and wage earners in large numbers turned to political figures like Jimmy Carter and Ronald Reagan, whose political stance was anti-governmental, anti-activist.

How could this have happened? How could majoritarian leaders have failed to cast policies in forms responsive to the needs of the national constituency so carefully nurtured in prior generations? How could so astute a politician as Lyndon Johnson fail to see that his programs did not respond to the common problems of the nation's majority—especially as his own political convictions had been formed out of the majoritarian hopes and fulfilled promises of the New Deal?

In important part, the majoritarian failure in the 1960s stems from the same source as its initial success, and that is the collaboration with functionalists in the design of the Great Society. For one thing, the emphasis in the Great Society programs on solving specific, limited problems was reinforced by the general tendency of functionalists to see problems as amenable to managed solutions—to solutions based on the knowledge and skills experts can command. Experts can calculate the numbers of calories, square feet of living space, or frequency of pediatric visits necessary to a certain standard of health; they can calculate the numbers of teachers and books, the amount of equipment and supplies necessary to a certain level of learning, the numbers of job openings requiring particular skills and the hours of training necessary to impart those skills. Therefore experts are likely to prescribe such programs as policies for the cure of social ills.

But at a deeper level also—the level of fundamental belief —the influence of functionalists in the shaping of the Great Society narrowed its focus to limited and special problems. That is, functionalists looking at the troubles of the times did not see their cause in a general, wide-scale imbalance of power between managers and wage earners. Thus they did not see their solution in a general and wide-scale use of governmental power on the side of wage earners as a whole to right the balance. On the contrary, functionalists opposed the intrusion of political power in the economy as itself the enemy of functional efficiency— which, of course, they saw as the engine producing benefit for all. In their view, if some groups were *not* well served by the private economy, it was due to the vast complication that had developed in industrial systems and the inevitable aberrations that occur within them. For functionalists, then, the proper role of government was to deal with the aberrations—which, in the 1960s, meant locating pockets of poverty and providing the means for people to leave them.

In short, the general functionalist conception of wrongs and solutions, economic enemies and agents of deliverance, brought them to the conclusion that the troubles of the times *were* special cases. And dealing with such problems one by one was as far as they were prepared to go in supporting federal social action. Thus, if majoritarians were to cooperate with functionalists, this was as far as their joint venture could take them. The problems of the majority as a whole—the persisting and widening imbalance of economic power between the wage-earning majority and the managers—could not be addressed as a matter of governmental responsibility.

But the apparent common interest of managers and wage earners in addressing the problem of poverty masked the fundamental differences between the two groups. Thus when wage earners found that the Great Society programs were not helping *them,* they did not see this failure as caused by limits imposed by functionalist/Republicans in governmental action. Rather, much of the wage-earning constituency concluded that it was the use of governmental power as such that had failed, and they began to turn away from their long-held belief in the national government as their agent or protector in their dealings with the world of managerial power.

It was not only a narrow functionalist interest, however, that kept the focus of reform in the 1960s on the narrow range of special problems. Majoritarians themselves, along with functionalists, failed to see the size and scope of the problems facing the nation. They did not fully perceive the changes in technology, in the size and power of corporations, in patterns of investment, in international competition, or, more to the point, the impact of these changes on the security of wage earners. Partly, their vision was blocked by the very scope of the problems, which were not fully understandable to anyone, but in important part also it was blocked by the ever-present myth in its majoritarian version.

The myth of deliverance promises in general that hardships can be relieved and inequities resolved without undue loss to any interest, which means that conflict among the interests is not the cause of hardship and inequity. Rather, the cause is some disturbing force or evil that can be removed. But for such a force to be removable, it must be relatively limited in scale, in all versions of the myth, including that of the majoritarians—even though their interest forces them to identify evils that are broader in scope than those defined by functionalists or localists.

In the 1930s, although faced with the large-scale hardship of the Great Depression, majoritarians had succeeded in identifying a fairly limited cause behind it in the excessive power and short-sighted selfishness of economic royalists. That is, they concentrated, not on the structure of economic power as the basic problem, but on the misuse of power by selfish or uncomprehending magnates. This made it possible to devise remedies within the scope of the myth—the remedies of regulating abuses or balancing excessive power.

But the majoritarians of the 1960s could not identify economy-wide issues in such a limited way because the nation's economic life had become too complicated. They had no such convenient villains as Roosevelt's royalists, his money changers in the temple, the piratical, ruthless entrepreneurs who could be stymied and forced to reform through securities and exchange regulations, minimum wage laws, and collective bargaining.

Economic issues had actually been more complicated in the 1930s than the diagnosis of economic royalism implied. Then, too, as the study commissioned by Roosevelt had found, economic power was becoming concentrated in fewer and fewer corporations, and such concentration threatened even then to defy the balancing mechanisms being devised. But majoritarians a generation later faced a situation in which the managerial decisions of huge companies had greater impact than the deliberate decisions of elected lawmakers on vast areas of American life —wage levels, the economic health or decay of whole regions, suburbanization and its effects on the quality and equality of education, the quality of air and water as affected by manufacturing wastes. Further, by the 1960s, the operations and decisions of the largest firms had become multinational, extending their influence worldwide, making them still more powerful laws unto themselves.

These were the kinds of forces Kennedy was trying to define in a manageable way in his Yale speech—the cumulative effect of decisions made in huge corporate bureaucracies on the welfare of the nation's work force—but he could not develop the implications of his own thesis, because they would have carried him beyond the boundaries of the myth and therefore beyond the boundaries of thought and solutions broadly acceptable to Americans. What he did, therefore, was to take note of problems that strained the limits of the myth by their enormity, but then to reduce them to solvable size. He acknowledged the vulnerability of workers to such complex forces as technological change and the pressures of world markets, then placed such problems back within the compass of deliverance by calling them "technical," a matter of "practical management." By this he meant the rational and cooperative discussion of problems by all concerned —management, labor, and government.

But the larger concept of ongoing discussions among these three groups about economy-wide policies was not merely a proposal for technical or practical cooperation. The logic of the idea went far beyond the level of cooperation on specific social problems that functionalists would outline as proper for public and private sectors to undertake jointly. Cooperation among management, labor, and government on large-scale problems— if it meant anything at all—implied national economic planning. That is, it implied the necessity for deliberate decisions concerning the running of the economy, the agreement among management, labor, and government on priorities they would observe, the acceptance of some disadvantage or cost in some sector to avoid unacceptable harm in others.

Or, to put it another way, ongoing public-private cooperation, involving management *and* labor on the private side, implied the absence of a natural, unplanned balance in the private economy—that balance by which, in mythic terms, all participating groups would benefit. If such a balance were naturally possible—as the myth promises it is—there would be no need for the major economic actors to engage in a perpetual process of negotiation, cooperation, and management of their differences. Thus, the scope of problems Kennedy was discussing led him toward the concept of planning, but, as planning flies in the face of the myth of deliverance, it is a concept he could not even formulate. It was still outside the political frame of reference for Americans, outside any range of conceivable choice.

Unable to locate an economy-wide enemy within the bounds of the myth, Kennedy's successors found pockets of poverty, special cases, groups with special needs. More specifically, as Johnson defined it, the enemy was a lack of *opportunity* suffered by racial minorities and other underprivileged groups and thus was a problem for which solutions could be readily devised. If people lacked opportunity because they lacked salable skills, the government could fund programs teaching the needed skills, and likewise provide other needed services and subsidies.

But by focusing on lack of opportunity for people suffering extreme disadvantage, the designers of the Great Society failed to see that lack of opportunity was general. The entire structure of the economy was changing in the direction of an increasingly segregated work force consisting of highly skilled people on the one hand and providers of menial services on the other. And it was changing in the direction of a reduced work force—the displacement of workers by sophisticated machines creating a corps of permanently unneeded workers. Such structural change is clearly not a problem for minorities only, although the problems of undereducated, underprivileged minorities are worse than those of other wage earners. It was the larger context, the structural context, of the problems of wage earners that the anti-poverty programs did not address.

The failure of the Great Society, then, was not that it tried to do too much, that it went too far with governmental activism. Its failure was that, holding out the traditional majoritarian promise to the nation's wage earners as a whole, it did too little —and exacted payment from the wrong people.

VII

Vietnam: Failure of the Majoritarian Mission

The lost promise of the Great Society produced bitterness among Americans, some shaking of the long-held American certainty that social problems need only be identified to be solved. But even more shaking and more divisive for Americans was the bitter experience in the 1960s of the war in Vietnam.

In important ways, the two stories, both epic failures of policy, were intertwined. Most obviously, the demise of the Great Society, while a consequence of its own weaknesses, was hastened by the budgetary claims of the war. At a deeper level, the connection between the two lay in the fundamental causes, the common root, of their failure.

Both were majoritarian initiatives, undertaken in political alliance, and seeming philosophic accord, with functionalists. But in both cases, majoritarians and functionalists, while using the same language to back the same policies, held different assumptions about the nature of the problems they were confronting, and their differences confused their joint effort.

More generally, policies in both arenas failed because policy makers misperceived the problems they were attempting to solve —saw them as narrower, simpler than they were, as a wide range of intransigent complication was screened out by the myth of deliverance. That is, both the war on poverty and the war in Vietnam were expressions of a politics of deliverance in that both tried to achieve broad-scale change through the removal or control of particular, limited problems. And both failed, ultimately, for that reason.

The majoritarian cast to policy in Vietnam is confused by the fact that the first definitive involvement there by the United States was in 1954, during the Eisenhower administration, when the prevailing foreign policy was not majoritarian but functionalist— the militant, anti-communist functionalism of John Foster Dulles. There had been some involvement even earlier in the form of aid to the French, who were attempting to retain their colonial hold on Vietnam against the armed resistance of a communist-led nationalist movement, headed by Ho Chi Minh. But it was in 1954, when the French Army was defeated and Ho Chi Minh's forces established a government in the northern area they controlled, that the United States began its serious commitment.

Even after their defeat in the North, the French still held the South of Vietnam, but they had determined, nonetheless, to withdraw from the country altogether. Their departure would have left the South as well as the North open to control by Ho Chi Minh's communist government, a situation that Eisenhower and Dulles did not want to accept. The United States, therefore, backed the establishment in the South of a non-communist Vietnamese government to succeed the French, and provided that government with economic and military aid from 1954 on.

In making the tiny country of Vietnam a stake in their general policy of resistance to communism, United States officials were not so much concerned with Ho Chi Minh's movement as with the extension of Chinese communist influence throughout Southeast Asia—or more broadly with communist expansion in Asia jointly orchestrated by China and the Soviet Union. That is, the American involvement in Vietnam in 1954 was part of a more general strategy for the containment of Sino-Soviet power. This general strategy was accepted by the Kennedy administration and it became the basis for the Kennedy-Johnson policy in Vietnam as well.

How, then, was the 1960s war in Vietnam a majoritarian initiative—if it followed a functionalist strategy, already laid down, for the containment of communism? How did the Kennedy-Johnson policy differ from that shaped by John Foster Dulles? The answer is that the two approaches did *not* differ on the goal of keeping as much of Asia as possible, including South Vietnam, free of communist rule. But the thinking of majoritarian policy makers in the 1960s *did* differ from that of functionalists on the purposes, the ends that would be served by keeping communists out of power—and ultimately, therefore, the two groups differed on means.

For functionalists in the period following the Second World War, anti-communism was part of a more general American mission to keep international transactions of all kinds moving openly, free from arbitrary, disruptive national controls. Keeping communists out of power was especially important to this goal because the total controls imposed by communist states on economic and political life were the worst possible disruption of efficiency, of functional logic in international exchange. Thus functionalists backed policies of aid to non-communist governments and, where necessary, military action by the United States to prevent a threatened communist takeover of governmental power or to remove a communist government that had gained power. But, as discussed in Chapter V, this essentially negative role—guarding against communist rule—represented for functionalists the extent of the American national mission. It was, in their view, all that the American government should do. The positive work of international relations, the *building* of efficiently working systems of worldwide exchange, was the province of *functional* institutions—private corporations or international organizations, private or public.

The majoritarian mission, on the other hand, was broader. The ultimate goal, a world open to unlimited exchange, was the same, as was the short-term tactic of keeping communists out of power. But the national role of the United States, in the majoritarian scheme, included active American efforts to build and protect strong democratic nations throughout the world. In the Truman administration, this mission had been expressed in the protection of the democracies of Europe through the Marshall Plan and NATO and in efforts to build democracy in the non-industrialized world on the base of economic development—the concept behind the Point Four program. That is, where function-alists assigned the positive role of building international systems to functional, mainly private institutions, majoritarians sought a world order based on healthy, responsible nations and assigned responsibility for developing such an order to the already strong and healthy nations—the United States foremost among them.

After 1960, with the election of John F. Kennedy, the ma-joritarian mission calling for active national engagement in a wide range of foreign disorders was focused primarily on the non-industrial Third World. Or rather, the Third World was the arena for policies that were distinctly majoritarian, that called for American engagements abroad differing from those sought by functionalists. The reason was that, by the 1960s, the majoritarian interest in bolstering strong democracies had been substantially fulfilled in Europe. All that remained, in addition to the con-tinued containment of communism, was to bolster and promote among those democracies the economic linkages that produced benefits for all—through policies such as the ratification of United States membership in the Organization for Economic Cooperation and Development in 1961 and passage of the Trade Expansion Act in 1962.

But the establishment of strong democracies was far from a reality outside the industrial world. Most of the countries of Asia and Africa were just emerging from a century or more of colonial rule. The Latin American countries had long since achieved polit-ical independence, but their economies, like those of the recently colonial states, were still based primarily on agriculture or mining and thus still suffered chronic disadvantage in relation to indus-trial centers. Throughout the Third World, poverty, illiteracy, and lack of capital with which to effect change precluded the possibility of effective popular government. Instead, most non-industrialized nations were under some form of authoritarian rule, often ineffectual and unstable, and ever vulnerable to dis-order or serious violence. Vietnam, with its internal turbulence and particularly its division between northern and southern sections of the country, was part of this general situation. And it was to this situation that the incoming Kennedy administration turned with its majoritarian impulses and energies and hopes for constructive change through the agency of American national effort.

Shortly after taking office, Kennedy proclaimed the coming years the Decade of Development, by which he meant a period for fostering economic growth throughout the Third World, and he quickly set in motion a variety of policies designed to advance that general purpose. He launched in the Alliance for Progress an ambitious development program for Latin America. He also established the Peace Corps. Further, he sought to separate economic and military aid budgets as they went through Congress so that the purposes of the two were not confused, and he proposed long-term instead of annual appropriations for development aid so that recipients could do the kind of long-term planning that modernization and industrialization required.

Kennedy's first major message to Congress on foreign aid clearly set out the new agenda. Many less developed countries, he said, are "on the threshold of achieving sufficient economic, social and political strength and self-sustained growth to stand permanently on their own feet," and long-term aid allowing planning for long-term goals will help to put them " 'into orbit' —bringing them to a state of self-sustained growth where extraordinary outside assistance is not required."[1]

This was the older Truman conception of building a world of independent nations through development aid but ramified by a decade of academic attention to development economics, attention that had produced fairly precise theories about the process of industrial growth on an agrarian base. The foremost development theorist was Walt Rostow, whose *Stages of Economic Growth* described the necessary and often difficult steps an agrarian people had to take on the road to development. But, the theory promised, if the process was followed, the economy would inevitably reach a point of "takeoff"—the point at which a nation could generate its own capital and join the world of trading nations on natural and mutually beneficial terms.[2] Rostow had been an adviser to Senator Kennedy and moved with him as a special assistant to the presidential office, where he supplied the expertise and direction for the Kennedy aid program.

The image of taking off, going into orbit—as the astronaut John Glenn actually did early in the Kennedy administration—was an exuberant rendering of the myth of deliverance. Crippling poverty would seem to belie the myth, but the development theory defined poverty as a temporary, remediable condition—in this sense parallel to the Kennedy-Johnson poverty programs at home. The development remedy was not without painful cost —a great deal of money from those in the developed countries who had it and a great deal of effort from those in the developing world who did not. But this expenditure would not be permanent. As with the domestic programs, at the point of takeoff there would be deliverance from pain.

Thus the Kennedy program was a classic expression of the myth of deliverance and its mechanism for deliverance was classically majoritarian—the use of political authority by the donor nation to transfer capital to other nations. Further, it placed trust in public as well as private authority in the recipient states to see that the capital was used for the benefit of the majority, not minorities that might represent, as Kennedy said, either the "entrenched privilege of the right" or the "subversive conspiracies on the left."[3]

But as Kennedy's remarks on the Right and the Left indicated, economic development in the 1960s could not take place in a political vacuum. There could not be an ideal linear movement from an agrarian base to economic takeoff and then to the development of democratic institutions that placed in the majority the power to control self-serving minorities. Rather, the Third World was subject at that time to immense pressures of competition among groups seeking to control the process of change—political competitors within each country, but also the competing great powers. Just as the United States and the Western nations wanted to construct an open world order of democracies, the Soviet Union and its allies wanted to construct an international communist order, and the Third World was inevitably a stake for these opposing movements. Therefore, American development policies had to take into account the likely operation of Soviet or other communist influence in areas the United States sought to aid.

Concern with the problem of communist competition in developing countries sharpened in the earliest weeks of the Kennedy administration in response to a speech delivered by Soviet Premier Nikita Khrushchev just days after Kennedy's inauguration. Khrushchev, in a highly pointed talk, declared that nuclear dangers precluded making gains for communism throughout the world by direct military means. But, he said, the communist states could still extend their influence, especially in the underdeveloped world, by providing aid for groups waging wars against pro-Western and Western-dominated governments —wars of national liberation.

This message from Khrushchev was reinforced directly for Kennedy a few months later when the two leaders met for personal talks in Vienna. Kennedy, reporting to the American people on his return from Europe, described in sober terms the magnitude of the gulf he perceived between the United States and the Soviet Union. Khrushchev was certain, Kennedy said, that in the Third World "the revolution of rising peoples would eventually be a Communist revolution" and that the Soviet Union could advance this cause by engaging in wars of liberation "through guerillas or insurgents or subversion." The communist theory, Kennedy went on, was that a "small group of disciplined Communists could exploit discontent and misery in a country where the average income may be $60 or $70 a year, and seize control, therefore, of an entire country without Communist troops ever crossing an international border."[4]

That is, the general assumption that the Soviet Union was an expansionist power and that it was actively seeking converts in the developing countries had become sharpened to a conviction that the Soviet leadership was embarking on a newly deliberate campaign of subversive engagement in wars of liberation. Thus, Kennedy said, American strategies for economic development in the Third World had to be combined with a strategy for counteracting communist subversion that might be going on at the same time.

The most important element in the future political direction of new and poor countries, Kennedy stressed, was still their development of economic strength, and American aid for that process was crucial—to foster industrial and agricultural growth and also to establish programs encouraging "better administration and better education, and better tax and land distribution." With strong economies and broadly based governments, the newly developed nations would not be prey to subversion or to any communist threat except invasion, "and that threat, we know, can be stopped."[5]

But where subversion was already a reality, it had to be counteracted and controlled so that development policies had a chance to work. To deal with this problem, Kennedy outlined a new and special military strategy. In general, Kennedy was a proponent of increasing the American capacity for conventional warfare, opposing the primary reliance of the Eisenhower administration on a nuclear arsenal for purposes of deterring war. He accepted, and during his campaign advocated, the arguments of military leaders such as General Maxwell Taylor that the nation should be able to respond more flexibly to threat than by nuclear war or nothing. In addition, as a means of dealing with the specific strategy of communist subversion outlined by Khrushchev at Vienna, Kennedy advocated developing quickly a special capacity for counterinsurgency. One part of the plan was to equip the armed forces of developing countries for anti-insurgent warfare, and the other, to develop an American force —the Green Berets, as they were later known—especially trained to combat military subversion.

That the United States could successfully counter the new menace of Soviet-backed insurgencies and guide a process of long-term development, Kennedy had no doubt. "[We] have the talent and the resources to do it, if we will only use and share them," he insisted.[6] This was majoritarianism at its most energetic. First, the Kennedy design would have the United States become deeply engaged in shaping the process of economic development in poor countries. And through counterinsurgency tactics, Americans would burrow yet more deeply into the internal life of troubled nations in order to locate forces—Soviet-supplied forces—disrupting a natural and healthy process of growth. That is, deliverance from the abusive power of subversive forces and from the oppression of poverty would be accomplished through the active agency of the American *nation*. The United States as a nation would be playing essentially the same role in the poor countries of the world as majoritarians would have it play at home—the role of an active power balancer.

Kennedy's programs were passed for the most part—the Alliance for Progress; the Peace Corps; a new Agency for International Development (AID), consolidating aid programs previously scattered throughout the government; the budgetary separation of economic and military aid; and the new counterinsurgency force, the Green Berets, as well as a substantial buildup in equipment and weaponry for counterinsurgency campaigns. But behind the apparent acceptance of the Kennedy approach—an activist majoritarian approach to the problems of the Third World—there was great built-in ambivalence of purpose. Both localists and functionalists, for their different reasons, maintained the opposition they had mounted in the Truman years to publicly financed foreign development policies. Thus while they accepted the establishment of new development agencies, they did not fund the agency programs at levels anywhere near the administration's requests.

Kennedy tried to build support for foreign aid by setting up a blue-ribbon commission to study it. The commission was headed by General Lucius Clay and weighted heavily with figures from the business world in the hope that the commitment of the nation's capital managers to internationalism would lead them to support international development through the proposed aid programs—and that their support would lead Congress in the same direction. But Kennedy reckoned without the force of functionalist ideology. The commission report was unenthusiastic about public funding for development, especially in the long term. The only dissenter was the one member representing the wage-earning constituency, George Meany, president of the AFL-CIO.

Since the late 1950s, the AFL-CIO had supported greater economic and technical aid for Latin America and also the elimination of quotas and tariffs restricting raw material imports from

Latin America in the interest of stabilizing the commodity markets crucial to underdeveloped economies. As a member of the Clay Commission, Meany dissented from the majority conclusions on the grounds that the aid levels recommended were too low, that Africa was not given sufficient attention, and that excessive reliance was placed on private development capital.[7] But organized labor, while a formidable constituency, could not alone move Congress along majoritarian lines.

There was more support, more funding, for the military side of the program. Localists could agree to the military pursuit of an actual communist enemy, especially if, as Kennedy insisted, the enemy was a subversive agent of the Soviet Union. And functionalists, still following the Dulles approach to the control of international communism, were actively enthusiastic about counterinsurgency, because these sophisticated techniques promised to control communist expansion with a level of force small enough to be controlled by rational professionals. It promised the possibility of defining targets and neutralizing or removing them with virtual surgical precision and without the long-drawn-out involvement that becomes vulnerable to pressures from an emotional electorate.

With support from all three constituencies, the special counterinsurgency force had grown by 1964 to more than 100,000 men and included, as Lyndon Johnson reported, "six special action forces on call around the world to assist our friendly nations," "five brigade-size backup forces ready to move into instant action," and 344 teams in 49 countries training local military forces "in the most advanced techniques of internal defense."[8]

Thus by the mid-1960s the majoritarian Presidents had constructed an elaborate policy for carrying their mission to the Third World, but it was a policy full of dangerous contradiction. Its long-term political aim—the development of strong, independent nation-states, a "world of diversity" as Kennedy said—was not shared by the functionalists, whose backing was crucial for any sustained internationalist program.[9] The economic development component of the mission was unsupported by both functionalists and localists and was inadequately funded. And although the sophisticated military component was well funded and developed and had support from all three groups, each had different assumptions about the purposes it was supposed to achieve.

The major testing place for the majoritarian mission of the 1960s, with all of its internal ambivalence, was, of course, Vietnam. The Kennedy administration picked up the problem of Vietnam seven years after the establishment of a separate government in the South, a government headed by a pro-Western leader, Ngo Dinh Diem, and supported heavily by American aid. The Diem government, from the beginning, faced resistance to its authority from a variety of forces and factions—an incipient educated middle class seeking democratic institutions, Buddhists seeking to protect traditional social ways (Diem was a Roman Catholic), local power holders ranging from large landowners to organized brigands, and the National Liberation Front or Vietcong, a nationalist, peasant-based movement with ties to Ho Chi Minh in the North.

Ho Chi Minh's ultimate aim was to extend his authority through the entire nation, but his strategy after defeating the French in the North was to play a waiting game for the South, assuming the Western-supported government there would ultimately collapse under the pressure of local factionalism. By 1958 and 1959, however, the Vietcong in the South was beginning to feel the pressure of Diem's army and began to strike back militarily, with aid from the North including supplies and irregular forces—mainly southerners who had chosen to go North in 1954. And North Vietnam, in turn, received support for the effort in the South from both the Soviet Union and China.

The problem facing Kennedy in 1961 was that the Diem government was on the verge of collapse. Its authority was relatively secure in the cities, but the Vietcong held much of the countryside. Leaders in the Kennedy administration saw the conflict in Vietnam as a clear manifestation of Khrushchev's declared intent to advance the communist cause throughout the Third World by aiding insurgent movements. And there was strong

consensus among those dealing with foreign affairs that it was
vitally important to foil the communist advance in Vietnam as
a means of foiling the larger communist strategy. Vietnam, they
thought, was a "test case" for the tactic of subversive aggression,
as the Berlin blockade and the Korean invasion had been tests of
American willingness to resist communist advances by open
force.

Thus the primary enemy in South Vietnam, as Kennedy and
his advisers saw it, was the element of outside communist involvement in the insurgency. But looking at the problem from
a majoritarian point of view, they were concerned with another
enemy, or evil, in the picture as well. The secondary evil was the
misuse and abuse of power by the government of South Vietnam.
In this view, to the extent that the insurgency was locally based
and supported, it should have been controllable by the South
Vietnamese government and army. But these institutions were
seriously defective because the government, from 1954 onward,
was not broadly based; it was dominated by cliques—a family
clique under Diem—and part of its attention was chronically
consumed by the need to protect itself from challenge by other
power-seeking groups. Unconnected to large segments of the
society, and distracted by power struggles, the government could
not carry out its basic functions effectively. It could not sys-
tematically collect taxes, provide services, or police roads and
towns, and the lack of effective government perpetuated the
turbulent conditions that outside communist states could exploit.

The conclusion of the Kennedy advisers was that any policy
in Vietnam would have to deal with both evils—outside intervention and internal power abuse—at the same time. As secretaries Rusk and McNamara reported to the President in November
1961, the United States would have to supply military aid to help
stop "the flow of men and supplies from North Vietnam," but
it would also have to insist that the government of South Vietnam take the internal measures necessary to put itself in "a
position to win its own war against the guerillas."[10]

The upshot of the policy review carried on under Kennedy
in 1961 was that the administration formally decided by the end
of November to increase substantially the number of American

units in South Vietnam as well as levels of support services and equipment. By the end of the year, there were over 2,500 American servicemen in Vietnam, 11,000 by the end of 1962, and nearly 17,000 by November 1963, when Lyndon Johnson became President on Kennedy's death.

As for internal measures for broadening the base and effectiveness of the South Vietnamese government, the United States pressed on Diem a variety of administrative reforms and also an elaborate plan called the strategic hamlet program. This program was first devised in detail by a British military consultant to Diem, a person with experience in the defeat by the British of a communist-led insurgency in Malaya. The heart of the plan was a policy of "clear and hold," which called for clearing the Vietcong out of a particular area by military means, then holding the area through efficient and enlightened civilian organization. Civilian police would keep the people of the area secure from a return of the Vietcong and political officials would ensure that the people could support themselves economically, and would ensure also the provision of whatever services were needed in particular areas—such as education, health care, or flood control.

In the Kennedy administration, Roger Hilsman, head of the State Department's Bureau of Intelligence and Research, formulated a strategic hamlet plan based on the British model, and the Hilsman plan won the enthusiastic support of the President and of General Maxwell Taylor, then chairman of the Joint Chiefs of Staff. The Defense Department study of the war (the Pentagon Papers) notes that President Diem also liked the plan, but not because he shared the American faith in organizing social strength at the grass roots. What Diem liked was that the plan called for substantial American aid for civilian programs which would necessarily be under his direct control.[11]

That is, the Kennedy planners expected the program to produce an ever-widening engagement of government and people in common efforts and thus ever-widening popular support for the government. But Diem had no intention of seeking to build strength on popular support—nor perhaps did he have the capacity for doing it, even had he wanted to. One serious flaw in the strategic hamlet plan as a program appealing to the populace was

212 DREAM OF DELIVERANCE

that it required peasants to move from their homes to hamlets that could be effectively protected from the Vietcong. Many peasants, attached to their own villages and burial grounds, had to be moved forcibly and their homes burned to prevent their returning, which generated hostility toward the government, not support.

This particular program ended with the death of Diem by assassination, just weeks before Kennedy, too, was killed in the fall of 1963, but the Johnson administration's review of the Vietnam situation in the year following Kennedy's death produced continued adherence to both parts—military and political/economic—of the counterinsurgency strategy.

In the first place, the focus on outside communist aid to the insurgency as the key problem remained strong. In March 1964, President Johnson ordered preparations for "retaliatory action" in North Vietnam as it became necessary,[12] action which was taken in August of that year in the confused incident of the Gulf of Tonkin. Claiming that the North Vietnamese had made unprovoked attacks on American ships in the Gulf of Tonkin, the United States retaliated with several bombing raids over North Vietnam. And Johnson asked for a Joint Resolution from Congress authorizing the President in aiding South Vietnam "to take all necessary measures to repel any armed attack against the forces of the United States and to prevent further aggression."[13] Congress passed the resolution almost immediately and with little debate by the overwhelming votes of 416–0 in the House and 88–2 in the Senate—although, as later events would show, the apparent unanimity of support for the presidential policy was misleading.

In the short run, however, there was little opposition. On December 1, 1964, Johnson approved a plan to bomb North Vietnam as a means of forcing its withdrawal of support for the Vietcong insurgency. The bombing began in February 1965. It was followed in the summer of 1965 by the direct introduction of American combat troops, whose numbers ultimately reached a level of half a million.

At the same time, the other part of the strategy—the battle for "the hearts and minds" of the people—also gathered strength.

In June 1965, the President told Congress that an increased military effort in Vietnam was essential, but not by itself enough. Aid for economic and social development throughout Southeast Asia was crucial, he said. The message was a request, subsequently passed, for $89 million to finance such projects as the development of the Mekong River basin, the building of electrification cooperatives in South Vietnam, and imports to Vietnam of iron, steel, cement, chemicals, pesticides, and trucks to expand factory production and provide materials for low-cost housing.[14] And the emphasis on internal development continued even as the military dimension of the war increased. Three successive presidential conferences with Vietnamese officials in 1966 and 1967—in Honolulu, Manila, and Guam—stressed the importance of building the grass-roots institutions through which the government could effectively protect the people so that the people could begin to work with confidence for a better future.

The term for this part of the war in use by 1965 was "pacification," but that term did not convey the larger purposes of counterinsurgency, as Secretary of Agriculture Orville Freeman said at the Honolulu conference. Freeman suggested "social construction" as a better alternative and proposed yet more energetic engagement in village life: for example, through a "joint training program for the village and hamlet chiefs," including "some background in the philosophy, purpose and aims of government, and the techniques of governing and administration."

Also in Honolulu, the ever-ebullient Johnson gave the Vietnamese officials a pep talk on the importance of grass-roots reform, telling them that he would want answers in the succeeding months addressed to how they had "built democracy in the rural areas." And in looking at the goals set at the conference for such efforts as the development of handicrafts and light industry and the spread of rural electrification, he would want to know: "Are those just phrases, high-sounding words, or have you coonskins on the wall . . . ?"[15]

By 1966, however, and certainly by 1967, the evidence was mounting that the American policy was *not* producing the results its planners intended. On the military side, the Vietcong, aided by regular army units from North Vietnam, were far more difficult to dislodge from the countryside than Americans had anticipated, partly because the enemy forces were highly elusive. They would disappear before an American advance and then return unless the area was heavily occupied by armed troops.

As for pacification, or social reconstruction, or revolutionary development, as the economic and political rebuilding programs finally came to be called, all of the effort and aid poured in produced little by way of better living conditions or effective social systems connecting people at the grass roots to the central government in Saigon.

Back in the United States, the war policies—calling increasing numbers of Americans into military service, costing increasing millions of dollars, producing little in measurable results— began to come under serious question. On the streets there were student protests and peace marches, and there was also official questioning—hearings held by the Senate Foreign Relations Committee and the Armed Services Committee, and the long review conducted by the Department of Defense, the results of which would later be published as the Pentagon Papers.

By the spring of 1968, it was clear that even with 500,000 American troops, the government of South Vietnam could not maintain its authority anywhere but in major cities and even that was more and more uncertain. Faced with the choice of increasing American forces or cutting American losses and seeking a way out, President Johnson accepted the advice of a widening group of advisers that there was no longer any hope of swift victory, that staying in meant fighting an unpredictably long, dirty war of attrition, the main burden being carried by American troops.

Johnson knew that such a commitment, such a posture—the mighty United States hounding the people of a tiny Asian country with sophisticated, devastating weaponry—was becoming increasingly intolerable to the American public. And so he decided not to ask Congress for the higher troop levels the military was requesting and not to approve widened bombing targets. On the contrary, he announced on March 31, 1968, a major cutback in the campaign of bombing in the North.

The actual winding down of the American military engagement in Vietnam took place under the Nixon administration, the last ground troops coming out in 1973 with the signing of the Peace Accords with North Vietnam, but Johnson's decision in 1968 marked the end, the defeat, of the Vietnam policy as initially conceived—its purposes, the assumptions behind it, the hopes its planners held for victory. None of the American designs or expectations for Vietnam had been fulfilled or would be. With the defeat of South Vietnam by the North in 1975 and the establishment of a united communist state, all that remained of the American effort was the vast destruction it left behind.

Why was the failure so complete? How could a policy shaped by the highly able, highly knowledgeable planners in the Kennedy and Johnson administrations and funded unstintingly by Congress fall so wide of the intended mark in its actual operation?

Part of the reason, as always in important American policies, was a degree of confusion built into the policy by the conflicting visions and purposes of the groups behind it. And once the commitment had been made and Americans dispatched to Vietnam, all three major groups—including the localists—*were* behind it, as the lack of opposition to the Gulf of Tonkin resolution testifies. All three had agreed to its broad charge to the President "to take all necessary measures" against "armed attack" or "further aggression" in South Vietnam. In retrospect, however, it is clear that the different groups, while united in opposing communist expansion, had different conceptions of what "all necessary measures" meant—and further, did not fully grasp the extent or depth of their differences.

What majoritarians meant was the panoply of military and economic strategies that expert advisers had been designing from the time Kennedy took office, the complicated strategies aimed simultaneously at short-run counterinsurgency and long-run nation building. But nation building was by no means what localists or functionalists meant by measures necessary to fight communism in Vietnam or elsewhere. Neither of these two groups shared the majoritarian belief in building the internal strength of nations as the key strategy of defense against communism.

The localist conception of "necessary measures" rested on attitudes that had been evolving for some years in the localist camp, attitudes accepting a greater degree of activism in world affairs than the tradition of the group had generally entertained. The vote of the Gulf of Tonkin resolution itself signaled the change, in that the resolution delegated wide discretion to the President in policy making on Vietnam, with no objection from the localists. Traditionally they had demanded a strong congressional role in matters involving war in order to be able to restrain the President from committing the nation to engagements they opposed. As late as 1957, localist senators had forced a two-month debate over a request by President Eisenhower for discretionary authority to fight communist aggression in the Middle East.[16] But between 1957 and 1964 they had changed their minds. They were willing to concede congressional authority and to fight communism in distant arenas in defiance of their own long-held traditions. Why?

The answer lies, not in any increased trust in the executive, but in increasing mistrust of Congress—the Congress that had by 1964 come to reflect a majoritarian-functionalist outlook that was involving the nation in domestic and foreign ventures appalling to the localists. And further, their acceptance of the Gulf of Tonkin resolution did not represent acceptance of executive authority as such, but a new willingness to accept the authority of the military.

In the past, localists had been wary of the military as a dangerous source of advocacy for foreign interventions and entanglements, but ironically, by the 1960s, it was the military that seemed more likely than either the presidency or Congress to safeguard the distance localists wanted to maintain between the United States and the rest of the world. That is, the basic position of the localists had not changed. They still wanted to avoid foreign entanglements, the linkages to other nations, the esoteric networks of cooperation enthusiastically sought by the other groups and generally accepted in the postwar period by strong majorities in Congress. The approach of most military leaders to foreign problems, on the other hand, was based on assumptions about the world far more congenial to localists.

For one thing, localists found in the military sympathy for their conception of what an enemy must be. For military leaders and localist politicians alike, a particularly infuriating trait of both majoritarian and functionalist officials was their tolerance for ambiguity in relations with others. After the Second World War, localist senators had wanted to know why the administration was continuing Lend-Lease aid to the Soviet Union while asking for aid to Greece and Turkey to prevent a Soviet takeover through communist insurgencies. With the advent of the Kennedy administration, the inconsistencies were even more maddening.

In 1960, for example, the Soviet Union demonstrated its hostility to the United States by extending its economic and military protection to the government of Fidel Castro in Cuba and, in 1962, began to build a missile base there. Localists could understand and approve the Kennedy administration's attempt in 1961 to overthrow Castro in the abortive invasion of the Bay of Pigs, and to call a showdown with the Soviet Union in the missile crisis of 1962. They could not understand, however, the logic of Kennedy's experts in seeking, at the same time, Soviet cooperation in long-range arms limitation.

Senator Strom Thurmond of South Carolina insisted that there could be no such thing as a power or a political system that was partially hostile, partially friendly. Rather, he said, "the threat to our survival demands a national recognition of the global communist conspiracy." That is, the enemy, for Thurmond and the localists, was a group of communist states that, led by the Soviet Union, were deliberately seeking to extend their power by subversive military means. And as a clearly definable military threat, they should be, and *could* be, met and defeated militarily.[17]

The implication for foreign policy in this highly concrete conception of the enemy was that controlling such an enemy, by military means, was *all* the United States needed to do by way of international engagement. Where majoritarians and functionalists sought to involve the United States in firm multilateral relations, localists sought to defeat the enemy and return home. Senator Barry Goldwater of Arizona, the unsuccessful Republican candidate for President in 1964, expressed this outlook graphically in a comment praising the military establishment. Americans should not deplore the military-industrial complex, he said, but "should thank heavens" they have it. "That complex gives us our protective shield. It is the bubble under which our nation thrives and prospers. It is the armor which is unfortunately required in a world divided."[18] In mythic terms, the military was for localists an agent of deliverance from the impossible tangles involved in close relations with other nations—the deliverance of Americans to the "bubble" in which they could run their own affairs as free as possible from outside pressure and confusion.

Localists voting for the Gulf of Tonkin resolution, then, were supporting activist but not internationalist measures in Southeast Asia. They were willing to delegate authority to the President in order to allow him to conduct a *military* campaign, the point of which was to avoid continuing international entanglements. Richard Russell of Georgia, a quiet power in the Senate and an important localist voice from 1933 to 1970, underscored this distinction in moving remarks about the qualms he had felt in approving that resolution.

He had earlier opposed sending military advisers to South Vietnam, Russell said, because "by instinct and inclination, I must confess that I am an isolationist. I do not believe that the might and power of the United States can bring about the millennium. I do not believe that any number of treaties . . . will absolutely clear up all the strife among the peoples of the world, of different nationalities, different races, and different creeds." He added that he deeply regretted also the necessity to grant great power to the President. "I am a congressional man," he said. "I have stood here for more than thirty years and deplored—almost wept over—the slow erosion of congressional power that has placed this body in a position inferior to the other branches of the Government."[19]

But Russell, as well as other localists, had accepted the President's depiction of Southeast Asia as a target of Soviet-led communist aggression, in the course of which the North Vietnamese had fired on American ships. They accepted the strategy of defeating aggression before the communist world came to outweigh the non-communist. And they saw this strategy in clear-cut military terms—find the enemy forces and destroy them.

Thus the localists, while doubtful of the majoritarian mission of political change abroad, were not at all doubtful of the need to defeat enemies and they were scornful of those who were. Russell's remarks on the Gulf of Tonkin resolution were made in a 1966 Senate debate over a motion to limit the military authorization bill for that year. It was a motion proposed by Wayne Morse of Oregon, one of the two senators who had voted against Johnson's resolution in 1964. Morse argued that the 1966 authorization was constitutionally improper because the amount of money requested would allow the President discretion to widen drastically the scope of the war in Vietnam without Congress passing on it as a matter of policy. Russell opposed Morse and defended the authorization, calling the constitutional argument "a fictitious issue" arising out of some kind of "infection that is today making this country quiver and hesitate" in the face of an enemy.[20]

It had been Russell, during the Cuban missile crisis several years earlier, who had expressed the strongest congressional criticism of the same kind of hesitation in President Kennedy's inclination to blockade Cuba instead of taking direct military action as the Joint Chiefs of Staff advised. According to Robert Kennedy, Russell told the President that "he could not live with himself if he did not say in the strongest possible terms how important it was that we act with greater strength than the President was contemplating."[21]

Russell deeply believed that American society could function best if the nation were detached from the quarrels, demands, and confusions of the rest of the world and if the states remained as detached as possible from the authority of the federal government. In this scheme of things, Congress should be the protector of the states, and so Russell was "a congressional man," a backer of congressional power. But Congress, too, had become a victim of the debilitating "infection" rampant in the country and was no longer capable of performing its functions with clarity and decisiveness. It quivered and hesitated.

The military, on the other hand, had a clear conception of the enemy and clear strategies of response. The localists, therefore, were willing to follow the military lead. They were willing to support military missions against communism abroad in order to keep Americans safely detached from the troubles of others. Thus

they supported President Johnson's stand in Vietnam, but with
purposes in mind that would inevitably come to clash with the
administrative policies their support had helped to set in motion.

Functionalist differences with the majoritarian mission in
Vietnam were more subtle, harder to detect, at least during the
Kennedy years and through the point of Johnson's broad-scale
commitment to Vietnam in 1964. In fact, both administrations
were made up of majoritarian *and* functionalist policy planners,
and in foreign policy there were broad areas—especially in relations with the industrial world—where differences between the
two groups were slight. As to relations with the Third World,
the two shared a broad correspondence in outlook on the policy
of counterinsurgency—if for different reasons.

The outstanding functionalist advocate of counterinsurgency in both the Kennedy and Johnson administrations was Secretary of Defense Robert McNamara. Kennedy had recruited
McNamara into public office from the presidency of the Ford
Motor Company, a position he had only recently attained after
a career in industrial management that would have gladdened the
heart of Frederick Winslow Taylor. A graduate of the Harvard
Business School in the late 1930s, he worked briefly in the accounting firm of Price, Waterhouse, then returned to Harvard to
teach accounting at the Business School in the fall of 1940. With
the outbreak of war, he was recruited with several other business
professors to set up a system of statistical control for the mush-
rooming growth of the Air Corps. He spent the war primarily
"getting the proper number of men to mesh with the right
amount of equipment at the appointed hour." This meant, in
effect, setting up accounting systems on a formidable scale to
serve the most crucial kind of national need—military effectiveness in wartime.

After the war, McNamara and several other officers who had
together managed the impressive growth and performance of
American air power decided to stay together and offer their
services as a management team in some growing area of the
business world. They were taken on by Ford, which was at that
time "a model of inefficiency" but became under the new managers, using advanced statistical techniques of cost, asset, and reve-

nue control, a strong competitor to General Motors. Throughout his career at Ford, culminating in the presidency of the company, McNamara gained a reputation for long days, hard work, precise, non-emotional analysis of problems, an extraordinary memory for complicated data, and a strong sense of responsibility—both his to the company and the company's to the society.[22]

He brought these same qualities to government service as Secretary of Defense, formulating them himself as a philosophic commitment to the use of reason as the basis for social organization of all kinds—public and private. In a 1968 essay on the phenomenon of student protests against reigning authorities generally during the preceding few years, he discussed the antagonism of the young to what they saw as the dehumanized approach to social problems affecting the United States—the heartless, computerized, oppressive responses of huge bureaucracies throughout the society, in universities, corporations, and government alike.

McNamara admitted the dangers of over-bureaucratization but asserted that even greater danger lay in any undermining of reason as the shaper of policy. The society suffers, "not from overmanagement, but from undermanagement," he said, adding emphatically, "To undermanage reality is not to keep it free. It is simply to let some force other than reason shape reality. That force may be unbridled emotion; it may be greed; it may be aggressiveness; it may be hatred; it may be ignorance; it may be inertia; it may be anything other than reason. But whatever it is, if it is not reason that rules man, then man falls short of his potential."[23]

Committed to reason and managerial prowess as the key to social order generally, McNamara analyzed the problem of Vietnam in the early 1960s and came to the same conclusions Dulles had in similar situations a decade earlier. Communist-led insurgents were progressively undermining the effectiveness of the non-communist South Vietnamese government. The insurgents were being supported in this effort by the communist government of North Vietnam, which was guided and supported in turn by both China and the Soviet Union. The aim of the communist intervention was to displace Western-oriented governments throughout Southeast Asia, starting with South Vietnam. What was necessary, then, was to relieve the pressure imposed by communists on the government of the South so that its officials could carry out their difficult function more effectively. This meant seriously increased military aid from the United States to the embattled government and finally direct American engagement in combat against the persistent communist forces.

Weighed only lightly in McNamara's analysis, far too lightly as critics of his policy would later demonstrate, was the political disposition of the people generally in South Vietnam—the apathy or hostility toward the Saigon government of a variety of groups in the cities and villages of different regions, the ties of the people to various dissident leaders and causes, and their likely hostility to an army of foreign, and especially of white, soldiers.[24]

It was not that McNamara was unaware of the lack of loyalty or the absence of even a sense of connection to their government on the part of the South Vietnamese people as a factor in the overall problem. Rather, his lack of focus on the internal politics of South Vietnam stemmed from his conviction that this was a problem to be left to the South Vietnamese government itself. That is, unlike majoritarian planners, McNamara drew a mental line between the campaign to neutralize outside communist intervention in the politics of South Vietnam—which he regarded as a proper American mission—and a campaign to reform the internal political structure of the South—which he thought Americans should *not* be doing. This difference, however, was blurred in the early years of the war by the common language of counterinsurgency. The point at which their meanings actually diverged was not clear until well after the deep engagement in Vietnam began with the Gulf of Tonkin resolution.

The differences that would later surface and contribute to confusion in the war policy were forecast by one functionalist voice in the Johnson administration—a functionalist entering an early dissent to the Dulles-defined excursion of the managerial constituency away from its traditional emphasis on non-military approaches to international affairs. This was Under Secretary of State George Ball. A lawyer from Chicago, Ball had spent most of his professional life in private law practice, but had always been engaged as well in issues of public affairs. He spent several years in Washington agencies in the early New Deal, and during the Second World War served as a lawyer in the Lend-Lease Administration. There he formed what would become a long-lasting personal and political association with Jean Monnet, then the head of a joint British-French supply mission but later the apostle of European functional unification.

In 1946, Ball joined a Washington law firm and continued his association with Monnet, working extensively with him in drafting the Schuman Plan (the European Coal and Steel Community) and in the early planning for the Common Market. This commitment on Ball's part to international functional planning never faltered. He worked actively with the Council on Foreign Relations beginning in 1948, when he became a member, and his law firm served as United States representative for several of the European institutions he had helped to set up—Coal and Steel, Euratom, and the Common Market.

Joining the State Department under Kennedy, Ball was primarily interested in promoting firmer linkages between the United States and the countries of Europe, linkages that treated economic and political problems as matters for joint analysis and ultimately for joint, not separate, national decision making. For example, he was the main proponent of a Kennedy administration plan for a multilateral force, or MLF, that would have added to the NATO system nuclear weapons operated under joint European-American control. The weapons in question were a type of Polaris missile and were to be carried by surface ships with mixed crews from various NATO countries. The decision to use the missiles, Ball said in a 1963 speech, "would be exercised through some form of executive body representing the participating nations."

The beauty of the MLF for its promoters was that it would give Europe a nuclear deterrent not wholly dependent on American decisions, but its greater beauty was that the exercise of multilateral cooperation in itself would serve, in Ball's words, to promote a "gradual and constructive evolution . . . toward greater unity in Europe and closer partnership between Europe and the United States." The ultimate point of close American-

European cooperation, Ball said in 1965, was to allow that broad community, representing 90 percent of the industrial strength of the non-communist world, to build for the future a rational, peaceful order—"a role that is something new and unique in history, a role of world responsibility divorced from territorial or narrow national interests."[25]

According to the *New York Times* edition of the Pentagon Papers, George Ball "makes his first appearance in the Pentagon history as the Administration dissenter on Vietnam" on November 24, 1964, as a member of a National Security Council select committee reviewing recommendations from various parts of the government addressing the deteriorating situation in Vietnam. From that point to July 1965, when the decision to send substantial ground troops became firm, Ball argued against increased military commitment and for settlement of the conflict by an international conference, even at the price of admitting the communist-led Vietcong to some degree of power in South Vietnam.

In arriving at his conclusions, Ball was responding more than McNamara to the older, pre-Cold War principles of functionalism—the insistence on building and strengthening institutions capable of carrying out the complicated social and economic functions that linked all peoples in an increasingly industrialized world. The military defeat of communism in Vietnam, even if that were possible, would not advance American interests very far, Ball thought, because Vietnam lacked the institutions necessary to build the functional order McNamara assumed could follow the defeat of the Vietcong. The United States, he said in later commentary on the war, had been transfixed in the 1960s by the concept of rationally planned "nation building." But Vietnam, a "poor, agrarian Oriental society, built around the family and the village," could not provide the "institutional bricks" for building a modern economy and political structure that could link the country to a larger international order.[26]

Further, Ball reflected more than McNamara the enduring functionalist sensitivity to the role of the irrational, the emotional in politics—the concern underlying the functionalist insistence on placing authority in calm, rational, disciplined professionals in the first place. In Vietnam, Ball thought the element of will and fervent purpose on the part of the Vietcong and North Vietnamese would prove more significant than the material losses American military power could inflict. He also feared, rightly as it turned out, the emotional pressure at home for increasing troop levels as the war wore on to avoid the humiliation of loss and to legitimate the American deaths already incurred.[27]

George Ball left the government in September 1966, having lost the battle over Vietnam, both the battle to keep the United States out of Vietnam militarily and the battle he carried on for almost a year to keep the level of engagement low. But within the functionalist camp generally, the Ball position was not lost. Rather, as the war continued and widened, far beyond the scope its planners first anticipated, functionalists generally came to question and then to move away from acceptance of military strategies for Third World problems.

George Kennan, for example—a professional diplomat himself and strong advocate of the professional as opposed to the political conduct of foreign affairs—testified in 1966 hearings before the Senate Foreign Relations Committee that the American military commitment in Vietnam should be drastically limited. He suggested reducing military objectives there to the occupation and defense of limited enclaves, strong points where the authority of the South Vietnamese government had a reasonable chance of operating.

The United States should not dissipate its resources and goodwill through close involvement in the conflicts of new nations, Kennan said. Such nations "with shallow traditions of national life" are inevitably "going to fight with each other," and Americans could not further any clear aims through intervention in such quarrels because there will be "right and wrong on both sides." The United States should "try to keep these local conflicts from doing great damage to world peace," he concluded, but otherwise should concentrate its energies in areas of the world where natural grounds for natural (functional) relations were in place—the industrial world, including Europe and Japan.[28]

Of particular importance to the war policies in Vietnam, however, was the fact that by late 1966 the key functionalist

within the administration, McNamara himself, began to question
the premises of his own policy. First, he ordered a Defense
Department study of the entire history of American involvement
in Southeast Asia (the Pentagon Papers) in order to gain greater
perspective on the problem. Then he began to conclude that the
distinction he had thought possible, the distinction between outside intervention in the insurgency in South Vietnam and internal
political conflict, could not be maintained. Increasingly, he saw
the two as inextricably intertwined, and this meant a military
campaign could not be effectively directed at outside forces alone.
That is, the insurgency could not be ended by precise and neat
strategies such as pinpoint bombing of supply routes from the
North, because the forces behind the insurgency were deeply
entrenched in the South. They were part of the society of the
South as well as the North. The only kind of military campaign
that could defeat such an insurgency would be a long, large-scale
war of attrition, a war against the whole people, which
McNamara was not willing to accept.

In his position as Defense Secretary, McNamara did not
advocate abandoning the involvement in Vietnam. He thought
it would be useful to minimize military pressure from the North
in order to give the government in the South more time to
strengthen its position. But from late 1966 on, he argued within
the administration against strategies depending on greater and
greater levels of gross force and for reliance instead on forms of
combat that would keep the war as precise and surgical as possible. He recommended the construction of an electronic barrier
between North and South as a means of reducing the flow of
supplies to the Vietcong. As for internal reform and pacification
in the South, he continued to argue that this was a Vietnamese
responsibility, that the American role was only to advise and that
the only helpful enhancement of this role would be improvement
in the management techniques Americans used to impart their
advice.[29] And he argued strongly against pressing the war against
the North—again, because of his newfound conviction that the
North was not the seat of the real enemy.

This point—the question of the proper strategy against the
North—became a matter of intense and bitter conflict between

functionalists and localists on the conduct of the war. The argument between the two was joined and their positions articulated in hearings before the Senate Preparedness Investigation Subcommittee in August 1967. At these hearings, McNamara stated for the first time in public his increasingly iconoclastic position within the administration as an advocate of limiting the war. Specifically, he argued against heavy reliance on bombing in North Vietnam as a means of ending the fighting in the South. This strategy would not work, McNamara insisted, because the North was not in full control of the insurgency. It was not the main source of its motivation and supplies.[30] The Joint Chiefs of Staff, on the other hand, testified strongly in favor of increased bombing in the North.

The subcommittee was chaired by John Stennis of Mississippi, long an advocate of localist positions on security affairs, and the committee report came down solidly for the Joint Chiefs— specifically disputing McNamara's concept of the enemy as intrinsically rooted in the South. The report stated squarely that "the enemy [North Vietnam] has been hurt in his homeland" and that "the pressure should be increased and not reduced to persuade him that his continued support of the war in South Vietnam is definitely not in his best interests." And it specifically recommended increased bombing for the purposes of "closing the port of Haiphong [the major port of entry for Soviet supplies], isolating it from the rest of the country, striking all meaningful targets with a military significance and increasing the interdiction of the lines of communication from Red China."[31]

Strom Thurmond, speaking in the Senate in the fall of 1967, stated the localist position on this point even more directly. "This is not a civil war. This is a war by the Communists to take over the world. . . . Who started this war; who came into South Vietnam; who inspired these guerillas; who is supplying these guerillas; who is giving leadership and training to the guerillas and the Vietcong? It is the Communists of the Soviet Union and Red China and North Vietnam." Elsewhere Thurmond charged that the United States was withholding that use of military force which "should strike fear into the hearts of any aggressor anywhere in the world." And specifically in Vietnam, "leadership which . . . glories in exhibitions of unnecessary restraint" had the nation "bogged down in a war that is draining away our life's blood."[32]

What emerges from this tangled history is that the three major constituencies in American politics were all behind the war effort in Vietnam, but by 1967 they were fighting clearly different wars with different enemies and different strategies.

Majoritarians and functionalists were agreed, by then, that the primary enemy was chaos and conflict *within* South Vietnam, but they drew different conclusions from this premise. Majoritarians wanted to fight the chaos with strategies of pacification and social reconstruction. Functionalists, represented by McNamara, were willing to fight the intervention by the North in order to buy time for the beleaguered South. But if, with this degree of help, the government of the South still could not function, then McNamara—along with Ball and Kennan—was prepared to accept the fact that the United States could carry on no useful relation with that country. That is, the grounds for functional relations simply did not exist, and the United States could not itself create them.

On this point—the futility of deep involvement in the internal problems of the South—functionalists and localists were agreed. And they were jointly opposed to the majoritarian insistence on such involvement. But functionalists came to their opposition *in spite of* their belief that the internal enemy in the South was the real enemy. Localists, on the other hand, saw the real enemy in the North and therefore insisted—vitriolically—on the need to carry the battle there.

President Johnson was in anguish by the end of 1967, with his early expectations of victory frustrated and his advisers in increasingly wide disagreement. His reaction, as the depth of differences revealed itself, was to remove McNamara from office, later explaining privately that the Defense Secretary had been on the verge of a nervous breakdown due to personal doubts about the war he held responsibility for directing. "Two months before he left he felt he was a murderer and didn't know how to extricate himself," Johnson said.[33] Whether or not that was true, McNamara acted immediately on his functionalist principles, taking on responsibility, at his own request, for organizing economic development in the Third World through an *international* agency—as president of the World Bank.

McNamara's leaving did not prove to be a victory for the localists, however, because Johnson continued to maintain most of the restrictions McNamara had imposed on carrying the war to the North. He did not extend significantly the bombing of northern targets or allow the mining of northern harbors. Rather, he continued the majoritarian effort to defeat the insurgency in the south until, in the spring of 1968, he, too, became convinced of the futility of this strategy and began the American withdrawal.

To some extent, all three strategies—majoritarian, functionalist, and localist—were followed in Vietnam. But no single strategy was put into full effect, uncompromised by the others, and this fact laid the basis for much of the postwar rancor over Vietnam. As no one group was given full rein for its approach, each could maintain the assumption after the defeat that *its* strategy was right and that the defeat was due to the mistakes—or betrayals—on the part of others.

The final tragedy of Vietnam, however, is that all three were wrong. Certainly, the conduct of the war suffered from the differences among American policy makers, but no one of the approaches, carried out in its full logic, could have produced a vastly different result, because all three were flawed by the premise of the myth of deliverance—the premise that conflicts are inherently resolvable.

Starting with this idea, all three groups formed the assumption that the unresolved trouble in the south—the inability of a succession of governments to maintain order—must be caused mainly by outside interference. And because of Khrushchev's declaration of intent to conduct subversive wars, along with the evidence of Soviet aid to North Vietnam, all three groups identified aid from the North as the alien element destabilizing the situation. Thus the conclusion followed logically that excising the abnormality—the interference from the North—would reduce the problems of the South to solvable size. Further, blocking the success of outside subversion in Vietnam would convince the leaders of communist states, most importantly the Soviet Union, that campaigns of subversive aggression would not pay.

But what the mythic view of the problem obscured was the depth of the internal conflict—the deep differences between cities and mountain and delta people, Catholics and Buddhists, sympathizers with the West and the East, and cultural and nationalist resistance to all outside influence. The myth obscured the indigenous strength, in the South, of the nationalist-communist cause represented by the Vietcong—strength demonstrated by the ability of the insurgents to sustain themselves even when supplies from the North were cut to a trickle by the bombing of roads and bridges. Most significantly, however, the need imposed by the myth to see an outside troublemaking agent as the cause behind continuing disorder in the South blinded Americans to the fact that the internal conflict in Vietnam involved the whole country, across the artificial barrier that the Geneva Conference had drawn in 1954.

The North was not an alien element in the situation. The communists—North and South—were one contending interest in Vietnam, and by 1965 they had been fighting for twenty years to advance their cause, to unify Vietnam under Vietnamese—and communist—rule. Further, they were intransigent; their differences with rival groups were so wide that there was no chance of resolution as long as communist forces and nationalist groups allied with them had the capacity to fight. Whether their cause was just or unjust was beside the point; the impact of the North on the South could not be eliminated by techniques primarily designed to eliminate an outside intervening force. Ho Chi Minh's movement was deeply entwined in the politics of the South by history and by conviction and it could not be removed except by massive annihilation—even more massive and devastating to the Vietnamese people and their land than the damage that in fact was done.

Functionalists proved on the whole more sensitive than the other groups to the disruptive force of conflicting interest in Vietnam and to the play of powerful emotions in the conflict. Fear of such forces is, after all, at the base of functionalist ideology, the source of their insistence on reasoning professionals as the agents of deliverance for all societies. This outlook led some, such as George Ball, to oppose American engagement in Vietnam altogether, and it led Robert McNamara to recognize, sooner than many administration members, the intricacy of the conflict and the degree of destruction it would take to end it. Still, most functionalists—McNamara foremost among them—were sufficiently blinded by the myth to believe, at the outset, that American planners could *manage* the conflict, could distinguish outside interference from internal factionalism. And they believed that removing the outsiders—the abnormal disruptive force—from the situation would allow normal stabilizing processes in the South to work. By the time McNamara decided this was not the case, the American commitment had become too large and complicated to reverse.

The localist version of the myth, on the other hand—which identifies an enemy always as a clear-cut malevolent force—produced the conviction held by localists from beginning to end that the only enemy of consequence in Vietnam was a Soviet-led communist force bent on aggressive expansion. And with this conviction in mind, localists insisted throughout the war on a strategy of destroying the enemy by destroying its primary agent—the communist government of North Vietnam. Of all three conceptions of an enemy to the United States in Southeast Asia, the localist was furthest from an appreciation of the depth of trouble there. And it was the most dangerous conception of the three because it called for an intensified military campaign, virtually an all-out war on the North. Then, the refusal by Johnson to follow such a strategy produced among localists a dangerous bitterness—accusations reminiscent of the McCarthy era against officials who *chose* not to defeat the communists when it was possible to do so.

Finally, however, the failure in Vietnam was a majoritarian failure. It was the majoritarian version of the myth more than the others that impelled the engagement there and broadened it to encompass an army of half a million Americans. Majoritarians made the same mistake as the others in assuming that the North was the primary enemy, underestimating the depth and complication of conflict running through the society, North and South.

And this was so in spite of the fact that the majoritarians from the outset defined internal conflict in the South as an important part of the problem. That is, they recognized its importance but not its profundity. They thought the United States could solve the problem of communist intervention in the South militarily —by cutting off supplies from the North and by seeking out communist forces in the South and destroying them. *And* they thought the United States could significantly improve the effectiveness of the government of South Vietnam through the logic of the development process and political reform. Economic growth would begin with development aid and teachers of development techniques and it would produce a higher standard of living—which in turn would produce loyalty to the government responsible for it. Political reform would begin with the establishment of institutions—such as an elected parliament—giving the people some connection to their government, some control over it and therefore greater faith in it.

But the majoritarian plan did not begin to address local conditions and complications. Vietnam was an agrarian culture with loyalties fixed in the locality—in the village, the family, or in some regions, the tribe. And it was by ancient tradition a society governed by hierarchies. The rules defining the right and wrong uses of power were far from those of the democratic United States, and the idea of shifting power to the people through constitutions, parliaments, votes, and seminars for local hamlet chiefs was simply inapplicable—even if there had been no insurgency to contend with, communist or otherwise.[34]

Certainly, the strategies for economic development and political liberalization pressed by American officials found little sympathy within the central governments in Vietnam from Diem onward. For these officials, theories of subversive aggression, counterinsurgency, test cases of communist will, as well as the more esoteric theories of economic growth, were beside the point. They were fighting to stay in power and, for many, retaining power meant little more than retaining access to the immense possibilities for building fortunes through various forms of graft in the chaos of war.

But corruption aside, Americans and Vietnamese were operating with widely different purposes and assumptions. The story that unfolds, document by document, in the Pentagon Papers indicates that the two sets of officials, with wholly different visions in their minds, could barely communicate, let alone cooperate effectively.

Thus majoritarians went into Vietnam with a broader conception of the enemy than the other two groups, but with no greater sense of reality. They recognized the importance of an internal as well as an external dimension to the struggle but thought that *both* could be solved with a broad enough plan. They sought deliverance from outside aggression *and* deliverance from political chaos, both of which they assumed could be accomplished fairly readily once the culprits in each situation were located.

But the source of trouble in Vietnam was not an abnormality that could be readily excised. It could not be bombed out of existence, as the localists sought to do, or managed according to functionalist plans, or transformed through the benign development process envisaged by majoritarians. The trouble in Vietnam could not be solved by the removal of abnormal elements or the reversal of abnormal conditions because the conflicts producing trouble were deeply interwoven in the society, shaped by its culture and history. The conflicts were themselves a norm, and the American mission, the majoritarian mission of rapid reform, could not force them to yield.

Finally, the focus of all three groups on the significance of outside aid led to misperception of the importance of the Soviet Union in the Vietnamese picture. The larger American strategy in Vietnam was to foil the Soviet policy of intervention in wars of national liberation, but the strategy would work only if Soviet aid to the Vietnamese insurgents was so central and substantial as to make the failure of Soviet objectives a serious loss to the U.S.S.R. But this was not the case. The success of Soviet involvement in local insurgencies depended on strong local forces in play whose sympathy the Soviet Union might win with timely supplies of arms and other needed material. Even if the local group receiving communist aid were defeated, its protector had lost little and would not be deterred by the loss from trying again elsewhere. The American strategy of discouraging subversive aggression by making it too costly simply did not apply where the costs were borne primarily by local forces. Again, it was the blinder of the myth that prevented Americans from seeing how intransigent, how unwilling or unable to resolve their differences peacefully, local forces could be.

VIII

Reaction: Carter's Functionalism, Reagan's Localism

The story of American politics in the period following the experiments of the 1960s is a story of reaction. In part it is a story of reaction by wage earners against leadership that seemed to betray the promise of majoritarianism— the promise of deliverance through the active use of national political power at home and abroad. In the presidential elections of 1968 and 1972, great numbers of workers deserted majoritarian candidates—Hubert Humphrey and George McGovern—who held out the traditional promise and insisted on its validity.

This reaction—of majoritarians against their own tradition —was essentially negative. It did not produce any widespread reshaping of programs and directions. Indeed, it could not. Fixed between the interests of wage earners and the myth of deliverance, the majoritarian vision could not extend beyond the concept of a fairly easy to achieve power balance—a balance struck by the agency of government between the powerful few and the powerless many. Thus when the balancing mechanism did not work as expected, the majoritarian constituency was left in a state of confusion and uncertainty.

More coherent reaction, the pressing of programs based on

235

different premises, came from the other constituencies—the localists and functionalists, whose belief in their own approaches was
only confirmed by majoritarian failures. Both groups gained in
political strength with support from disaffected majoritarians, and
each in turn captured the presidency and attempted to enact its
own programs as public policy—the functionalists with Jimmy
Carter, the localists with Ronald Reagan.

That is, the policy direction of the Carter administration and
then that of Reagan were *reactions* to the politics and failures of
majoritarianism, but they were not deep-seated reactions of the
nation as a whole, not sea changes in the whole American populace. Rather, the core policies of each were rooted in the interests
of particular constituencies. Each expressed an alternative political vision compounded of the myth of deliverance and a particular economic interest. As such, both policy ventures—Carter's
functionalism and Reagan's localism—would suffer, as did the
ventures of majoritarians, from undercutting by the other interests. And, more important, both would suffer, and ultimately fail,
from the false premises of the myth.

But, to backtrack, how did these movements of reaction take
shape? What, precisely, were their alternative perspectives and
programs, and what was the course of their failure?

The strongest and most immediate reaction to the 1960s
experiments came from the localists, who opposed from the
beginning the majoritarian initiatives in domestic affairs and
especially the programs brought into being by the Office of
Economic Opportunity. Once established in 1964, the OEO
drew to Washington hundreds of sociologists, psychologists,
economists, nutritionists, urbanologists, and educators demanding
money from Congress to redress a long agenda of social wrongs.
However, since social issues including education had traditionally
been the province of the states, the OEO offensive was essentially
an attack on the kinds of social choices the states had been
making, and an attack on local control through an enlarged
federal role in designing social policy.

The Civil Rights Act was also an assault on local authority,
most especially in its enforcement procedures. With federal district attorneys in charge of prosecuting violations of the law and

with violators tried in federal as opposed to state courts, the interpretation and actual application of rules against racial discrimination would presumably be more stringent than they would be if administered by the states. By the same token, local control over local community relations would be seriously undercut, as Borah had strenuously pointed out in the debate over the 1938 anti-lynching bill.

As discussed earlier, localists of the 1940s and early 1950s had equated demands for national legislation on social issues with the threat of communism riddling the nation. They had seen the increasing insistence on national laws against racial discrimination and national standards for terms of employment as produced by communist propaganda insidiously fed into the society through innocent-seeming movies, books, and other instruments of the mass media. That is, they had seen a deliberately malevolent communist movement secretly orchestrating demands for the shifting of authority on social questions away from the base in local communities where it belonged.

In the 1960s, with majoritarians and functionalists enthusiastically cooperating in administrations committed to social activism, localists came to see that the primary enemy to local authority was not a hidden, conspiratorial force. Rather, there was a new enemy, clear to see in the political arena, stating its goals not only openly but with missionary zeal. This newly recognized threat to the localist cause was the professional expert, the social scientist who issued decrees from a university or Washington agency about every aspect of social life, from education and mental illness to inflation and counterinsurgency techniques. And experts were a highly dangerous enemy because their authority rested on special training and special knowledge difficult for ordinary citizens at the grass roots to challenge.

Strom Thurmond saw the emergent danger as a new form of socialism whose adherents do not call themselves socialists but believe nevertheless that "bureaucrats . . . are perfectly justified to use the organs and resources of government to remake social patterns, to propagandize for government control, to beat reluctant citizens down by force . . ." In line with such principles, power was being given over to a "creative elite," a "technological elite" in the interests of efficiency. But this was disastrous, Thurmond warned. "Despite the advantages of computers and programming, no central authority can ever have adequate information to plan for every locality," he said.[1]

These were the themes that carried another localist, Governor George Wallace of Alabama, out of the South and into a campaign for President in 1968 and again in 1972, when he won impressive percentages in several northern primaries before he was shot and paralyzed in an assassination attempt that occurred when he was campaigning in Maryland. Wallace, more crude and colorful than Thurmond, was also more successful in broadening the appeal of his attack on the Washington elite. "I don't want to be petted like a little poodle dog by a bunch of social engineers in Washington," he proclaimed. People dissatisfied with the Great Society in the North as well as the South loved his attacks on "this outlaw beatnik crowd in Washington" or the "intellectual morons" in the federal government. He declared himself absolutely opposed to "the ideal that believes government can manage the people and by management and manipulation bring about a utopian life."[2]

Localist mistrust of the expert, the federal bureaucrat, extended beyond domestic policy to foreign policy as well, where it seemed confirmed in the early 1960s, well before the Vietnam question arose, by disturbing signs of American loss of power and control over its own fortunes. The entire nation had, of course, been shocked by the advent of the first Russian Sputnik in 1957, which signaled the reality of Soviet long-range military power. Then, in 1960, Fidel Castro, having brought a revolutionary government to power ninety miles from the Florida coast, declared his attachment to Marxism, and in 1961 the United States failed in its badly conceived effort to overthrow him with an invading force of Cuban émigrés attempting to land secretly at the Bay of Pigs. In 1961 also, the Berlin Wall went up and the United States could do nothing about it.

In 1962, the United States succeeded in stopping the Soviet deployment of missiles in Cuba, but only at the price of promising not to threaten again the position of the Cuban government. At the same time, growing numbers of newly independent countries challenged the established American dominance of the United Nations and began to turn the General Assembly into a forum for attacks on American policies. Europe, with the Common Market in place, was no longer a poor cousin but a strong competitor and, following the imperious example of Charles de Gaulle, often refused to accept American political leadership. De Gaulle vetoed British entry into the Common Market in 1962, built an independent French nuclear weapons system in defiance of the United States, and later withdrew French troops and bases from NATO. The American balance of payments began to go into deficit in the late 1950s, and the first serious run on American gold reserves occurred in 1962.

The localist response to the uncertainties unfolding in the 1960s was the increased suspicion that the new power holders in the federal government were undermining American strength by their ambivalence, if not their femininity—"the sissy attitude of Lyndon Johnson and all the intellectual morons and theoreticians he has around him," as George Wallace said.[3] This mistrust of intellectuals in government, heightened by the experience of Vietnam, was important in the turning of localists to political alliance with the military, as discussed in Chapter VII.

Even more important, however, in the reaction of localists to political events of the 1960s was a growing unity among them —and by the same token, a growing disunity between majoritarian and localist elements within the Democratic Party. Outraged by the direction being set by majoritarian leadership, localist Democrats—southern Democrats mainly—began in 1964 to leave the party to join the localist ranks of Republicans. Of course, southern Democrats had for years resisted the majoritarian influence within the Democratic Party by voting with Republicans against social and economic programs pushed by labor and minorities, but the passage of the Civil Rights Act precipitated a definitive party break with an impact on national politics that spread far beyond congressional voting patterns.

The first important defector was Strom Thurmond, then a Democratic senator from South Carolina, who announced in September 1964 that he was leaving the Democratic Party to become a Republican. Thurmond had for years been a major voice in the southern Democratic opposition to northern Democratic initiatives on civil rights. In 1948, as governor of South Carolina, he had been the presidential nominee of the States' Rights Party, hastily formed by Southerners to counter President Truman's support for a civil rights program in that election. However, for Thurmond to engage in a third-party stratagem to put pressure on northern Democrats was a far different matter from turning Republican himself.

In spite of increasingly sharp differences between North and South in the Democratic Party, it had been accepted until the 1960s that both sides stood to gain from continued coalition. For the North, southern votes were crucial to elect Democratic Presidents and to form the majorities necessary to control Congress. For the South, Democratic Party membership ensured the chairmanship and thus control of important congressional committees because of the long-standing seniority rule in both houses of Congress. That is, as long as chairmen were appointed by length of continuous service in the House or Senate, the positions would frequently go to Southerners whose political longevity was protected by one-party elections. And the Southerners also enjoyed the protection of the Senate cloture rule, which allowed them to carry on filibusters as long as one-third of the Senate was willing to vote against closing debate—which was usually the case.

In 1964, however, the protective rules system failed for the South. The Deep South senators began their filibuster as usual when the Civil Rights bill came to the floor of the Senate and the northern Democrats, as usual, submitted a motion for cloture. The Southerners needed 32 votes to defeat cloture, but this time, with Lyndon Johnson in the presidency and determined that the bill should pass, they had no regular Democratic support. Besides their own 18 votes, they had only 11 others—5 Democrats from Arizona, Nevada, Tennessee, and West Virginia and 6 localist Republicans.

In the face of virtually united opposition to the South on civil rights within the Democratic Party, and increasingly vigorous attack by northern Democrats on other organizational rules, like seniority, that had traditionally protected southern power in Congress, the logic of the Democratic alliance began to collapse.

"The Democratic Party has abandoned the people," Thurmond declared as he announced his change of allegiance, adding, "It has repudiated the Constitution of the United States. It is leading the evolution of our nation to a socialistic dictatorship."[4] By 1985 there were 9 Republican senators from the Deep South out of a possible 18, and 30 Republican congressmen out of a total of 80.

The more dramatic impact of shifting party loyalties in the South, however, has been in the realm of presidential politics. In 1964, having lost their monumental battle with the North on civil rights, five southern states—Alabama, Georgia, Louisiana, Mississippi, and South Carolina—voted Republican for Barry Goldwater of Arizona rather than the apostate Lyndon Johnson of Texas. Southern states had occasionally voted for Republicans before. Florida, Virginia, and North Carolina had voted for Herbert Hoover rather than the northern Catholic Democrat, Al Smith, in 1928, and Florida and Virginia voted against another northern Catholic, John Kennedy, in 1960. However, these earlier defections were specific responses to a particularly objectionable candidate and not indicative of basic shifts in voting behavior as 1964 turned out to be.

In 1968, no southern state voted Democratic in the presidential election. Five voted for former Alabama governor George Wallace, running as an American Independent; the four others, Florida, North Carolina, South Carolina, and Virginia, voted Republican and provided the electoral vote margin for Richard Nixon's defeat of Hubert Humphrey. Four years later, Nixon carried the entire South along with the rest of the country except Massachusetts and Washington, D.C., when the Democratic candidate was the Great Society proponent George McGovern.

The functionalist reaction to the politics of the 1960s was less immediate and less clear-cut than that of the localists, and necessarily so, as functionalists had participated as allies in the Kennedy and Johnson administrations. They had worked with majoritarian leaders to shape the Great Society programs and also the counterinsurgency stratagems of the Vietnam War. Still, as the Great Society faltered and the conflict in Vietnam defied the controls fashioned by American planners, important parts of the functionalist constituency began to separate themselves from the majoritarian alliance.

This movement was most clearly evident in foreign policy, crystallized by the shock of failure in Vietnam. With Robert McNamara, functionalists generally took the lesson of Vietnam to be that political conflict in developing countries could not easily be resolved by force. It was not simply a matter of isolating and removing communist movements run from the outside. Rather, the tangle of internal trouble besetting new or industrially developing nations was such that no degree of American military intervention could deliver these areas quickly from disruption into efficient functional relations with others. In short, the experience of Vietnam convinced much of the functionalist constituency that John Foster Dulles had been wrong. The use of force to control communism in the Third World would not work; rather, the times called for an application to the developing countries of older functionalist principles—the slow building of functional connections through investment and trade, as such connections became possible.

Early evidence of the functionalist rejection of Cold War principles in the aftermath of Vietnam was an extensive shake-up, in the early 1970s, of both personnel and policy in the Council on Foreign Relations. In 1969, the senior members of the Council met for a two-day conference to review the purpose and direction of the Council in response to the "growing feeling that the premises underlying our foreign policy in the middle and late 1940s are no longer fully applicable and that new concepts must be developed."[5] Then, between 1970 and 1972, important organizational changes ensued. The chairmanship of the board of directors passed from John McCloy to David Rockefeller. A new seniority bylaw displaced from the board a number of longtime directors even before the end of their terms, and such committed advocates of international cooperation and organization as Paul Warnke, Michael Blumenthal, Marshall Shulman, and Cyrus Vance took their places. Bayless Manning, former special assistant to George Ball as Under Secretary of State, became Council president, and the editorship of *Foreign Affairs* changed hands from Hamilton Fish Armstrong to William Bundy.

After this point, the focus of Council study projects and discussion groups was no longer divided, as it had been during the 1950s and 1960s, between concern with the protection of Western institutions against Soviet threats on the one hand and more general international cooperation on the other. Rather, the post-1970 topics for study reflect a wholehearted devotion to the analysis of world problems in functional and global terms, the exploration of "such major trends as the explosion of knowledge, vast scientific and technical developments, changed mass communications, growing economic integration . . . and the growth of population."[6]

As for relations between the United States and the Soviet Union, discussion groups concerned themselves, not with finding ways of countering Soviet pressures and threats, but with defining areas in which long-term cooperation between the superpowers could occur. George Kennan provided the keynote for this theme in a 1972 *Foreign Affairs* article called "After the Cold War: American Foreign Policy in the 1970's." His thesis was a flat declaration that the largest postwar issue—the political configuration of Europe—had been settled and, that being so, "there are today no political issues between the Soviet Union and the United States which could conceivably be susceptible of solution by war, even if the state of weaponry had not made any major military conflict between the two powers unthinkable."

Acknowledging that instability in Asia and the Middle East and difficulties with development in the Third World generally were dangerous problems, Kennan still insisted that neither the United States nor the Soviet Union could resolve these problems or even make significant gains through war. Therefore, he said, the United States, instead of wasting its energy in anti-Soviet efforts that could produce no advantageous change, should turn to addressing problems susceptible of steady, positive change through "constructive statesmanship," such as preserving the natural environment worldwide or discouraging the growing reliance of new, small states on nationalist strategies to protect themselves and promote particular interests.[7]

In 1974 the Council confirmed its new clarified focus on the building of world order with plans for a broad three-year cycle of study called the 1980s Project. The announcement of the project drew a parallel between its conception and the War and Peace Studies the Council had done for the government during the Second World War. For both, the ultimate purpose was to shape a vision, to instruct the nation about reliable principles of order, "to break out of the inhibitions and the constraints on thinking" that have molded an unsatisfactory foreign policy.

Included in the outmoded approaches the project was to challenge were not only the anti–Soviet fixation of the Cold War, but also the "institutional components of the post–World War II era, such as the GATT, the IMF, and NATO," which "increasingly seem out of gear with changed conditions." What the project would address were new "clusters of interrelated problems" emerging in the evolution of a new international system. Such problems included "management of the international economy; global poverty; management of the environment; and of the new 'common'—the oceans, the seabeds and space; and interstate violence, including arms control."[8]

The themes were the old ones, problems conceived in functional, not political terms—poverty, the environment, seabeds, space. And solutions to the problems would be found through proper management—*management* of the international economy, *management* of the environment, etc. However, if the new functionalist outlook had old roots, its application to new conditions took members of the Council into somewhat new political terrain. The aim of the Council from its inception was to bring the influence of reason to bear on the processes of policy making within the United States, and specifically to resist unreason in the form of parochialism in American politics—mainly the localist impulse to disengage the United States from outside connections or to engage only defensively as in the anti-communist policies of the Cold War. Thus while the functionalist vision was global, its policy focus, before the 1970s, was national. After 1970, the mission to educate Americans in the ways of reason remained the focus of Council activity, but Council members became increasingly concerned with the need to deal with problems of interdependence by shaping common, reasoned attitudes toward such problems throughout the industrial world.

The response of Council leaders, most prominently its board chairman, David Rockefeller, to the need for cross-national understanding of world problems was characteristically institutional —the formation in 1973 of the Trilateral Commission, "A Private American-European-Japanese Initiative on Matters of Common Concern," as it titled itself. Its founding purpose was to bring together managers and professionals engaged in international exchange from all three regions to identify common needs and define policies, global policies, that would serve those needs. American members from the business world came from such firms as Lehman Brothers, the Bendix Corporation, Time Inc., Deer and Co., the Chase Manhattan Bank, Brown Brothers Harriman, and CBS.

The Commission's techniques for achieving its purposes were the same as those practiced for years by the Council on Foreign Relations and the Committee for Economic Development, essentially educational techniques designed to influence the thought of decision-making elites. It sponsored conferences that brought members from the three areas together, published a journal, *Trialogue,* to report on meetings and conferences, and published also, at the rate of about three a year, reports similar to those of the CED on the results of study projects dealing with particular international problems.

The first of these reports, called Triangle Papers, presented the findings of the Trilateral Monetary Task Force on the problem of renovating the world monetary system, and each subsequent report tackled problems similarly cast in global terms, each defining yet another aspect of the supranational, managerial approach to global issues the Commission sought to propagate. There were, for example: *Energy: The Imperative for a Trilateral Approach* (1974); *OPEC, the Trilateral World, and the Developing Countries: New Arrangements for Cooperation, 1976–1980* (1975); *A New Regime for the Oceans* (1976); *Seeking a New Accommodation in World Commodity Markets* (1976); and *Collaboration with Communist Countries in Managing Global Problems: An Examination of the Options* (1977).

The Trilateral Papers, taken as a whole, present what can only be described as a design for deliverance—the creation of an order for the future that would accomplish, however slowly, deliverance for all of the world's people from the evils of material want and of violence in the process of distributing the world's goods. That is, the purposes and policies of the Commission, while on one level a blueprint for a world congenial to the interests of multinational corporations, are also a clear formulation of the functionalist version of the American myth of deliverance. A 1977 paper, *Towards a Renovated International System,* spells out the mythic underpinning of Trilateralist thought in logical detail.

The international system under examination in the paper is that of cross-national interdependence, the system of links connecting the industrial states to others in various ways—closely to other industrialized countries; significantly but less closely to the developing world; and increasingly but least closely to the communist world. The concern of the study was to define the issues blocking easy cooperation within each set of interdependent relations—obvious and vast differences in political interest blocking cooperation between East and West; equally divergent economic interests dividing North and South; and among the industrialized countries, national welfare concerns taking the form of economic protectionism operating at odds with efforts to achieve common solutions to common problems. All of these blockages, the report warned, operate to prevent finding solutions to such dangerous and pressing issues as nuclear proliferation, ecological breakdowns, desperate poverty in parts of the globe, and the insistent demand everywhere for economically just societies.

The writers of the report, however, affirmed the possibility of overcoming blockages and establishing grounds for cooperation even against the odds they described. The key to this achievement, they said, was the "shared conviction" that rational cooperation in solving functional problems "maximizes overall gain and increases the welfare of those involved." The report went on to identify this concept, rightly, as a conviction with "philosophic roots" that "go back to the 18th century notion of progress," to the idea that "the human condition as a whole could be improved through human efforts to master parsimonious nature." This meant, the report stated approvingly, "a revolution-ary departure from the age-old notion that one man's gain must be another man's loss, or that one group could improve its condition only by robbing or exploiting other groups." The report characterized the older, pessimistic concept in modern terms as "zero-sum thinking" and its opposite, the belief in mutual maximum gain, as "positive sum thinking." And it as-serted that in spite of failures and setbacks, "the conviction that positive sum behavior is the most rational approach to interna-tional affairs has become the prevailing concept among Western political and intellectual elites."[9]

The systems defined in the various Triangle Papers for posi-tive conflict resolution were direct descendants of those formu-lated by turn-of-the-century American Progressive and scientific reformers. Problems should be defined and analyzed in terms of function and not political jurisdiction. Their solution should not be piecemeal or crisis-oriented but systemic, encompassing the interrelated parts of highly complicated issues. The locus for decision making should be shifted away from the political arena to functional institutions dealing with problems in terms of ongoing professional analysis, and most important, the decision makers themselves should be functional experts basing judgments on knowledge, not politicians negotiating solutions on the basis of power.

Ideally, in the international sphere, professional experts would deal with specific problems, whether of seabed resources, monetary policy, or arms control, as international civil servants employed by international functional institutions. Short of the ideal, however, the Trilateral approach urges the increased prac-tice of international consultation among national officials respon-sible within their own governments for a particular policy area. The key point, stressed by a Triangle Paper, *The Problem of International Consultations,* is that such cross-governmental discus-sions should not be filtered through diplomatic officials present-ing and arguing for whatever position their political heads of government have taken. Rather, "the critical element is contin-ual, direct and mutually respectful contact between responsible functional officials." This would give the experts from various nations a chance to arrive at a common professional position before the political position of their governments forms and hardens.

The same report advocates involving national politicians, legislators especially, in the consultative process—not to bring to the professionals the knowledge and interest of the politician, but to the politician the logic of the professionals. "No matter how careful, extensive and well-intentioned the consultation among administrative officials," the report stated in a tone of some exasperation, "any consensus or agreement can be frustrated by legislators, who do, and must, reflect the primarily domestic concerns of their constituents."[10]

This distinction between careful consultation among functional officials and the "primarily domestic concerns" of legislators points up again the cleavage in basic beliefs among the interest-based groups in American politics on the issue of decision-making authority. For localists, of course, the "domestic concerns" of a legislator's constituents are the only legitimate ground for the exercise of public authority. But for functionalists, they are virtually illegitimate, at least in conditions of highly advanced industrialism where the domestic concerns of one nation are deeply intertwined with those of others. In such conditions no rational policy for responding to domestic issues can be devised that does not take into account their entire reach, across national boundaries.

The Trilateral answer to Cold War issues, the group having eschewed Cold War politics, was simply to apply functionalist principles to East-West conflicts as far as the principles would go. Triangle Paper #15, *An Overview of East-West Relations,* stressed the importance of working diplomatically, not to force the Soviet Union into positions the West wants, but to influence the choices affecting the West that the Soviet Union necessarily makes in the normal course of its political processes. Through continuing discussions that "shape the alternatives facing its negotiating partners in such a way as to make one internal choice more rewarding to them than the other," the report writers insisted, the West could make real gains in arms limitations, human rights, cultural exchange, and economic cooperation.[11] Unstated, but implied, was the mythic assumption that under the stormy surface of East-West political relations, the natural grounds for beneficial exchanges of all kinds lay waiting to be discovered and put to use.

The first political product of the various reactions against majoritarianism was the election in 1968 of Richard Nixon to the presidency. And it was essentially a vote *against* the Kennedy-Johnson direction in policy, as Nixon did not himself represent a clear alternative direction. A lawyer from California, Nixon had been in national politics most of his adult life—as congressman, senator, then Vice-President under Eisenhower. He had built this career largely by serving the Republican Party organization, which meant courting both its major constituencies—functionalist and localist—rather than articulating a program, a call to action, based on the beliefs of one of them. That is, whereas the leadership of most Presidents consists of articulating one version of the myth—even while holding together a coalition of several interests—Nixon's lay mainly in building the strength of his party. And under his leadership, the Republican Party was ready in 1968 to capitalize on the growing national disaffection for majoritarian Democrats.

Paradoxically, Nixon's strength, his preoccupation with consolidating party power, led eventually to his political downfall. Having condoned illegal interference with election processes in 1972, and also obstruction of the judicial investigation of that interference, he was forced to resign the presidency in 1974. While in office, however, the Nixon administration served as a channel for both localist and functionalist reactions to the politics of the 1960s.

It served localists by scaling down funding requests for Great Society programs. "We are approaching the limits of what government alone can do," Nixon said in his first inaugural address. And in his first State of the Union message he articulated an even more explicit localist message. "It is time for a New Federalism," he declared, "in which after 190 years of power flowing from the people and local and state governments to Washington, D.C., it will begin to flow back to the States and to the people of the

United States."[12] In several instances, Nixon refused to spend money Congress had already appropriated for programs begun in the Great Society years.

In foreign policy, however, Nixon gave effect to the functionalist approach with a turn in the early 1970s to the stance in world affairs being urged in those years by the Council on Foreign Relations and the Trilateral Commission—a stance based on principles of cooperation rather than contention, even with communist countries. In the State of the Union address calling for a New Federalism at home, he announced that abroad the United States was "moving . . . from an era of confrontation to an era of negotiation." A month later he developed this theme in a Report to the Congress on United States Foreign Policy for the 1970s. Beginning with the premise that the communist world was no longer monolithic, that it had been broken up by conflicting nationalisms, he expressed firm American confidence "that tensions can be eased and the danger of war reduced by patient and precise efforts to reconcile conflicting interests on concrete issues."[13]

Pursuing what were popularly called policies of détente with the communist world, Nixon traveled to China and began the establishment of diplomatic relations with its government, which since 1949 the United States had refused to recognize. He also traveled to Moscow for a summit conference in 1972 and signed there a joint Soviet-American commitment to peaceful coexistence—which took immediate form in broadened trade and in negotiation for an agreement limiting the construction of strategic armaments.

Continued widespread mistrust of majoritarians served Nixon well in the 1972 election, as the Democrat, George McGovern, pleading for a return to the Great Society, was routed nationwide. But the Watergate scandal following the election and the revelation of abuses of executive power by the Nixon White House produced a reaction against the Republican Party generally, and in 1976 the presidency was regained by the Democrats with the election of Jimmy Carter of Georgia.

But Carter was not a Democrat in the traditional mold. He was the first Democratic President in the century who was not a majoritarian by conviction and who did not win the presidency preaching the majoritarian promise. He had the support of many majoritarians who traditionally voted Democratic, and as a Southerner, he also had localist support. In fact, he won back for the party, at least temporarily, the straying southern states. His convictions, however, and the leadership he offered were functionalist, and his election represented the continued strength of the reaction against majoritarianism.

One mark of Carter's functionalism was his membership in the Trilateral Commission, which he had joined as governor of Georgia and as part of the emerging leadership of what was coming to be called the New South. It was a South with greatly expanding industry and commerce, moving out of regional isolation, beginning to integrate itself into the economic and political patterns of the nation as a whole. Carter's Trilateral connection carried that logic one step further, into a vision of international integration, the organization of people linked through similar enterprises into cross-national functional patterns.

Carter's Trilateralism, however, was only one aspect of a commitment to functionalist principles that had informed his political enthusiasms from the beginning of his career. In describing and explaining his political philosophy, Carter formulated principles virtually indistinguishable from those of Herbert Hoover—not the Hoover of the anti–New Deal rhetoric, but the voluntarist Hoover, the engineer-philosopher who would govern the nation through techniques of efficiency. Carter, like Hoover, had been trained as an engineer. He was graduated from the United States Naval Academy in 1946 and served until 1953 as an officer and engineer, much of that time on submarines, the last year in Admiral Rickover's atomic submarine program. He left the Navy to take over his family's peanut-farming business and ultimately to enter politics. As a politician, Carter continued to employ engineering concepts and an engineering vocabulary, including Hoover's watchwords—efficiency, function, and the elimination of waste.

In his book *Why Not the Best?*, presenting himself to the nation as a presidential candidate, Carter outlined the major issues facing the nation in two questions: "Can government be honest?"

and "Can government be competent?" His answer to the first, the general prescription of sunshine laws enforcing openness in all parts of the governmental process, reflected the localist heritage that was an important, although not dominant, element in his political makeup. The longer, fuller, more complex answer Carter offered to the second question made clear both his greater interest in it and the essentially functionalist basis of his political outlook. "Tight, businesslike management and planning techniques" were necessary to make the "mechanism of our government . . . understandable, efficient and economical," he said. He called for reorganized bureaucracies and for long-range planning based on all relevant data as the basis for policy making.[14]

The primary enemy of efficient organization in government, for Carter, was the historic enemy of the managerial constituency, the operation of politics as functionalist managers define the term—that is, the exertion of power to influence decision making in government for the benefit of a particular interest, without regard for the effect of such action on the community as a whole. Thus opposition to efficiency in government, Carter warned, can always be expected from "special interests, selfish bureaucrats, and hidebound elected officials," who seek to use public authority and wealth for private or special benefit. Carter's deep disgust for special-interest politics, recalling that of functionalist forebears like Charles Evans Hughes, appears in the language he used habitually to describe its practitioners. He pictures them repeatedly in speeches and essays as inhabiting "dark corners," coming out when no one is looking, scuttling back when "exposed to public scrutiny and debate."[15]

The final mark of functionalism in Carter's thought was his belief that efficiency, along with long-range planning, was *all* that was necessary to good government. Asked during the 1976 campaign how he would feel about members of his administration leaking to the press stories of internal policy differences, Carter discounted the likelihood of serious differences arising. Rather, he was confident that "my normal careful, methodical, scientific or planning approach to longer-range politics . . . would serve to remove those disharmonies long before they reach the stage of actual implementation."[16]

That is, he assumed that social programs scientifically planned to meet clear and proper public needs, in the full light of available knowledge, would not conflict with each other. Further, if their long-term purposes and logic were clearly explained, such programs would meet no serious opposition in his administration or in the nation, only the opposition of special interests seeking to preserve special benefits. Thus the combination of science in planning and science in administration, if allowed to operate uncorrupted by low politics, would serve the society as agents of deliverance.

Carter's functionalism, once he assumed the presidential office, took the form in domestic affairs of resistance to additional interventions by the federal government in areas of social trouble —such as inadequate welfare for the unemployed and the unemployable; inadequate health care, housing, and education for the poor; or discrimination against racial minorities and women. Carter did not reject governmental responsibility in such areas, but his enthusiasms and priorities did not run to direct use of government funds as the balancing factor for groups without power to help themselves. Rather, his first response to social needs was to seek the streamlining of government programs already in place in the interests of efficiency and then to rely on long-range structural reform—in taxation, for example, and energy—to render the private sector more open to disadvantaged groups and generally more equitable.

These proposals, however, had little legislative success. Carter's distaste for politics and special interest—rooted in his functionalism—translated into suspicion and misunderstanding of Congress, and these attitudes translated quickly into chronic lack of legislative cooperation, from Democrats, who held a majority in both houses, as well as Republicans. As a result, his major programs—government reorganization, tax reform, and energy development—were amended out of recognition before emerging from Congress.[17]

The shaping influence of functionalist ideas on the foreign policy of the Carter administration was, if anything, greater than it was on domestic policy, and ultimately just as unpersuasive to Congress and the general public. Carter's commitment to functionalism, although it was not named as such, was clear in the numbers of like-minded Trilateral Commission members he appointed to positions important to foreign policy making, both political and economic. The Trilateralists included Cyrus Vance, Secretary of State; Harold Brown, Secretary of Defense; Michael Blumenthal, Secretary of the Treasury; Richard Cooper, Under Secretary of State for Economic Affairs; Fred Bergsten, Assistant Secretary of the Treasury for International Economic Affairs; Samuel Huntington, Assistant Secretary of Defense for International Security Affairs; Richard Holbrooke, Assistant Secretary of State for East Asia and Pacific Affairs; Zbigniew Brzezinski, head of the National Security Council; Paul Warnke, Chief Arms Limitation Negotiator and Director of the Arms Control and Disarmament Agency; and also Carter's Vice-President, Walter Mondale.

The major foreign policy efforts of the Carter administration, at least until its involuntary preoccupation with American embassy officials and others taken hostage in Iran during Carter's last year in office, were firmly Trilateral in their direction. Some were efforts to reduce directly the element of political or military power in various sets of international relations. These included the withdrawal of American troops from Korea, begun in 1977, and the 1978 Camp David negotiations with Egypt and Israel, resulting in a treaty that normalized relations between the two former enemies. Other initiatives—notably the ratification in 1978 of the Panama Canal Treaties—aimed to place the relations of the United States with small neighboring countries on functionalist grounds of common interest rather than American hegemony. And in foreign economic policy, the Carter administration made strenuous efforts to reduce trade barriers and increase American contributions to multilateral development agencies and banks.

The long-standing functionalist commitment to arms control was expressed energetically in a number of policies: a 1977 initiative that would have greatly broadened the scope of arms limitation negotiations between the United States and the Soviet Union, and when that failed, the continued negotiation and final signing (but not ratification) of the second Strategic Arms Limitation Treaty (SALT II) in 1979; the imposition in the 1978 Nuclear Nonproliferation Act of tighter safeguards on uses of exported nuclear materials; attempts (not finally successful) to limit international traffic in conventional arms through ceilings on United States exports and negotiations for cooperative international limits; and early attempts (also finally unsuccessful) to reduce the level of American defense expenditures generally.

The functionalist character of the Carter foreign policy appeared also in the administration's habitual reliance on diplomacy as opposed to force or threats of force in response to issues demanding immediate attention as they arose. Confronting the problems of Soviet aid and protection for Ethiopia, the buildup of Cuban troops in Angola, and Marxist influence in Rhodesian and Namibian nationalist movements, the Carter government did not impose punitive measures on the Soviet Union or throw American weight into the African conflicts on the anti-Soviet side. Rather, as Secretary of State Vance told the House International Affairs Committee, the administration increased economic aid to Africa while warning the Soviet Union of American concern about its activities. It also discussed this concern with European allies as well as Arab, African, and other non-aligned nations, and generally chose to "rely on our long-term strengths in Africa developed over the years of trade, aid, investment and cultural exchange." All of these relations, Vance said, "bind us to Africa in enduring and mutually beneficial ways."[18]

But for all the internal clarity and coherence of the Carter administration policies, and the alternative they offered to the majoritarianism of the 1960s, Carter was not a popular President. Indeed, by the end of his term in office, he had offended, or seriously confused, all three major constituencies—which meant he entered the election of 1980 with no firm political base, except the presidency itself. In part, Carter suffered this unhappy fate— and ultimately electoral defeat—due to deficiencies in political skill. But essentially his difficulties were the inevitable consequence of the anomalous political position he had occupied from the beginning. He was a functionalist in a party historically composed of majoritarians and localists. He had been elected because localists and some majoritarians were seeking an alternative to the course set by Presidents Kennedy and Johnson, but neither group was quite prepared to find in a Democratic President the ideological heir of Herbert Hoover.

The most distressed constituency, not surprisingly, was that part of the Democratic Party still committed to some form of majoritarianism, and opposition from this group mounted as its members came to understand the depth of Carter's contrary convictions. Joseph Califano, Carter's Secretary of Health, Education, and Welfare, resigned in the face of the President's insistence on welfare reform based on efficiency, not increased expense. George Meany, president of the AFL-CIO, declared to the union's biennial convention in 1977 that Carter was no better for labor than the Republicans had been. But the most dramatic expression of differences between the President and majoritarian Democrats emerged in the 1980 primary election campaigns. There, Senator Edward Kennedy of Massachusetts carried on a months-long denunciation of the President's policies in an attempt to displace Carter as the presidential nominee, in the name of the Democratic tradition John Kennedy had represented.[19]

Localists, on the other hand, appreciated Carter's domestic approach, but were outraged by his foreign policy. Carter, as a functionalist, wholeheartedly abjured the localist concept of a malevolent enemy loose in the world and, moreover, embraced international connections (localists would say entanglements), creating political and economic obligations far beyond the grasp and control of ordinary citizens. For localists, this approach smacked, as always, of a behind-the-scenes sellout of the nation and its people by powerful business interests. This sentiment poured out in the bitter Senate fight in 1978 over the ratification of the Panama Canal Treaties. The purpose of the treaties was to set up cooperative arrangements leading to the eventual transfer of sovereignty in the Canal Zone from the United States to Panama—in localist terms, another "giveaway" of American resources.

Localist resistance to the treaties was led by Jesse Helms, Republican senator from North Carolina. "Those of us who cannot fathom any legitimate reasons for disposing of the Canal Zone and the Panama Canal are asking," Helms declared, "what is the quid pro quo?" And there being no legitimate reason, recognizable to localists, why the United States should engage in transfers of power and property to another country, Helms suggested that there must be illegitimate ones. It is to the interest of the financial world, he said, to have the United States taxpayers bail out Panama as they have other Third World countries who cannot make good on their debts, and the entire treaty scheme, in Helms's view, was being "orchestrated . . . by financial institutions and multinational corporations." It was being foisted on the American people by the enormous conglomerate of power operating through the federal executive—"the President of the United States, the entire foreign policy apparatus, the power structure of academics, businessmen, and bankers, and the most powerful voices of the media."[20]

Sixty-eight senators ultimately voted to approve the treaties, a margin of only one vote beyond the two-thirds necessary for ratification. Of the 32 opposed, 25 were from the localist heartland, and 3 more from the Midwest, making the opposition nearly 90 percent localist or semi-localist. The vote was a signal of localist defection that was to cost Carter dearly in the 1980 election—in which he lost the entire South except for his native Georgia.

The final wound to Carter's presidency, however, was the no-win political situation caused by the taking of American diplomatic hostages in Iran in November 1979. The first response of the Carter strategists was to rely as usual on quiet negotiations. This tactic provoked denunciatory attack from those—localists primarily—who were scornful of withholding forceful pressure in dealing with an enemy. Then, with the hostages still in captivity six months after the event, and the 1980 election campaign underway, the administration turned to military measures—an air rescue mission—in an attempt to end the crisis.

The mission did not succeed in reaching the hostages and therefore did not mute the demands for a further use of force. But it did cause an erosion of support for Carter within the one group—the functionalist constituency—still generally supportive of his policies. Most notably, the rescue mission produced the resignation of Secretary of State Cyrus Vance, who stated publicly, if decorously, that he was resigning in protest against the Carter decision to deal with a tense international conflict through force. For Vance, this was too serious a reversal of the functionalist vision of deliverance that he shared with Carter but that Carter, under political pressure, had been forced to modify.

Several weeks after his resignation, Vance reiterated, in a commencement address at Harvard University, the functionalist principles from which he would not depart. He set out in careful detail the vast array of conflicting interests around the world and insisted that the cause of trouble and violence confronting the United States lay in the fact that those conflicts existed. They could not be wished away or forced away, he said. But he concluded, in the functionalist heart of his message, that these troubles, immense as they were, could be overcome. Complexity could be sorted out and conflict resolved if nations would only rely on peaceful negotiations as the medium of settlement—that is, if authority to resolve conflict were vested in the patient, skilled, professional negotiator. If the nation followed this prescription, Vance said, "there need be no insurmountable barriers to our progress" and any failure would be "a failure not of opportunity but of seeing opportunity; a failure not of resources but of the wisdom to use them; a failure not of intellect but of understanding and of will."[21]

This message—the advocacy of professionalism in policy making, the reliance on reason to produce solutions for the problems of the day—was applauded at Harvard. But Carter's attempts to follow it in both its foreign and domestic applications had encountered in other constituencies equally strong—and opposing—convictions. And at the end of a single term, Carter was defeated for reelection by the Republican Ronald Reagan.

Reagan's victory expressed the long-gathering localist revolt against both majoritarians and functionalists, and specifically the gathering of localist dissenters within the Republican Party. Southern defections from the Democratic Party in presidential elections since 1964 had taught Republicans that the South was a winnable stake, with the right Republican. And the right Republican had to be someone more appealing to localist interests than whatever Democrat was running.

Choosing a candidate in 1980 in the light of this experience, Republicans gave heavy weight to southern preferences and produced in Ronald Reagan a candidate whose call for a return of power to ordinary citizens and local governments made him strongly appealing to rural and small-town constituencies. This put Reagan in a position to capture the localist West, Southwest, and South. In addition, as governor of California, he had staked out ground which localists and the traditional managerial wing of the Republican Party could occupy jointly, the general ground of freedom from governmental interventionism. Thus he was not so completely identified with rural interests as to preclude functionalist Republican support as well.

As it happened, in the surprising returns of 1980, Reagan swept most of the country, taking not only the South (with the exception of Carter's Georgia) but also the traditionally Democratic states of the North and Northeast, as disaffected Democrats voted Republican in those areas. In spite of Reagan's country-wide success, however, the localist base of his strength is clear in the margins by which he won in various regions. In the entire North and Northeast, the margins were close, and in most states, the votes of other anti-Reagan candidates, if added to Carter's, would have tipped the vote the other way. In the localist West and Southwest and in three midwestern states (Indiana, Iowa, and Kansas), the returns were heavily pro-Reagan. In the South, except for Virginia, the Reagan majorities were small, but, again, his opponent was a Southerner, so that even close votes stand as strong evidence of enthusiasm for Reagan in that historically localist area.

The same pattern of strong localist support for Reagan appears in his 1984 reelection as well. Although he won by a much larger margin across the country than in 1980, his margin was substantially larger in localist territories than elsewhere—averaging about 64 percent in the South, Southwest, and West taken together, and about 58 percent in the other regions combined. At the extremes, it was over 70 percent in Wyoming, Utah, and Idaho, and under 55 percent in Massachusetts, New York, Pennsylvania, and Rhode Island.

Reagan was in some ways an unlikely carrier of the localist

message. Although born and brought up in a small midwestern town in the early decades of the century, he left that territory for the city to become first a sports announcer on radio in Des Moines, Iowa, and then a movie actor in Hollywood. Furthermore, in his early years, he considered himself a Roosevelt Democrat, applauding the labor legislation of the New Deal as well as its localist agenda. He first became deeply involved in politics as president of the Screen Actors' Guild in the late 1940s, a time when the Guild and other movie industry unions were riven by conflicts among conservatives, liberals, and communists over organizing rights. It was a time when controversy within the industry was complicated and heightened by congressional investigations of communist influence in movie making generally.

Reagan emerged from this contention, by his own account, with a changed set of political convictions. Central among them was a perception of communism in the United States as a serious threat to individual freedom and the certainty that extensions of federal government authority also threatened freedom by reducing the area of individual and local community choice. His career shifted in the 1950s to public relations work with the General Electric Corporation, but it was public relations with a political message—the message of freedom from governmental restraints, for the individual and for the economy.[22]

In the 1960s, Reagan turned to politics in his own right and was elected governor of California in 1966 and 1970, bearing the same message he had been preaching for a decade in the business world, which was a call for a return of authority to the common people, to limited government, and to local government. His program, although developed in the service of one of the nation's largest corporations, was unambiguously localist in its terms. It stressed the value of free enterprise—the common ground of localists and managers—but its most insistent theme was opposition to the idea that "a few men in Washington know better than we do what is good for us and know better than we do how to spend our money."

In his inaugural message as governor in 1967, he said that for years "you and I have been shushed like children and told there are not simple answers to complex problems which are beyond our comprehension." But, he insisted, the answers *are* simple. Government cannot provide everything everyone wants and it must cut spending back to the level of income. The implication is that it does not take experts to do that. Similarly, in his speech accepting the Republican nomination for President in July 1980, he said, "We are going to put an end to the money merry-go-round where our money becomes Washington's money, to be spent by the states and cities only if they spend it exactly the way the Federal bureaucrats tell them to." And in his January 1981 inaugural address, he declared, "It is my intention to curb the size and influence of the Federal establishment and to demand recognition of the distinction between the powers granted to the Federal Government and those reserved to the states or to the people. All of us . . . need to be reminded that the Federal Government did not create the states; the states created the Federal Government."[23]

Several years later, Reagan cast the same issue in the enduring terms of the myth of deliverance. The Great Society programs, he said, were an "abuse of power," comparable to the excesses of George III in the taxes and regulations he imposed on the American colonists before they rebelled in 1776. The excesses of the 1960s, Reagan went on, were "subtler" than those of the British Crown, but still they were interventions of government "where it is neither competent, nor needed, nor wanted by the mass of Americans."[24]

Once in office Reagan acted quickly to translate his ideological convictions into national policy. In June 1981, he won from Congress a budget for the following year with drastic reductions in the scale of established government programs, including those for social security, welfare, medical aid, veterans' benefits, and education—programs, in the view of the Reagan people, that many Americans had come to regard, wrongly, as "entitlements." Reagan also won a substantial tax cut, which he regarded as the most direct possible technique for transferring power from the government to the people.

But the greatest enthusiasm of the Reagan administration, beyond reduced spending, was for a long-range effort called "the new federalism." In the face of some alarm on the part of state governors, including Republicans, Reagan launched a program in his 1982 State of the Union message for solving the problem of unbalanced federal-state authority "with a single, bold stroke" by transferring $47 billion in federal programs to the states. It was Reagan's ultimate prescription for deliverance from the primary domestic evil of the 1980s as he saw it—the "maze" or "jungle" of federal programs so overgrown and tangled that they were out of control, stifling the American economy, and worse, the spirit of the American people.

The most fervent backers of Reagan's dismantling of federal responsibilities were, not surprisingly, political leaders from the localist regions of the nation, people regarded before Reagan's victory as peripheral figures in Washington, eccentrics endlessly insisting on what had seemed an outgrown style of politics—in the Senate, Jesse Helms of North Carolina, Paul Laxalt of Nevada, Orrin Hatch and Jake Garn of Utah, Malcolm Wallop of Wyoming, and the elder statesmen of the group, Barry Goldwater of Arizona and Strom Thurmond of South Carolina. And each of Reagan's programs that passed Congress did so with a margin of Democratic votes from localist regions added to a complement of loyal Republicans.

For example, Reagan's program passed an early Senate test, a May 1981 vote to cut cost-of-living increases for social security and other retirement benefits, by a margin of 49–42, a victory possible only because Senate Republicans were joined in favor of the measure by 6 Democrats, 5 of whom were from localist regions. A month later, in the nominally Democratic House of Representatives, a key vote allowed the President's budget to go through as a package, so that his spending reductions could not be voted on program by program with a greater chance of their being defeated or changed. The winning margin of 217–210 was provided by 29 Democrats voting with Republicans, and 26 of the 29 pro-Reagan Democrats were from the localist heartland —15 from the South, 10 from the Southwest, 1 from the West.

A Senate vote in 1982 on an anti-busing bill provided an even more striking measure of localist sentiment behind the Reagan policies in that there was less than usual voting by party. The bill, restricting the jurisdiction of federal courts over public school integration programs, passed the Senate 57–37, with 36 of the 57 winning votes from localist territory—16 Democrats and 20 Republicans, 15 from the South, 21 from the West and Southwest.

As was the case with domestic policy, the large outlines of Reagan's foreign policy followed predominantly localist principles, most importantly in the conception of the enemy underlying his administration's approach to world affairs. Cyrus Vance and the other functionalists of the Carter administration had identified such forces as competition for scarce resources or imbalances of power between the industrialized and developing worlds as the causes of world conflict, the enemies or evils that must be controlled to achieve world order. And they had pressed, as the proper mechanism of control, broad multilateral agreements delegating the management of such problems to professionals. But the localists came into office with a different view. They saw economic and political problems in the world arena as matters that normally work themselves out through relatively simple processes that do not need expert management.

Indeed, localists cannot admit the necessity for the professional management of world problems without threatening their belief in deliverance through the devolution of authority, real authority, to the grass-roots level of the society. That is, to protect the claims of popular sovereignty, localists must maintain that there is no legitimate business or political judgment that ordinary sensible people cannot handle. They must dismiss the significance or even the reality of economic, social, or technological complications beyond the competence of people in local communities to understand and control.

Thus, in the localist world view, if transactions involving scarce resources or commodity trading with the Third World are *not* proceeding in a straightforward way, if instead they are surrounded by conflict and violence threatening world peace, it is not for lack of proper management, but because some force is deliberately causing trouble. That is, the localist enemy in world affairs is not some amorphous environmental force, but a deliberate wrongdoer. And with the election of Reagan to the presidency, this conviction—that the intentional, wrongful search for power and plunder is the *primary* cause of conflict in the world —was elevated to the basis for national policy. Specifically, national policy began to be shaped on the premise that all serious trouble in the world was the result of deliberate wrongdoing by the Soviet Union.

Reagan forecast the shift to a localist foreign policy in his speech accepting the presidential nomination in July 1980. His remarks on international affairs in that speech dealt exclusively with the theme of ill will or malevolent intent in enemies abroad. He made several specific references to the Soviet Union as a threat to American interests and then unspecified references to a "dictatorial foreign power," "adversaries large and small [that] . . . seek to confound our resolve," "a hostile foreign power," "tyrants," "those who would wish us ill," and "those who would destroy freedom." At no point in the address did he refer to threats stemming from large amorphous conditions or conflicts in interest. As President, Reagan reinforced this conception of the enemy as a deliberate wrongdoer in a major speech depicting Soviet leaders as "the focus of evil in the modern world" and their policies as "the aggressive impulses of an evil empire."[25]

Reagan's emphasis on evil or malevolence necessarily placed responsibility for trouble in the world on national leaders personally—a localist habit going back to William Jennings Bryan and his accusations against "ambitious monarchs" and "professional man-killers" as the forces behind war, as opposed to ordinary, peace-loving citizens. Reagan developed this idea explicitly in a homely parable about the likely conversation that would occur if two ordinary couples—"Ivan and Anya and Jim and Sally"— were to meet without a language barrier. They would probably talk about their children, he said, and their work and bills and hobbies. The moral of the story was that "people don't make wars." Their governments do. "If the Soviet Government wants peace," Reagan said, "then there will be peace." The implication was, of course, that all that stood in the way of peace was the unpeaceful intent of the Soviet leaders.[26]

Another enduring localist theme carried over into Reagan's approach to foreign policy was the explanation of conflict, where no clear-cut enemy appeared on the scene, in terms of conspiracy, of hidden or disguised enemies. Thus, for Reagan's policy makers, when violence erupted in Central America or the Middle East in the absence of a Soviet presence, the explanation was subversion—trouble caused long-distance, directed and financed by the Soviet Union. Of course, majoritarians and functionalists had accepted a theory of subversion also in the 1960s. But the experience of Vietnam had convinced many in these constituencies that contentions in poor countries were rooted primarily in poverty itself and the conflicts it produces—conflicts that the Soviet Union might seek to influence but could rarely cause by itself. The localists, however, continued to see violence in which local communist forces were involved as produced mainly by Soviet direction, even if carried out, as Reagan said, by "the use of surrogate forces."[27]

And Reagan made it clear that in talking about subversion he meant literal conspiratorial deceit. For example, he said that when Nicaraguan communist forces—the Sandinistas—failed in their first attempt to unseat the long-established Somoza government, they were addressed by the Cuban communist leader, Fidel Castro, and instructed in the fine points of international deception. "He told them . . . to form a broad alliance with the genuinely democratic opposition to the Somoza regime," Reagan said. "Castro explained this would deceive Western public opinion, confuse potential critics and make it difficult for Western democracies to oppose the Nicaraguan revolution." More generally, Reagan attributed insurgencies throughout Central America to "Cuban and Nicaraguan aggression aided and abetted by the Soviet Union."[28]

The final target of Soviet aggression, in the localist view, is the United States itself. And holding this sense of literal threat to American borders, localists in office focused much of their concern on communist movements in Central America. "It is so close," Reagan said. "San Salvador is closer to Houston than Houston is to Washington, D.C." Therefore, he went on, communist subversion in Central America "poses the threat that 100 million people from Panama to the open border in our south could come under the control of pro-Soviet regimes." Again, the most threatening pro-Soviet regime in the region was Cuba, which Reagan likened to "a roving wolf " that "looks to peace-loving neighbors with hungry eyes and sharp teeth."²⁹

Conceiving of the major problem the nation faced in international relations as a deliberate campaign of worldwide aggression by Soviet leaders and their proxies in other communist nations, the Reagan administration designed a foreign policy based primarily on military force. The overall strategy was to build up American military strength, conventional and nuclear—to seal up what Reagan in his first term called a "window of vulnerability" in American defense. In his second term, he extended into space the concept of sealing up porous defenses, proposing to develop a space-based missile system (popularly called Star Wars) that would serve as "a security shield that will destroy nuclear missiles before they reach their target."³⁰

Responses to specific problems as they arose were also primarily military, with the problems receiving the most acute attention being those in the Caribbean and Central American regions that were, as Reagan said, so close to home. Just weeks after taking office in 1981, Reagan's first Secretary of State, General Alexander Haig, told the House Foreign Affairs Committee that a strategy of "international terrorism" sponsored by the Soviet Union included a "hit list" for Central America.³¹ And thereafter the administration began to request increased military aid for governments facing dissident opposition and to increase the size and activity of the Southern Command, the American military forces organized to operate in the southern regions of the hemisphere. In October 1983, an American force conducted a surprise invasion of Grenada, a small island nation in a state of governmental upheaval. The administration first explained its purpose as the rescue of American citizens, mainly medical students, in Grenada. But on October 28, Reagan stated that the deeper danger had been an imminent occupation of the island by Cuba. Grenada was not the "friendly island paradise" it seemed, Reagan said. Rather, it was "a Soviet-Cuban colony being readied as a major military bastion to export terror and undermine democracy," and the United States "got there just in time."³²

In the same period, the Reagan administration undertook also to aid insurgent forces seeking to overthrow the Sandinista government of Nicaragua—a government characterized by Reagan as "Cuba's Cuba," a sub-proxy of the Soviet Union. Such aid included, in 1984, participation by the Central Intelligence Agency in the mining of Nicaraguan harbors in an attempt to prevent Soviet supplies from reaching the Nicaraguan government. This was a tactic American military leaders, joined by localist politicians, had repeatedly urged during the Vietnam War. They were frustrated at that time by majoritarian leaders who did not think, as localists did, that the war effort would be substantially affected by blocking Soviet supplies, since majoritarians did not think, as localists did, that the primary motive and energy for the effort was coming from the Soviet Union. Under Reagan, in Nicaragua, the localist theory and strategy prevailed and the mines were laid.[33]

Localist beliefs prevailed also in the Reagan administration's response to a suit filed by Nicaragua in the International Court of Justice, a suit claiming that the United States was violating the United Nations Charter by using force, including the mining of harbors, in an attempt to overthrow the Nicaraguan government. Anticipating the suit, the United States announced on April 8, 1984, that it would not submit to the World Court's jurisdiction on disputes involving Central America for the following two years. Historically, of course, localists back to William Borah had resisted submitting questions of national policy to international court jurisdiction at all.

Reagan's approach to world issues, then, represented a clear ideological shift from the approach through cooperation and negotiation that had been practiced by the Carter administration. Like Carter, however, Reagan faced difficulties in pursuing the policies he favored due to ideological differences within the coalition supporting his presidency. Localists in general applauded his tough stance toward the Soviet Union and his call for building military strength, but the functionalist component of his administration demurred.

By long tradition, functionalists do not share the localist faith in the primacy of military solutions, but do place faith in a strong economy. When Reagan's defense budgets raised already phenomenal national deficits to new heights, thus keeping interest rates high and the dollar overvalued in international markets, voices within the managerial world began to express concern. In April 1983, the presidents or chief executives of over 360 major corporations, banks, and professional firms, as well as 68 former government officials, sponsored a two-page advertisement in *The New York Times* urging cuts in Reagan's budget proposal for the following year, but most pointedly in his defense budget. And the same group made the same appeal in the following year as well. The language of the managers was conciliatory, but their message implicitly challenged the basic premise of Reagan's foreign policy—its conception of the enemy as primarily a military aggressor requiring primarily a military response. For functionalists, high interest rates disrupting investment and international trade were an enemy at least as serious as the military machinations or intentions of the Soviet Union.[34]

Several years of governing had thus forced the profound differences between localists and functionalists to the surface and threatened the continuity and coherence of Reagan's localism as the prevailing guideline for policy. But the ultimate weakness of Reagan's policies—and Carter's—went beyond the inconsistencies imposed by differences among the policy shapers. In both domestic and foreign realms, the alternatives to majoritarianism offered first by Carter's functionalists and then by Reagan's localists suffered from the same flaw—the flaw of mythic belief—that ran through the policies each sought to displace.

Majoritarians, attributing inequities in American society to excessively concentrated economic power, had attempted to end inequity by using the government to shift power. They had sought through rules and taxes and appropriations to reduce corporate power and enhance that of wage earners and people working in local economies—to achieve deliverance through power balancing. And they had sought to solve international problems by replicating this same system abroad. That is, assuming that conflicts and violence in other countries were also caused by excessive power concentrations—economic and political— they sought to fight such concentrations by promoting the same power-balancing techniques in other countries that they relied on at home. In the Third World, this had meant promoting political change and engaging deeply—in Vietnam, violently—in the process of change because the new nations did not have national political structures capable of restraining excessive and oppressive power.

The majoritarians of the 1960s did not achieve their goals, in spite of massive governmental expenditures at home and abroad, because the balance they sought—the point of balance at which excessive power is under control, allowing all groups to receive fair returns—is not possible to achieve. There is no such point of balance. The majoritarians had held out high hopes, asked for considerable sacrifice, then could not deliver. But neither could functionalists or localists. Subscribers themselves to the myth of deliverance, they attacked majoritarianism, not for its false premise, but for its faulty techniques. The majoritarians were wrong, each of these groups insisted, not for promising deliverance, but for relying on the government to achieve it. Both promised deliverance themselves by *reducing* the power and significance of the national government at home and using it differently abroad.

On economic questions at home, functionalists and localists alike saw governmental intervention as injuring a system that would work fairly for all if allowed to work according to its own logic. For functionalists, that logic was complicated and could be released only by careful, expert management, the construction of complicated corporate systems in the private sector, with supplementary regulation and monitoring by experts in government. Thus the Carter administration came into office promising deliverance by taking politics—in the form of Great Society programs —out of the economy and using government only to enhance the ultimate goal of efficiency in the working of the economy—on the theory that an efficient economy would benefit all.

But even if Carter had managed to construct more solid support for his programs than he did, his approach would not have achieved the stability and equity that was its purpose. Enthroning efficiency would not have touched the problems of regional unemployment and poverty caused by the decline of old industries or of the widening gap in income and privilege between the highly educated or highly skilled and all others. In an increasingly technological economy, following principles of functional efficiency would be good for the mechanized production of goods, and good for those controlling the productive systems and working in them, but not good for those—the unskilled or the irrelevantly skilled—not needed in the new economic arenas. And a governing system organized to promote economic efficiency would have no means—except to promote economic growth through more efficiency—to deal with groups and regions left behind by economic change. That is, a functionalist governing system, by definition cut off from the press of politics to the maximum degree, would have no means of measuring and addressing the needs of those outside the realm of efficiency. Finally, the functionalist theory of deliverance is false because no economic principles—even complicated ones—will automatically or naturally create work and distribute income fairly for all.

Reagan's system of automaticity—the simple return to a free market—was put into effect to a greater degree than Carter's and its failings as an agency for fairness were more clearly manifested. Capital managers, with resources freed by tax cuts and the removal of regulations, turned heavily to financial speculation and corporate merger rather than productive investment. And they turned as well to increased benefits for themselves—increases in their own incomes and in the level of corporate perquisites, from elaborate dining rooms and steam rooms to golf courses, company jets, and mountain hideaways. The menial-service sector grew to serve the richer rich, thus increasing the rate of employment, but increasing also the disparity of income and opportunity between rich and poor. Further, to the extent that the industrial sector increased, it was due largely to defense spending financed by federal deficits that constantly threatened the stability of capital markets.

An old-fashioned free market in the economic conditions of the 1980s could by no means produce fairness for all groups bargaining within it, but Reagan's policies, based on this premise, were accepted and tried out of the insistent, enduring *belief* that deliverance must be possible, that finding it is simply a matter of finding the right rules.

In foreign affairs, Carter's functionalism, with its recognition, again, of complication and its reliance on techniques of long-range negotiation, produced an atmosphere of goodwill and, more tangibly and dramatically, such accomplishments as the signing of a peace treaty between Egypt and Israel. But the functionalist promise of deliverance from foreign conflict, in spite of vast trouble and complication abroad, in effect denies the weight of complication even while admitting it. It underplays the defiance of reason by groups in conflict and their propensity to violence. Carter's emphasis on reason—and successes with it—left the administration and public alike unprepared for dramatic reverses—such as the Soviet invasion of Afghanistan and the seizure by Iran of American diplomatic hostages. These events seemed like the failure of a system rather than expected difficulties, and Carter suffered a loss of public confidence in not having prevented or quickly resolved either situation. That is, the belief in deliverance, creating unreasonable expectations, undermines success by inducing an unpreparedness for failure.

Of all failings in policy produced by the belief in deliverance, however, none is so serious, so dangerous as the lack of realism and the militarism of localist foreign policy. But paradoxically, the problem with localist policy, for all its emphasis on military strategies, does not lie in unrealistic schemes of military conquest or domination. Localists are not interested in building an American empire abroad because they are not interested in reforming the world—or at least they do not think that the use of power abroad by the American national government can accomplish that result. Their own experience of localities under siege has undoubtedly heightened their sensitivities to the intransigence of localities anywhere when subjected to outside pressure for change.

What localists want, faced with an unfriendly power strong enough to harm the United States, is to build "a security shield," in Reagan's phrase, a defense system capable of withstanding any attack, capable of allowing the United States to conduct its own internal affairs free from outside pressures and threats. Within this protected arena—"the bubble under which our nation thrives," Barry Goldwater called it—localists hope to find the undesigned, unregulated, untaxed, locally organized society, the free society, of their constant vision.

But it is precisely this peaceful vision that *is* the problem. Believing that such detachment, such simplicity is possible to achieve, they attribute any frustration of it to the deliberate wrongdoing of an enemy. Their vision and belief force them to deny the complications abroad that functionalists see, to deny the existence of indigenous conflicts likely to explode into violence whether or not Soviet communists or their proxies are there to light the match. Misinterpreting such complication and insisting instead on Soviet malevolence as the only or primary cause of trouble, localists under Reagan designed policies that decreased the possibility of long-term assistance to troubled areas and increased Soviet-American enmity. On both counts the policies increased the terrible prospects of war. In the localist conception of American relations to the world lay the worst betrayal yet of American hopes and values by the myth of deliverance from evil.

CONCLUSION

Beyond the Myth of Deliverance

The American promise is in trouble. The approaches to governing that have been ceaselessly put forward by our three major interests—localists, functionalists, and majoritarians—are inadequate to advance, in difficult times, the promised goals of maximum freedom and maximum equality for all. The shared myth that the entire society can be delivered from evil, pain, and loss screens out too large a part of problems that are now more complicated than any in our history.

In its consequent failure to provide policies which assure Americans progress toward broad social justice, the American system of belief threatens to produce rising uncertainty, disillusion, and recrimination. In its quest for what is not possible, and never was, it puts in jeopardy the essential promise of the nation, which is the achievement, through self-government, of the degree of freedom and equality that *is* possible in a world of limits. If, then, something is badly wrong with the system as it is, the question arises: What part of it can be changed, or ought to be?

One serious obstacle to the development of coherent, sustained policies advancing our central goals is the chronic conflict among the three major interests in the society. As no one interest

273

is predominant, at least two of the three major groups must cooperate for any important domestic or foreign policy to go into effect; but their cooperation is hobbled by their different political beliefs, their different conceptions of deliverance. Once launched, policies tend to fall into incoherence, often inner contradiction, and to be pursued fitfully, over short terms.

Still, change for the better—escape from incoherence—cannot occur by excising the interests at play. The fact of interest and the importance of interest as a component of political behavior is immutable. This was Madison's wise and timeless message in his *Federalist* paper no. 10. Socialists and communists seek to overcome the division of society into separate interests by nationalizing one of them—the managerial interest—so that policies can reflect the choices of wage earners alone (a separate agrarian interest is a problem rarely acknowledged and never solved in socialist theory or practice). But in wholly communized systems, like the Soviet Union and China, nationalization simply transfers control of capital from the private sector to government, where, backed by the power of the police and the military, capital managers have the most complete control possible over the labor force.

In partly socialized and democratically run systems, managers of nationalized enterprises do not have the luxury of total control over labor and are in fact subject to wage earner pressure through the ballot box, but the goals of the two interests are still intrinsically opposed. Managers must, by their function, seek to maximize discretionary control over the capital in their charge and manage it as productively as possible. This means resisting worker control and the demands of workers for higher returns to them, whether the profit motive is in play or not.

Factions or interests are immutable because they are rooted in economic functions which may change in certain particulars as technologies change, but do not change in their basic purposes, in their different goals and needs, and in the fact of their competition with each other. Therefore, change in the working of American government may be possible, but it cannot occur through wishing away conflicts in the essential economic interests of different interest-based groups.

What can change, what must change if we are to escape from the cycle of self-delusion, misconception of problems, and seriously inadequate policies, is the way each group *understands* its purposes. And since the system of understanding held by each derives from the myth of deliverance, it is our attachment to the myth that must change. We must give it up. We have always asked how we can achieve a condition of mutual gain. We must now begin to ask how we can decently allocate the pain of unavoidable loss.

Of course, there never, in fact, has been a time marked by mutual gain, and all social policies have, in fact, been policies allocating loss, but we have not understood them that way. We have expected from them deliverance from loss and have been angry, confused, frustrated, and suspicious of betrayal when their promise has not been fulfilled. And with each major disappointment, we have gone off in search of different ways around the limits we refuse to recognize.

But the limits are real. We cannot all come out ahead. There is no natural complementarity of interests. In spite of President Reagan's inaugural promise in 1981, we could not emerge from his economic reform "with no one group singled out to pay a higher price." It is inevitable, no matter what the policy, that some will gain, others will clearly lose, not just in the short run but in the long run as well. And abroad, no policies of opposition to Soviet power will deliver the United States to a noncontentious world open to peaceful progress. Even if the Soviet threat were removed, profound contentions everywhere would remain. We would still face worldwide competition for resources and face also the conflicts inevitable in the process of industrial development in some parts of the world. And we cannot avoid the scarcely less painful adjustment in the already developed nations to the constraints, especially the limits on growth, inherent in post-industrial economies.

Both developing and developed countries, moreover, must begin to deal with the immense and unprecedented fact that the production of needed goods is becoming less and less dependent on human labor. That is, during the industrial development of England, Europe, and the United States, intensive labor was necessary, but now, the organization of new resources and products, as well as the continued production of the old, can take place, increasingly, through the contributions of the skilled middle and upper classes alone, and for their benefit alone. Thus new forms of production could leave millions of unskilled people in Third World countries where they have always been, outside the money economy, and the less skilled workers even in the most advanced industrial countries in poorer and poorer straits.

The conflicts inherent in such radical change—conflicts between industrial and non-industrial areas and among classes and groups of workers within industrial countries—cannot be resolved through the exercise of even the most determined goodwill and rationality. Or rather, they cannot be resolved without the acceptance of tangible loss on the part of some of the parties.

A politics based on the recognition of limits, the expectation of inevitable conflict in interests and inevitable loss, is not a happy prospect. It would mean that the largest political issues for the society would be deciding on priorities in both domestic and foreign policy—whose welfare, whose long-term interest, whose security is most in need of government protection—which in turn means recognizing the real loss implicit in each possible policy choice and then deciding where loss *will* fall, who must bear it.

A politics of loss allocation is especially difficult for a democracy because it means that the people ultimately must accept the pain of imposing loss on themselves. To do that, to use democratic processes to allocate loss, means that there must be some consensus among the people about whose claims are more compelling, whose are less. But how can there be such consensus if people are divided, as I argue they are, by undissolvable differences in economic interest? If people cannot believe in solutions that will produce gain for all interests, then they must accept the fact that some contending party—workers, managers, localists—must lose some of the battles some of the time in their continuing conflict. But if this is true, if all interests must face the continuing prospect of serious loss, what would prevent the nation's political life from degenerating into class war? How could we live in peace with each other without a reconciling myth?

I hope we can find ground for social peace in the commitment to the goals that underlie the myth of deliverance—the desire for liberty and the desire for equality and the belief in the rightness of these goals that all major groups in American political life have shared from the beginning. The myth has allowed us to believe that we could totally attain both goals, that the advancement of full individual liberty would not conflict with the advancement of full equal rights and opportunities, that we could all make our own choices without impinging on the choices and chances of others—as long as the proper safeguards were in place against abuses of power. Without a myth, we would have to maintain a commitment to liberty and equality knowing that they conflict—knowing that we cannot always exercise our liberty to avoid loss but must sometimes accept loss in the interest of others and in the interest of a decent future.

Such a commitment is necessarily extremely difficult. It raises, in fact, the problem that has always lurked at the heart of political systems founded on the value of individual liberty. This is the conflict between the fullest possible operation of individual will and the need for social rules curbing the choices of powerful groups so that the less powerful may also exercise free choice. For a society committed to liberty not to violate its own first principle, its members must willingly accept the need for restrictions that promote conditions of freedom for all.

But the problem, as the nation's founders knew, is to build a delicate balance of liberty and restriction on the imperfections of human nature. Human beings are not, by nature, wholly angelic or altruistic; rather, they are perpetually divided between concern for others and concern for self. Therefore, their capacity for sacrifice, for acceptance of loss, is not unlimited. But how much sacrifice free people will tolerate is a question so far without an answer. No one knows.

Historical experience surely suggests, however, that the degree to which people will accept responsibility for the welfare of others depends very much on whether they are convinced that their sacrifice is required and whether sacrifice seems fairly distributed and whether the result of sacrifice turns out to be what is promised or close to it. It is on this last point that the myth does us particular damage, because it promises deliverance but deliverance never occurs. That is, the myth has made it easy to ask all groups in the society to look beyond their own immediate self-interest in making decisions, because it has promised those who do a better result than they would achieve through selfish, shortsighted behavior. It has asked for small sacrifice always with the promise of larger gain.

But when the promise is not fulfilled for all parties, people have lost faith to the point that, as problems and losses have grown larger, faith in the system itself has been shaken. People in all three interests have come to see the government—the definer of needed sacrifice—as something wholly apart from them, not responsive to their will, operating in the interest of the officeholders themselves or of the powerful interests which, in various ways, can buy support for their needs. In this general view, government authority becomes something that has no moral claim on the individual, that is evaded where possible, used to promote self-interest where possible, obeyed only where necessary or convenient.

Public authority that asked more and promised less would stand a better chance of operating with the consent and support of the people. Asking more might mean higher taxes for more extensive social services, better public education, better public facilities, or more extensive controls on the choices—including the investment choices—of the largest corporations because of the breadth of their social impact. Beyond regulation and services, asking more might mean the assumption by government of responsibility for creating new forms of work. As computers and robots take over more and more of what has previously been human work, we could become a society made up of engineers and drones. In order to employ the non-engineers, we will have to tax robot-produced income and then decide what work needs doing and organize it.

Promising less would mean *not* promising a future of greater and greater individual choice, especially economic choice, not promising greater and greater equality occurring through some automatic, effortless progression. Both goals will require great effort to advance because steps toward one usually require compromise of the other—generally the restriction of liberty in the form of higher taxes to pay for programs designed to equalize opportunity for others. Given the natural inclination of people to avoid sacrifice, to maximize their own income and choices, steps toward broadened opportunity are hard to take. But commitment to liberty still requires that the society move toward equality only at the pace supported by its citizens. The alternative is to try to advance equality through non-democratic measures, to break through the selfishness of the privileged by compulsion, and the dangers here are proven. Governmental authority not subjected to democratic checks inevitably serves itself at the expense of its supposed goals.

Our political task, then, is to set social priorities and allocate losses democratically. But how? By what techniques? What is usable for a new politics of loss allocation out of the governing principles developed historically by majoritarians, functionalists, and localists?

In part, the principles of all three groups should be retained, because in part all three have rightly identified enemies to liberty and to equality. The localists are right that huge bureaucracies— private or public—become self-serving power structures and that in many instances people would be better served by smaller units —smaller corporations, smaller and more local governmental agencies. Functionalists are right that vastly complicated modern economies require organization through reason and through professionalism and that crude exertions of governmental power in intricate economic systems can cause unnecessary loss.

But both localist and functionalist approaches to governing are usable only in part. Localism does not sufficiently admit the facts, the size, the complexity of modern economic systems. Not everything can be run from the grass roots. Functionalism, on the other hand, fails as a total governing system because while recognizing the claims of complexity, it does not admit the claims of democracy. It relies, in effect, on elite rule. It has no place where the people generally can register their needs, or their values, where hard social choices must be made.

Of the three systems, majoritarianism comes the closest to what is needed for a democratic politics capable of allocating loss.

It is a governing system that accepts both modern complexity *and* democracy. Majoritarian programs have failed because their goals have been shaped too simplistically by the myth of deliverance. Unburdened by the myth, the majoritarian techniques of measuring national mandates through national election processes, of entrusting primary leadership to the President as a nationally elected official, offer—however crudely—a means of handling great complication democratically. A President can explain complication and the issues it produces and can choose among alternatives, again explaining why. And then a national electorate can approve or disapprove.

Ultimately, however, it is not political technique but political morality that will make the difference. Ultimately we must rely on what seems impossible—the willingness of people to move by means of majority decisions toward finally unreachable goals. We must hope to move toward the fuller realization of liberty and equality knowing that we cannot fully achieve both, but knowing also that there is nothing else, beyond survival, worth trying to achieve.

To give up a politics of deliverance, to accept a politics of allocating loss, is a bleak prospect. The future for political leaders who attempt to frame issues in these terms will be predictably hard, but the consequences of continuing to search for deliverance from pain, seeking enemies and answers in mythic terms, are fast becoming even worse. However bleak the new politics of reality may be, it is our only choice. We can, however, embrace the necessity and accept it, not as a sentence of doom, but as a chance to gain some measure of real choice over our fate—the next adventure for Americans as inheritors of a great promise.

Bibliographical Essay

The conflict between the goals of liberty and equality—between individual freedom and the need of the community to protect the freedom of all—is the central tension in American politics. In addressing this large problem, I have drawn from, and joined, a long historical dialogue. Listed here are books that have been especially suggestive to me as contributions to the dialogue, as it relates to twentieth-century issues.

Louis Hartz, *The Liberal Tradition in America* (New York: Harcourt, Brace & World, 1955), remains the classic work on the subject, both a historical and a critical inquiry into the weakness of national community values in the United States.

Writers in the early years of the century projected optimistic resolutions to the individualist/communitarian dilemma, from a variety of viewpoints. These include Herbert Croly, *The Promise of American Life* (New York: Macmillan, 1909) and *Progressive Democracy* (New York: Macmillan, 1914); John Dewey, *Liberalism and Social Action* (New York: Putnam's, 1935); Mary Parker Follett, *The New State: Group Organization the Solution of Popular Government* (New York: Longmans, Green, 1918); Herbert Hoover, *American Individualism* (Garden City, N.Y.: Doubleday, Page, 1923); Rexford Tugwell, *The Trend of Economics* (New York: F. S. Crofts, 1924) and *The Industrial Discipline* (New York: Columbia University Press, 1933); and Thorstein Veblen, *The Engineers and the Price System* (New York: B. W. Huebsch, 1921).

The literature of advocacy later in the century is more sober and complicated. The most optimistic theorists are the celebrators of a pluralist politics, those who believe that liberty and equality are both best advanced by the wide dispersal of power among competing groups—voluntary associations, lobbies, parties, corporations, federal, state, and local public authorities. See David Truman, *The Governmental Process* (New York: Knopf, 1951); Robert Dahl, *Modern Political Analysis* (Englewood Cliffs, N.J.: Prentice-Hall, 1963) and *After the Revolution? Authority in a Good Society* (New Haven, Yale University Press, 1970).

Those arguing that more centralized authority is necessary for any coherent governing principles to prevail include Reinhold Niebuhr, *The Irony of American History* (New York: Scribner's, 1952); Theodore Lowi, *The End of Liberalism* (New York: Norton, 1969); and Samuel P. Huntington, *American Politics: The Promise of Disharmony* (Cambridge, Mass.: Harvard University Press, 1981).

Several writers find, as I do, the conflicting claims of individual and community in the United States stalemated by systems of belief deeply rooted in American culture. See H. Mark Roelofs, *Ideology and Myth in American Politics: A Critique of a National Political Mind* (Boston: Little, Brown, 1976), and, more recently, Michel Crozier, *The Trouble with America* (Berkeley: University of California Press, 1984). For a discussion of American belief systems as tools of public manipulation by elites, see Thurman W. Arnold, *The Symbols of Government* (New Haven: Yale University Press, 1935) and *The Folklore of Capitalism* (New Haven: Yale University Press, 1937).

David M. Potter's deeply pessimistic *People of Plenty* (Chicago: University of Chicago Press, 1954) locates the dynamic center of American politics not in the promise of liberty and equality at all but in the promise of material abundance. Yet more radical critiques find liberty and equality as meaningful social goals defeated or seriously threatened by overweening corporate power. For example, C. Wright Mills, *The Power Elite* (New York: Oxford University Press, 1956); William Appleman Williams, *The Contours of American History* (Cleveland: World, 1961); and Gabriel Kolko, *Main Currents in Modern American History* (New York: Harper & Row, 1976).

Other critics of private power renew the communitarian argument with calls for democratically designed national controls on private managerial discretion. These include Grant McConnell, *Private Power and American Democracy* (New York: Knopf, 1966); Michael Harrington, *Toward a Democratic Left* (New York: Macmillan, 1968); John Kenneth Galbraith, *Economics and the Public Purpose* (Boston: Houghton Mifflin, 1973); and Michael Walzer, *Radical Principles: Reflections of an Unreconstructed Democrat* (New York: Basic Books, 1980) and *Spheres of Justice: A Defense of Pluralism and Equality* (New York: Basic Books, 1983).

Many historical works analyze the impact of these various schools of thought on American politics or trace the role of ideas and values in American politics generally. Ralph Henry Gabriel, *The Course of American Democratic Thought* (New York: Ronald Press, 1940), and Henry Steele Commager, *The*

American Mind: An Interpretation of American Thought and Character since the 1880's (New Haven: Yale University Press, 1950), are useful general histories of American political ideas. Michael Kammen, *People of Paradox: An Inquiry Concerning the Origins of American Civilization* (New York: Knopf, 1972), and John Diggins, *The Lost Soul of American Politics: Virtue, Self-Interest and the Foundations of Liberalism* (New York: Basic Books, 1984), focus explicitly on the ideological tensions of the early American experience with some analysis of their later manifestations. Richard Hofstadter, *Anti-Intellectualism in American Life* (New York: Knopf, 1970), portrays an American tradition of resistance to the power of ideas in American life, which is, in its political effect, a tradition of resistance to communitarian claims based on ideas.

A number of scholars examine the problematic character of the early twentieth-century reform movements, among them James Weinstein, *The Corporate Ideal in the Liberal State, 1900–1918* (Boston: Beacon Press, 1968); Robert H. Wiebe, *A Search for Order, 1877–1920* (New York: Hill and Wang, 1967); Charles Forcey, *The Crossroads of Liberalism* (New York: Oxford University Press, 1961); David W. Noble, *The Paradox of Progressive Thought* (Minneapolis: University of Minnesota Press, 1958); R. Alan Lawson, *The Failure of Independent Liberalism, 1930–1941* (New York: Putnam's, 1971); and Alan Brinkley, *Voices of Protest: Huey Long, Father Coughlin and the Great Depression* (New York: Knopf, 1982). Robert H. Wiebe, *The Segmented Society: An Introduction to the Meaning of America* (New York: Oxford University Press, 1975), and Helene S. Zahler, *The American Paradox* (New York: Dutton, 1970), are more general examinations of the unresolved tension at the heart of American politics. William Gerber, *American Liberalism: Laudable End, Controversial Means* (Boston: G. K. Hall, 1975), outlines the various schools of reform thought and supplies an extensive bibliography.

The following books are among the most interesting of those that trace the connections between American political values and American purposes and policies abroad. Ernest Lee Tuveson, *Redeemer Nation: The Idea of America's Millennial Role* (Chicago: University of Chicago Press, 1968), and Edward McNall Burns, *The American Idea of Mission: Concepts of National Purpose and Destiny* (New Brunswick, N.J.: Rutgers University Press, 1957), discuss the concept of the American mission to the world. Critics of a mission-based, or idealist, foreign policy include Charles A. Beard, *The Idea of National Interest* (New York: Macmillan, 1934); Robert Osgood, *Ideals and Self-Interest in America's Foreign Relations* (Chicago: University of Chicago Press, 1953); George F. Kennan, *Realities of American Foreign Policy* (New York: Norton, 1966), and Ernest May, *"Lessons" of the Past: The Use and Misuse of History in American Foreign Policy* (New York: Oxford University Press, 1973). The impress of domestic political culture on American perceptions of world problems is analyzed in Richard Barnet, *Roots of War: The Men and Institutions Behind United States Foreign Policy* (New York: Atheneum, 1972); Stanley Hoffmann, *Gulliver's Troubles or the Setting of American Foreign Policy* (New

York: McGraw-Hill, 1968); and, most recently, Robert Dallek, *The American Style of Foreign Policy: Cultural Politics and Foreign Affairs* (New York: Knopf, 1983).

The necessity for a new order of relations between domestic and foreign policy is addressed by a new generation of political economists concerned with protecting liberty and equality in a post-industrial economy. They advocate greater exertions of national public authority to ensure that nationally and internationally organized capital does not ignore or defeat the national social promise. See, for example, Barry Bluestone and Bennett Harrison, *The Deindustrialization of America: Plant Closings, Community Abandonment and the Dismantling of Basic Industry* (New York: Basic Books, 1982); Robert Kuttner, *The Economic Illusion: Prosperity and Social Justice* (Boston: Houghton Mifflin, 1983); Robert Reich, *The Next American Frontier* (New York: Times Books, 1983); and Lester Thurow, *The Zero-Sum Society: Distribution and the Possibilities for Economic Change* (New York: Basic Books, 1980). Thoughtful political commentaries on the same issues include James Chace, *Solvency, the Price of Survival: An Essay on American Foreign Policy* (New York: Random House, 1981); and Paul Tsongas, *The Road from Here: Liberalism and Realities in the 1980s* (New York: Knopf, 1981).

Notes

CHAPTER I

1. Mike Barnicle, Boston *Globe,* January 31, 1978, p. 15.
2. This breakdown of essential interests in the society parallels that used by Grant McConnell in *Private Power and American Democracy* (New York: Knopf, 1966) and R. Joseph Monsen and Mark W. Cannon in *The Makers of Public Policy: American Power Groups and Their Ideologies* (New York: McGraw-Hill, 1965).
3. For a similar definition and general discussion of political myth, see Henry Tudor, *Political Myth* (New York: Praeger, 1972).
4. "The Jefferson Bible," in *The Writings of Thomas Jefferson,* Albert Ellery Bergh, ed., Vol. XIX (Washington, D.C.: Thomas Jefferson Memorial Association, 1907), p. 15.

CHAPTER II

1. "Citizenship in a Republic," *The Commoner* 16 (July 1916), p. 5.
2. William Jennings Bryan, *The Commoner Condensed,* Vol. VII (Chicago: Henneberry Co., 1908), pp. 13–14.
3. Ibid., pp. 13–14, 44.
4. "An Industrial Peace Plan." *The Commoner* 20 (January 1920), p. 3.

5. Paolo Enrico Coletta, *William Jennings Bryan* (Lincoln: University of Nebraska Press, 1964–69), Vol. I, p. 388.

6. Included in Frederick W. Taylor, *Scientific Management* (New York: Harper & Bros., [1911] 1947).

7. Ibid., p. 30.

8. New York: The Engineering Magazine Co., 1917.

9. Charles Evans Hughes, *Addresses and Papers of Charles Evans Hughes, Governor of New York, 1906–1908* (New York: Putnam's, 1908), pp. 20–21.

10. Address, Carnegie Hall, July 31, 1916, *Addresses of Charles Evans Hughes, 1906–1916* (2nd rev. ed.; New York: Putnam's, 1916).

11. *The Autobiographical Notes of Charles Evans Hughes,* David J. Danelski and Joseph S. Tulchin, eds. (Cambridge, Mass.: Harvard University Press, 1973), pp. 134–35.

12. Address, Carnegie Hall, November 20, 1907, *Addresses and Papers of Charles Evans Hughes . . . 1906–1908,* p. 277.

13. "Hughes as Governor," *The Autobiographical Notes of Charles Evans Hughes,* pp. 344–47; see also Robert F. Wesser, *Charles Evans Hughes: Politics and Reform in New York, 1905–1910* (Ithaca, N.Y.: Cornell University Press, 1967).

14. Address, Federal Bar Association, Washington, D.C., February 12, 1931 (pamphlet), p. 5.

15. See Ruth L. Horowitz, *Political Ideologies of Organized Labor* (New Brunswick, N.J.: Transaction Books, 1978); Harold C. Livesay, *Samuel Gompers and Organized Labor in America* (Boston: Little, Brown, 1978); Louis L. Lorwin, *The American Federation of Labor: History, Policies and Prospects* (Washington, D.C.: Brookings Institution, 1933).

16. *Cabinet Government in the United States* (Stamford, Conn.: Overbrook Press, 1947); *Congressional Government: A Study in American Politics* (Gloucester, Mass.: Peter Smith, 1973).

17. August 7, 1912, in Woodrow Wilson, *The Crossroads of Freedom* (New Haven: Yale University Press, 1956), pp. 21, 22, 27, 30–31.

18. September 26, 1912, ibid., p. 280.

19. Commencement address, University of Tennessee, in Woodrow Wilson, *Leaders of Men,* T. H. Vail Motter, ed. (Princeton, N.J.: Princeton University Press, 1952), pp. 41–42, 50.

20. Labor Day speech, Buffalo, N.Y., September 2, 1912, *The Crossroads of Freedom,* p. 83.

21. Address, Sioux City, Iowa, September 17, 1912, ibid., p. 161.

22. Speech, New York Press Club, September 9, 1912, ibid., p. 130.

23. Address, Canton, Ohio, October 11, 1912, ibid., p. 420.

24. Pittsburgh, October 18, 1912, ibid., p. 455.

25. Arthur S. Link, *Wilson: The New Freedom* (Princeton, N.J.: Princeton University Press, 1956), p. 152.

26. Ibid., pp. 154–55, 173–75.

CHAPTER III

1. Letter to William Gibbs McAdoo, Secretary of the Treasury, November 17, 1914, in Woodrow Wilson, *The New Democracy: Presidential Messages, Addresses, and Other Papers (1913–1917)*, Ray Stannard Baker and William E. Dodd, eds., Vol. I (New York: Harper & Bros., 1926), p. 213.

2. Philadelphia, May 10, 1915, *The Papers of Woodrow Wilson*, Vol. XXXIII, Arthur S. Link, ed. (Princeton, N.J.: Princeton University Press, 1980), pp. 147–48. For further discussion of ethnic groups in American political life, see articles by Philip Gleason, Harold J. Abramson, William S. Bernard, Mona Harrington, Michael Walzer, and Edward R. Kantowicz in *The Harvard Encyclopedia of American Ethnic Groups*, Stephen Thernstrom, Ann Orlov, and Oscar Handlin, eds. (Cambridge, Mass.: Harvard University Press, 1980).

3. Address, Green Bay, Wisc., August 9, 1934, *The Public Papers and Addresses of Franklin D. Roosevelt*, Vol. III (New York: Random House, 1938), p. 370.

4. August 26, 1933, *The Public Papers and Addresses of Franklin D. Roosevelt*, Vol. II (New York: Random House, 1938), pp. 338, 340–42.

5. March 4, 1933, ibid., pp. 11, 14–15.

6. *Schechter v. U.S.*, 295 U.S. 495 (1935).

7. Address, New York City, April 25, 1936, *The Public Papers and Addresses of Franklin D. Roosevelt*, Vol. V (New York: Random House, 1938), pp. 177, 181.

8. Address, March 4, 1937, *The Public Papers and Addresses of Franklin D. Roosevelt*, Vol. VI (New York: Macmillan, 1941), pp. 113, 120; inaugural address, January 20, 1937, ibid., p. 2.

9. "Plan for Reorganization of the Judicial Branch of the Government," February 5, 1937, ibid., p. 55.

10. *NLRB v. Jones and Laughlin Steel Corp.*, 301 U.S. 1 (1937).

11. Marian C. McKenna, *Borah* (Ann Arbor: University of Michigan Press, 1961), Chapters 2 and 3.

12. Ibid., p. 49.

13. August 26, 1914, *Cong. Rec.* 51, Pt. 14 (63rd Cong., 2nd sess.), 14262.

14. Ibid.

15. August 4, 1914, *Cong. Rec.* 51, Pt. 13 (63rd Cong., 2nd sess.), 13233.

16. December 17, 1913, *Cong. Rec.* 51, Pt. 2 (63rd Cong., 2nd sess.), 1071.

17. June 7, 1933, *Cong. Rec.* 77, Pt. 5 (73rd Cong., 1st sess.), 5166–67.

18. June 13, 1933, *Cong. Rec.* 77, Pt. 6 (73rd Cong., 1st sess.), 5841–42.

19. July 29, 1937, *Cong. Rec.* 81, Pt. 7 (75th Cong., 1st sess.), 7794.

20. July 28, 1914, *Cong. Rec.* 51, Pt. 13 (63rd Cong., 2nd sess.), 12869.

21. January 7, 1938, *Cong. Rec.* 83, Pt. 1 (75th Cong., 3rd sess.), 141.
22. Leroy Ashby, *The Spearless Leader: Senator Borah and the Progressive Movement in the 1920's* (Urbana: University of Illinois Press, 1972), pp. 67–68.
23. See McKenna, *Borah,* pp. 116, 260, and Chapter 6 generally, and Walter Lippmann, *Men of Destiny* (New York: Macmillan, 1928), pp. 140–61.
24. For a sensitive discussion of Hoover's moral and political commitments, see Joan Hoff Wilson, *Herbert Hoover, Forgotten Progressive* (Boston: Little, Brown, 1975).
25. *Memoirs* (3 vols.; New York: Macmillan, 1951–52), Vol. I, p. 82.
26. Hoover was the first president of the American Engineering Council, founded to promote principles of scientific efficiency in the profession. See Samuel Haber, *Efficiency and Uplift: Scientific Management in the Progressive Era* (Chicago: University of Chicago Press, 1964), p. 48.
27. Quotations are all taken from one Hoover speech, "A Problem of Distribution," addressed to the National Distribution Conference, called by the United States Chamber of Commerce in Washington, D.C., January 14–15, 1925, and printed in a pamphlet, but the same analysis is found in addresses and articles by Hoover throughout his tenure as Secretary of Commerce and as President. It appears also in publications of the Department of Commerce during his secretaryship. See, for example, a pamphlet called *Elimination of Waste: Simplified Practice—What It Is and What It Offers* (Washington, D.C.: U.S. Government Printing Office, 1924), which contains instructions on how to set up studies of waste in particular industries in cooperation with the Department of Commerce. For further discussion of Hoover's theory and practice of voluntarism as the appropriate relation between government and business, see David Burner, *Herbert Hoover: A Public Life* (New York: Knopf, 1979), Chapter 9.
28. "A Problem of Distribution."
29. *The Challenge to Liberty* (New York: Scribner's, 1935), p. 131.
30. May 15, 1935, *Cong. Rec.* 79, Pt. 7 (74th Cong., 1st sess.), 7565, 7567, 7569, 7571, 7573.
31. For different appraisals of the NRA, see Hugh S. Johnson, *The Blue Eagle from Egg to Earth* (Garden City, N.Y.: Doubleday, Doran, 1935), and Leverett S. Lyon et al., *The National Recovery Administration: An Analysis and Appraisal* (Washington, D.C.: Brookings Institution, 1935).
32. Rexford Tugwell, *The Industrial Discipline* (New York: Columbia University Press, 1933), p. 223.
33. April 29, 1938, *The Public Papers and Addresses of Franklin D. Roosevelt,* Vol. VII (New York: Macmillan, 1941), pp. 305, 314.
34. John Kenneth Galbraith, *American Capitalism: The Concept of Countervailing Power* (Boston: Houghton Mifflin, 1952), p. 60.

CHAPTER IV

1. Annual message to Congress, December 4, 1917, *The Papers of Woodrow Wilson,* Vol. XLV, Arthur S. Link, ed. (Princeton, N.J.: Princeton University Press, 1984), pp. 194, 195.
2. Green H. Hackworth, ed., *Digest of International Law,* Vol VI (Washington, D.C.: U.S. Government Printing Office, 1943), p. 5.
3. Paolo Enrico Coletta, *William Jennings Bryan* (Lincoln: University of Nebraska Press, 1964–69), Vol. II, p. 252.
4. *World Peace: A Written Debate between William Howard Taft and William Jennings Bryan* (New York: George H. Doran, 1917), pp. 26, 66.
5. "They Want War Now," *The Commoner* 16 (January 1916), p. 2; "Raise the Money First," *The Commoner* 16 (January 1916), p. 2; address at peace meeting, Madison Square Garden, New York City, February 2, 1917, *The Commoner* 17 (March 1917), pp. 9–10.
6. Wayne C. Williams, *William Jennings Bryan* (New York: Putnam's, 1976), p. 413; "The Ostrich Illustration," *The Commoner* 16 (March 1916), p. 2.
7. Discussion of Bryan's emotional reaction to the *Lusitania* protest in Coletta, *Bryan,* Vol. II, pp. 337–43; quotation from resignation statement in Williams, *Bryan,* pp. 391–92.
8. Philip Jessup, *Elihu Root,* Vol. II (New York: Dodd, Mead, 1938), p. 373.
9. Address, Carnegie Hall, July 31, 1916, *Addresses of Charles Evans Hughes, 1906–1916* (2nd rev. ed.; New York: Putnam's, 1916), pp. 23 ff.
10. Letter, May 13, 1915, *Hoover-Wilson Wartime Correspondence,* Francis William O'Brien, ed. (Ames: Iowa State University Press, 1974), p. 10.
11. Note to German Foreign Minister, May 12, 1915, *The Papers of Woodrow Wilson,* Vol. XXXIII, Arthur S. Link, ed. (Princeton, N.J.: Princeton University Press, 1980), p. 176.
12. Shadow Lawn, N.J., November 4, 1916, *The Papers of Woodrow Wilson,* Vol. XXXVIII (Link, ed., 1982), pp. 613–14.
13. Address to the Senate, January 22, 1917, *The Papers of Woodrow Wilson,* Vol. XL (Link, ed., 1982), p. 538.
14. Address to Congress, April 2, 1917, *The Papers of Woodrow Wilson,* Vol. XLI (Link, ed., 1983), pp. 519, 523.
15. Annual message to Congress, December 4, 1917, *The Papers of Woodrow Wilson,* Vol. XLV (Link, ed., 1984), pp. 194, 195.
16. Speech, Washington's Tomb, July 4, 1918, *The Papers of Woodrow Wilson,* Vol. XLVIII (Link, ed., 1985), pp. 514, 516.
17. Address to Congress, April 2, 1917, *The Papers of Woodrow Wilson,* Vol. XLI (Link, ed., 1983), pp. 519, 523–25; address, New York City, March 4, 1919, *The Messages and Papers of Woodrow Wilson,* Vol. II, Albert Shaw, ed. (New York: The Review of Reviews, 1924), p. 651.

18. Address to the Union League Club, March 26, 1919, *The Autobiographi-cal Notes of Charles Evans Hughes,* David J. Danelski and Joseph S. Tulchin, eds. (Cambridge, Mass.: Harvard University Press, 1973), pp. 210–12.

19. Address, Montreal, September 4, 1923, in Charles Evans Hughes, *The Pathway of Peace* (New York: Harper and Bros., 1925), pp. 4, 7.

20. *Memoirs* (3 vols.; New York: Macmillan, 1951–52), Vol. I, pp. 449–50.

21. William E. Borah, *American Problems: A Selection of Speeches and Prophe-cies* (New York: Duffield, 1924), pp. 105, 109–23.

22. Ibid., pp. 67, 102–3.

23. Speech, May 30, 1916, *The Papers of Woodrow Wilson,* Vol. XXXVII (Link, ed., 1981), p. 126.

24. For list of states, see Chapter II, discussion of localism.

25. Merlo J. Pusey, *Charles Evans Hughes* (New York: Macmillan, 1951), Vol. II, pp. 419–20.

26. Address, New Haven, Conn., December 29, 1922, "Some Aspects of Our Foreign Policy," in Hughes, *The Pathway of Peace,* p. 57. For a thorough and provocative discussion of Hughes's approach to foreign policy gener-ally, see Betty Glad, *Charles Evans Hughes and the Illusions of Innocence: A Study in American Diplomacy* (Urbana: University of Illinois Press, 1968). Glad's study is written from the perspective of the realist school of political theory.

27. *The Council on Foreign Relations: A Record of Twenty-five Years, 1921–1946* (New York: Council on Foreign Relations, 1947), pp. 11–12; ibid., p. 29.

28. Letter to Edward M. House, September 17, 1935, in Franklin D. Roose-velt, *His Personal Letters, 1928–1945,* Vol. I, Elliott Roosevelt, ed. (New York: Kraus Reprint Co., 1970), pp. 506–7. (Originally, New York: Duell, Sloan and Pearce, 1950.)

29. Address, April 14, 1939, *The Public Papers and Addresses of Franklin D. Roosevelt,* Vol. VIII (New York: Russell and Russell, 1941), p. 198.

30. Address, Chicago, October 5, 1937, in *Peace and War: United States Foreign Policy, 1931–1941* (Washington, D.C.: U.S. Government Printing Office, 1943), pp. 385, 387.

31. Radio address, September 3, 1939, ibid., p. 484.

32. Radio address, October 12, 1940, in *Documents on American Foreign Relations,* Vol. III, 1940–41 (Boston: World Peace Foundation, 1941), p. 19.

33. Radio address, May 27, 1941, ibid., pp. 50–51.

34. Marion C. McKenna, *Borah* (Ann Arbor: University of Michigan Press, 1961), pp. 361–63. See also Robert James Maddox, *William E. Borah and American Foreign Policy* (Baton Rouge: Louisiana State University Press, 1969), p. 240, and Cordell Hull, *The Memoirs of Cordell Hull* (2 vols.; New York: Macmillan, 1948), Vol. I, pp. 649–50.

CHAPTER V

1. *Year of Decisions* (Garden City, N.Y.: Doubleday, 1955), pp. 50–51.
2. New York: Harcourt, Brace & World, 1955, p. 262.
3. Address, New York City, October 21, 1944, in *Documents on American Foreign Relations,* Vol. VII, 1944–45 (Princeton, N.J.: Princeton University Press, 1947), pp. 3, 5–6.
4. June 10, 1940, in *Documents on American Foreign Relations,* Vol. II, 1939–40 (Boston: World Peace Foundation, 1940), pp. 78–79.
5. January 6, 1945, in *Documents on American Foreign Relations,* Vol. VII, pp. 9–14.
6. Special message to the Congress on Greece and Turkey: The Truman Doctrine, March 12, 1947, *Public Papers of the Presidents, Harry S. Truman, 1947* (Washington, D.C.: U.S. Government Printing Office, 1963), pp. 176, 178.
7. Special message to the Congress Recommending Point 4 Legislation, June 24, 1949, *Public Papers of the Presidents, Harry S. Truman, 1949* (Washington, D.C.: U.S. Government Printing Office, 1964), pp. 329, 330.
8. Dean Acheson, *Present at the Creation* (New York: Norton, 1969), p. 415.
9. *One World* (New York: Simon and Schuster, 1943), p. 203.
10. The reports cited are all in the 1944 volume of *American Interests in the War and the Peace,* a bound but unpublished collection of the War and Peace Studies projects, Widener Library, Harvard University, Cambridge, Mass.
11. John Foster Dulles et al., *A Righteous Faith for a Just and Durable Peace* (New York: Commission to Study the Bases of a Just and Durable Peace, 1942).
12. *War, Peace and Change* (New York: Harper & Bros., 1939), pp. 117, 122–23; ibid., p. 126.
13. Leonard Mosley, *Dulles: A Biography of Eleanor, Allen and John Foster Dulles* (New York: Dial Press/James Wade, 1978), pp. 198–99.
14. *War or Peace* (New York: Macmillan, 1950), p. 6.
15. Council on Foreign Relations, *Annual Report 1946–47,* p. 30; *Annual Report 1947–48,* p. 20.
16. See, for example, Thomas K. Finletter, *Foreign Policy: The Next Phase* (New York: Harper & Bros., 1958), for the views of an active, influential member of the Council's board of directors, and Philip Mosely, ed., *The Soviet Union, 1922–1962* (New York: Praeger, 1963), a collection of articles on the Soviet Union published in these years in the Council on Foreign Relations journal, *Foreign Affairs.*
17. *Basic Aims of United States Foreign Policy: Study prepared at the request of the Committee on Foreign Relations, United States Senate, by Council on*

Foreign Relations, 86th Cong., 1st sess., Committee Print No. 7, November 25, 1959 (Washington, D.C.: U.S. Government Printing Office, 1959), p. 9.

18. Ibid., pp. 9, 18. Also the following reports of the Committee for Economic Development, published in New York: *Economic Development Assistance,* 1957, p. 18; *Cooperation for Progress in Latin-America,* 1961, p. 36; ibid., p. 35. For further references, see also two Council on Foreign Relations books: Charles D. Cremeans, *The Arabs and the World* (New York: Praeger, 1963), pp. 319–24, and Adolf A. Berle, *Latin America: Diplomacy and Reality* (New York: Harper & Row, 1962), passim.

19. April 16, 1947, *Cong. Rec.* 93, Pt. 3 (80th Cong., 1st sess.), 3498.

20. April 16, 1947, *Cong. Rec.* 93, Pt. 3 (80th Cong., 1st sess.), 3499.

21. March 4, 1948, *Cong. Rec.* 94, Pt. 2 (80th Cong., 2nd sess.), 2124.

22. *Congress and the Nation,* Vol. I (Washington, D.C.: Congressional Quarterly Publications, 1965), p. 1650.

23. Acheson, *Present at the Creation,* pp. 363–65.

24. Security Council Resolution, July 7, 1950: S/1588.

25. September 24, 1951, *Cong. Rec.* 97, Pt. 9 (82nd Cong., 1st sess.), 11945, 11948.

26. February 23, 1954, *Cong. Rec.* 100, Pt. 2 (83rd Cong., 2nd sess.), 2122–23.

27. Ibid., p. 2123.

28. January 28, 1954, *Cong. Rec.* 100, Pt. 1 (83rd Cong., 2nd sess.), 936.

29. February 15, 1954, *Cong. Rec.* 100, Pt. 2 (83rd Cong., 2nd sess.), 1728–1729.

30. January 28, 1954, *Cong. Rec.* 100, Pt. 1 (83rd Cong., 2nd sess.), 938, 944.

31. Acheson, *Present at the Creation,* p. 219.

32. *The New York Times,* January 18, 1961, p. 22.

CHAPTER VI

1. Harry Truman, *Memoirs,* Vol. II (Garden City, N.Y.: Doubleday, 1956), p. 182.

2. Statement carried on cover page of their annual reports.

3. Committee for Economic Development, 1971, p. 49.

4. Committee for Economic Development, 1978.

5. Committee for Economic Development, 1965, p. 12.

6. Committee for Economic Development, 1971, p. 31.

7. San Francisco, September 3, 1960, *Speeches, Remarks, Press Conferences and Statements of Senator John F. Kennedy, August–November 7, 1960* (Washington, D.C.: U.S. Government Printing Office, 1961), p. 95.

8. Bronx, N.Y., November 5, 1960, ibid., p. 901.

9. September 22, 1960, ibid., pp. 319, 323–24.

10. Los Angeles, September 9, 1960, ibid., pp. 189, 193; New York City, October 12, 1960, ibid., pp. 557, 561.

11. Arthur M. Schlesinger, Jr., *A Thousand Days: John F. Kennedy in the White House* (Boston: Houghton Mifflin, 1965), Chapter 25.

12. Address, June 14, 1956, in John F. Kennedy, *A Compilation of Statements and Speeches Made During His Service in the U.S. Senate and House of Representatives* (Washington, D.C.: U.S. Government Printing Office, 1964), pp. 1034–37.

13. Hobart Rowan, *The Free Enterprisers: Kennedy, Johnson and the Business Establishment* (New York: Putnam's, 1964), Chapter 6.

14. June 11, 1962, *Public Papers of the Presidents, John F. Kennedy, 1962* (Washington, D.C.: U.S. Government Printing Office, 1963), pp. 470–75.

15. Doris Kearns, *Lyndon Johnson and the American Dream* (New York: New American Library, 1977), p. 231.

16. New York: Coward, McCann & Geoghegan, 1974, pp. 263 and 233.

17. For an exasperated and informative discussion of the Community Action Programs, see Daniel Patrick Moynihan, *Maximum Feasible Misunderstanding: Community Action in the War on Poverty* (New York: Free Press, 1969).

CHAPTER VII

1. March 22, 1961, *Public Papers of the Presidents, John F. Kennedy, 1961* (Washington, D.C.: U.S. Government Printing Office, 1962), p. 205.

2. Walt Rostow, *The Stages of Economic Growth* (Cambridge, Eng.: Cambridge University Press, 1960).

3. Address, first anniversary of the Alliance for Progress, March 13, 1962, *Public Papers of the Presidents, John F. Kennedy, 1962* (Washington, D.C.: U.S. Government Printing Office, 1963), p. 223.

4. June 6, 1961, *Public Papers, 1961*, pp. 444–45.

5. Ibid., p. 445.

6. Ibid.

7. Carl Gershman, *The Foreign Policy of American Labor* (Beverly Hills, Calif.: Sage Publications, 1975), p. 8; Alfred O. Hero, Jr., and Emil Starr, *The Reuther-Meany Foreign Policy Dispute* (Dobbs Ferry, N.Y.: Oceana Publications, 1970), p. 62.

8. Commencement address, U.S. Coast Guard Academy, June 3, 1964, *Public Papers of the Presidents, Lyndon B. Johnson, 1963–64*, Vol. I (Washington, D.C.: U.S. Government Printing Office, 1965), pp. 741, 743.

9. Kennedy's speech on diversity was made at the University of California at Berkeley, March 23, 1962, *Public Papers, 1962*, pp. 263, 266.

10. *The New York Times* edition, *The Pentagon Papers* (New York: Bantam Books, 1971), pp. 150–51.

11. Senator Gravel edition, *The Pentagon Papers* (Boston: Beacon Press, 1971–72), Vol. II. pp. 142, 146–47.

12. *The Pentagon Papers* (*Times* ed.), pp. 283–84.

13. House Joint Resolution 1145, August 7, 1964, *Cong. Rec.* 110, Pt. 14 (88th Cong., 2nd sess.), 18471.
14. Special message to Congress, June 1, 1965, *Public Papers of the Presidents, Lyndon B. Johnson, 1965,* Vol. II (Washington, D.C.: U.S. Government Printing Office, 1966), pp. 607–9.
15. *The Pentagon Papers* (Gravel ed.), Vol. II, p. 552.
16. February 20, 1957, *Cong. Rec.* 103, Pt. 2 (85th Cong., 1st sess.), 2312–13; February 25, 1957, *Cong. Rec.* 103, Pt. 2 (85th Cong., 1st sess.), 2529.
17. Strom Thurmond, *The Faith We Have Not Kept* (San Diego: Viewpoint Books, 1968), p. 82.
18. Barry Goldwater, *The Conscience of a Majority* (Englewood Cliffs, N.J.: Prentice-Hall, 1970), p. 105.
19. March 1, 1966, *Cong. Rec.* 112, Pt. 4 (89th Cong., 2nd sess.), 4370–71.
20. Ibid.
21. Robert Kennedy, *Thirteen Days: A Memoir of the Cuban Missile Crisis* (New York: Norton, 1969), pp. 31–32.
22. Henry L. Trewhitt, *McNamara* (New York: Harper & Row, 1971), pp. 37–38, 41, and Chapter 2 generally.
23. Robert S. McNamara, *The Essence of Security: Reflections in Office* (New York: Harper & Row, 1968), pp. 109–10.
24. See especially Frances FitzGerald, *Fire in the Lake: The Vietnamese and the Americans in Vietnam* (Boston: Little, Brown), 1972.
25. George W. Ball, address, Washington, D.C., April 26, 1963, *American Foreign Policy Current Documents,* 1963, pp. 401, 403–4; address, Washington, D.C., March 16, 1965, *American Foreign Policy Current Documents,* 1965, pp. 428, 432–33.
26. George W. Ball, *Diplomacy for a Crowded World* (Boston: Atlantic/Little, Brown, 1976), pp. 51–52.
27. *The Pentagon Papers* (*Times* ed.), p. 450.
28. Kennan testimony generally, February 10, 1966, *The Vietnam Hearings* (New York: Vintage, 1966). Quotes from pp. 150–51.
29. See his draft memo for the President, October 14, 1966, *The Pentagon Papers* (*Times* ed.), pp. 542–50.
30. David Halberstam, *The Best and the Brightest* (New York: Random House, 1969), p. 644; Townsend Hoopes, *The Limits of Intervention: An Inside Account of How the Johnson Policy of Escalation in Vietnam Was Reversed* (New York: McKay, 1969), pp. 86–87.
31. Report issued August 31, 1967. Text of report in *The New York Times,* September 1, 1967, p. 10.
32. October 2, 1967, *Cong. Rec.* 113, Pt. 20 (90th Cong., 1st sess.), 27453; Thurmond, *The Faith We Have Not Kept,* pp. 64–65.
33. Doris Kearns, *Lyndon Johnson and the American Dream* (New York: New American Library, 1977), p. 336.
34. FitzGerald, *Fire in the Lake.*

CHAPTER VIII

1. Strom Thurmond, *The Faith We Have Not Kept* (San Diego: Viewpoint Books, 1968), pp. 127, 150.
2. George C. Wallace, *Hear Me Out* (Anderson, S.C.: Droke House, 1968), pp. 33, 55, 78, 69, 59.
3. Ibid., pp. 78–79.
4. *The New York Times,* September 17, 1964, p. 25.
5. Council on Foreign Relations, *Annual Report 1969,* pp. 12, 13.
6. Council on Foreign Relations, *Annual Report 1970,* p. 12.
7. *Foreign Affairs* 51 (October 1972), pp. 210, 220, 226–27.
8. Council on Foreign Relations, *Annual Report 1973–74,* pp. 1–3.
9. Richard N. Cooper et al., *Towards a Renovated International System,* Triangle Paper #14 (Trilateral Commission, 1977), p. 10.
10. Egidio Ortona et al., *The Problem of International Consultations,* Triangle Paper #12 (Trilateral Commission, 1976), pp. 15, 16.
11. Jeremy R. Azrael et al., *An Overview of East-West Relations,* Triangle Paper #15 (Trilateral Commission, 1978), p. 47.
12. Inaugural address, January 20, 1969, *Public Papers of the Presidents, Richard M. Nixon, 1969* (Washington, D.C.: U.S. Government Printing Office, 1971), p. 2; State of the Union address, January 22, 1970, *Public Papers, 1970* (Washington, D.C.: U.S. Government Printing Office, 1971), pp. 10–11.
13. State of the Union address, January 22, 1970, *Public Papers, 1970,* p. 9; First Annual Report to the Congress on United States Foreign Policy for the 1970s, February 18, 1970, *Public Papers, 1970,* pp. 116–22.
14. Jimmy Carter, *Why Not the Best?* (Nashville, Tenn.: Broadman Press, 1975), p. 147.
15. Ibid., p. 148.
16. *The New York Times,* July 7, 1976, p. A12.
17. Betty Glad, *Jimmy Carter: In Search of the Great White House* (New York: Norton, 1980), pp. 419–25.
18. *The New York Times,* June 20, 1978, p. A12.
19. Joseph A. Califano, Jr., *Governing America: An Insider's Report from the White House and the Cabinet* (New York: Simon and Schuster, 1981); Glad, *Jimmy Carter,* p. 437.
20. April 18, 1978, *Cong. Rec.* 124, Pt. 54 (95th Cong., 2nd sess.), 5783, 5756, 5781.
21. *The New York Times,* June 6, 1980, p. A12.
22. Bill Boyarsky, *Ronald Reagan: His Life and Rise to the Presidency* (New York: Random House, 1981).
23. Quotations, in order, are from Ronald Reagan, *The Creative Society*

(New York: Devin-Adair, 1978), pp. 74–75, 135, and 7–8; *The New York Times,* July 18, 1980, p. A8, and January 21, 1981, p. B1.

24. *The New York Times,* May 10, 1983, p. 19.
25. Speech accepting nomination, *The New York Times,* July 18, 1980, p. A8; speech to the National Association of Evangelicals, *The New York Times,* March 9, 1983, p. 18.
26. Speech on Soviet-American relations, *The New York Times,* January 17, 1984, p. 8.
27. Speech on Central American policy, *The New York Times,* May 10, 1984, p. 16.
28. Ibid.
29. *The New York Times,* March 20, 1984, p. 3.
30. Second inaugural address, *The New York Times,* January 22, 1985, p. A17.
31. *The New York Times,* March 19, 1981, p. 1.
32. *The New York Times,* October 28, 1983, p. 9.
33. *The New York Times,* April 9, 1984, p. 1.
34. *The New York Times,* April 6, 1983, and May 4, 1984.

Index

abuse of power. *See* power, abuse of

Acheson, Dean, 154, 156, 160

AFL-CIO, 191, 207–8. *See also* American Federation of Labor; CIO

agencies, regulatory, 43–4, 75–6, 172. *See also specific agencies*

Agency for International Development (AID), 207

agrarian interests, 10, 11, 23, 32–3
and New Deal, 71, 72–3
as political constituency. *See* localists

Agricultural Adjustment Act (1938), 12, 72, 172

aid programs. *See* foreign aid; social programs, domestic

Alliance for Progress, 203, 207

alliances, political, 59–60. *See also under* functionalists; localists; majoritarians

American dream. *See* liberty and equality, pursuit and promise of

authority
to control power and its abuse, 28. *See also* power, abuse of

of government. *See* government, authority and power of

of military (1960s), 216–17

of President. *See* President and presidency (U.S.)

for rule making, 20, 24–5, 97–8

as surrogate issue, 25, 63–4, 67, 81

for war-making, 116. *See also* Gulf of Tonkin resolution (1964)

American Federation of Labor, 51–2

American Society for the Judicial Settlement of International Disputes, 104

American Society of International Law, 104

anti-communism. *See* communism

anti-lynching legislation, 80

anti-poverty programs (1960s), 165, 184–6, 189, 190. *See also* Great Society program(s)

Ball, George, 222–5, 231, 242

Baruch, Bernard, 112, 142

A NOTE ABOUT THE AUTHOR

Mona Harrington was born in Lowell, Massachusetts, in 1936, and was educated at the University of Massachusetts and Harvard University, where she received a law degree and a doctorate in political science. She served as a lawyer in the State Department, taught political science, and raised a family of three children before turning to writing full-time. She is a contributor to *The Politics of Ethnicity* by Walzer, Kantowicz, Higham and Harrington (1982), and is currently executive director of the Alliance of Independent Scholars in Cambridge, Massachusetts.

A NOTE ON THE TYPE

The text of this book was set in film in a typeface named Bembo. The roman is a copy of a letter cut for the celebrated Venetian printer Aldus Manutius by Francesco Griffo. It was first used in Cardinal Bembo's *De Ætna* of 1495—hence the name of the revival. Griffo's type is now generally recognized, thanks to the research of Stanley Morison, to be the first of the old-face group of types. The companion italic is an adaptation of the chancery script type designed by the Roman calligrapher and printer Lodovico degli Arrighi, called Vincentino, and used by him during the 1520s.

Composed by The Haddon Craftsmen, Scranton, Pennsylvania

Printed and bound by Fairfield Graphics, Fairfield, Pennsylvania

Typography and binding design by Dorothy Schmiderer